EMMA WARREN

UP THE YOUTH CLUB

A Love Letter

faber

First published in the UK in 2025
by Faber & Faber Limited
The Bindery, 51 Hatton Garden
London EC1N 8HN
This paperback edition first published in 2026

Typeset by Faber & Faber Limited
Printed in England by CPI Group (UK) Ltd, Croydon, CR0 4YY

A CIP record for this book
is available from the British Library

ISBN 978–0–571–38922–3

2 4 6 8 10 9 7 5 3 1

UP THE YOUTH CLUB

Emma Warren has been documenting grassroots culture for decades. She is the author of *Make Some Space* (2019), which was a *MOJO* book of the year; *Steam Down* (2019), which was published by Rough Trade Books and named an *Irish Times* read of the year; and *Document Your Culture* (2020). *Dance Your Way Home* (2023) was a *Guardian* book of the year and inspired the 2025 summer series at the Southbank Centre.

A dual citizen of Ireland and the UK, she worked on staff at *The Face* and as the editorial mentor at youth-run Brixton publication *Live Magazine*. Her monthly radio show on Worldwide FM ran for six years.

Further praise for *Up the Youth Club*:

'A meticulous and fascinating consideration of youth spaces in all their forms. In times of increasing atomisation, its celebration of connection and community felt important' *Irish Times* (Book of the Year)

'An impassioned, thoroughly evidenced and engaging argument for the security of youth clubs' long term future . . . Warren's message is one of hope' Hugh Russell, *Buzz Magazine*

'Warren shows why youth spaces matter – not just for young people, but for all of us' Darren 'Loki' McGarvey

'A mixture of both heady nostalgia and a defiant call to arms – to let the Youth Club die is to erase a wonderful past and give up on a hopeful future – for all of us . . . At a time when individualism and social isolation has been exacerbated by the pocket-sized super-computers in every young person's hand, *Up the Youth Club* is a timely reminder of what we all truly crave as human beings – connection' Ben Bailey Smith

'As a critical and emotive analysis of the Youth Club's history, Warren's book is seminal. As an inspired trip down memory lane, *Up the Youth Club* is a passionate evocation of my childhood, a time where the very social interventions that made me were being underfunded and devalued . . . A necessary reminder of the power, function and enduring legacy of Youth Work in the UK' Courttia Newland

'Community, resilience, kindness and optimism against the odds – this is a story of people at their best' Richard King

'*Up the Youth Club* takes us to the beating heart and vibrant soul of the roots of our communities; our shared histories are interrogated, explored and celebrated so carefully and generously by Emma Warren. It is a triumphant call to action. I feel that in these stormy times, Warren is a lighthouse' Salena Godden

'Emma Warren is one of the great cultural historians of our time. Her work is rigorous, deeply empathetic and profoundly human' Aniefiok Ekpoudom

---

by the same author

MAKE SOME SPACE

STEAM DOWN

DOCUMENT YOUR CULTURE

DANCE YOUR WAY HOME

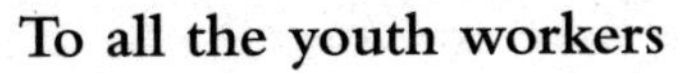

To all the youth workers

CONTENTS

INTRODUCTION
HELLO, WELCOME, COME ON IN

On the Northern Line, going south. A group of four get on and we're all standing together, at the window end of a grimy London Underground carriage. Three young teenagers are accompanied by a tall man who positions himself in the middle of the group, slightly back from what would be a rough semi-circle if we weren't on the Tube. No one's on their phone. I'm immediately interested and my radar switches on because I'm seeing something that I can't yet name. This is not a family group and they don't look like a lost portion of a school trip either, the adult's unlaced Timberlands at odds with a narrow interpretation of 'business dress'.

He's listening, actively, tuning in to the as-yet-unspoken. Around his neck is a lanyard that reads 'Wipers Youth CIC'. I've never heard of the organisation but the presence of this ID reveals the dynamic. The ties between this group are social and have been built between the young people and their youth worker. Wipers, I discover later, specialise in improving the confidence and self-esteem of vulnerable youth through mentoring. Their tagline is appropriate for this Tube carriage context: *A clearer vision for a safer journey.*

One of the Wipers group is telling the youth worker about an everyday example of interpersonal teenage drama, which in this case involves money. Listening, the adult draws another youngster into the conversation, recounting what's been said and seeking an opinion. He's a conductor, quietly indicating who should speak and noticing what might need to be said, with low-key authority that keeps him simultaneously on the teenagers' level and above it, offering off-hand observations instead of direct instructions.

Seamlessly, he steers the conversation around a gentle bend and another of the teens picks up the signal. Previously, this one has been silent, but he loves anime and can't help but glow when he's talking about it. He lights up, shifting from a kind of absence into presence simply by the opening up of space in which he can contribute with enthusiasm. Two stops pass as he recounts the entire plot of his favourite show, and it's lovely to hear because this youngster, who'll quickly be coded as troublesome above ground, is being childish in the best possible way, unselfconsciously. The group get off and I watch them walk up the platform. The youth worker is keeping time with the kids. He's solid yet mutable, able to meld gently with what's happening, utilising a kind of focus that appears softened and practical. For ten minutes, this man transformed the end of a Tube carriage into a youth club.

———

A central quality connects all the spaces in this book, whether they're attended by five young people or five hundred, in a shed or a purpose-built centre. A youth club, as far as I'm concerned, is a broadly warm and welcoming space where those who are in their second decade of life can gather regularly, in person, without compulsion, to do things they like doing, or to discover what they like doing, where restorative 'hanging out' is welcome. Some of these are officially designated, others less so. Youth clubs are places of mutual aid, not easily flipped into private profit, which makes them political too: not political with a big or small 'p', but with a wavy one, drawn with a borrowed felt-tip pen.

The titular space comes in many shapes and sizes. Some of you might have an image in your head, perhaps relating to your own experiences or to demographically familiar places containing pool tables or PlayStations. For others, they'll be cultural expressions of a distant past, like the coffee bars of 1950s Soho are for me. Youth clubs are a shifting entity, which adapts to whatever is available at a given moment in time. The youth club story has been acutely sensitive to changes in national, local and street-level politics; to culture as it arrives and leaves; and to ordinary community machinations in any given place. Sometimes they've been nationwide and plentiful; other times, as recounted above, they've been squeezed into the end of a Tube carriage. In their broadest sense, youth clubs are prismatic: you can look through them to see society from many different angles.

Youth clubs have been part of everyday life in the UK and Northern Ireland for over 150 years. Many people born before the start of the twenty-first century would have attended one, even as the youth service declined from the mid-1980s onwards. They've been maintained throughout history by a shifting and interconnected fascia of local authorities and voluntary or community organisations. Some have been run by the council in specially constructed buildings, attached to housing estates or schools. Others had a faith context, even if that was just someone in the congregation with keys and authority who'd allow local teenagers to stream through the doors.

Somewhere in the picture there will be adults, enabling access to whatever is on offer, and doing so through a unique dynamic. Motivated youth have repeatedly created spaces for themselves, by themselves: contemporary examples would be the skatepark or gathering places for rollerskaters, but even in these places, there are often helpful older people on the edges. Youth clubs can be sites of bonding across the generations, built out of choice.

Much of the existing discussion and documentation on the subject of youth clubs comes from the perspective of adult youth workers, with books, annual reports and articles discussing various aspects of their craft. Youth work has been much studied, but is abstract without spaces in which to enact it. I wanted to focus on youth clubs, in the broadest possible sense of the term, and try to understand what was happening when people attended them.

All societies have initiation rites, and many of ours have come adrift or been commercialised. I suspect that some of the necessary transition work that must happen between childhood and adulthood often takes place on weekday evenings, when teenagers can make noise, lounge about and experience an absence of structure alongside planned activities. The remaining survivor youth clubs, which operate in the tiny cracks available in hyper-capitalised towns and cities, show what's possible and provide a blueprint for the rebuilding. I say this believing that optimism can be a form of defiance. And, just to say it out loud, we don't need anything *back*, because we can't ever go back. The youth clubs of the 1930s wouldn't have suited the 1990s. We need what the conditions suggest now and in the future. In this way youth clubs are an aspect of creativity itself, improvised into existence, aiming for harmonics. Among other things, they have long offered an affordable, and mostly accessible, rite of passage.

All of this was broadly the same wherever you lived in mainland UK or the North of Ireland, although with some structural and cultural differences. For example, the Boys' Brigade was formed in Glasgow and fed into the foundations of Scottish youth work, much of which took place in schools. In Wales, many youth clubs had connections to community assets built and paid for by workers, often in mining communities. English history, meanwhile, meant time-rich wealthy people would often act as benefactors or volunteers. In Northern Ireland, the conditions were understandably unique. Each nation experienced phases in which government money flowed or was stemmed, with buildings and staff generated by committee reports, or removed and allowed to crumble.

It's easy to accept that youth clubs have an impact on society. Even those who refuse to fund them would probably agree that they have a role, even if it's just the worn-out trope of 'keeping kids off the street'. Spending this time immersing myself in youth club histories led me to an additional idea: that identifiable parts of sporting and cultural achievements across these islands owe a big debt to lively teenagers and youth workers sharing physical space, especially those catering to young people who don't have easy access to money or support within their family networks. Far from being an incidental place of leisure or charity, the youth club is an engine room.

Low and erratic funding has often meant that youth clubs have relied heavily on collective, grassroots resourcefulness. They are shaped by the young people who use them. Perhaps it's unsurprising, therefore, that they've long been innovative spaces, fostering talent, and in turn being reflected through popular culture. Whether it's TV show *Byker Grove*; The Smiths and their iconic representation of Salford Lads' Club on the cover of *The Queen Is Dead*; Stormzy's Merky FC in Croydon; Mercury Prize-winners Roni Size and Ezra Collective shouting out youth clubs across the decades; or spaces set up by or supported by boxers, from Henry Cooper to Anthony Joshua, youth clubs have had a cultural impact that has been almost entirely obscured.

Up the Youth Club is an attempt to give shape to the bigger story behind youth club life. It goes back further than I anticipated when I first set out. As I ventured back in time, I came across numerous descriptions that could have been cut and pasted from one era to another. The types of rooms set aside for young people, the activities taking place within them and the responses of young people to these spaces were extremely similar. The youth club struck me as a surprisingly stable set-up, holding tight in one form or another while those with structural power either ignored it or attempted to instrumentalise it, often as a way of containing or controlling the youth, and frequently valued only through the lens of crime reduction. The past is not a blueprint for what happens next, but it does offer examples and encouragement, illuminating possible futures. I'm inviting an emotional and imaginative response to these examples that I've selected, tiny shards from the vastness of the past: history as possibility.

Every writer has a relationship to their subject, even if they claim their interest is objective. Mine is familial: I spent most of my thirties as an informal youth worker, while friends, loved ones and family members have also done this work. My perspective isn't abstract. I know why it matters, and I continue to benefit from relationships forged in these spaces, whether they're friendships that have lasted since my own youth club experiences or ongoing bonds with people I first met as a mentor.

In the 1980s, my mum, Meg, ended up running a play-scheme in the London Borough of Bromley, on the edge of south-east London. Dropping my toddler brother off one day, she was told that the group was closing because there was no one to run it. She and her two friends, Beverley and Elaine, decided they'd take it on as volunteer leaders. Before long, she'd moved over to another club in Starts Hill with a very mixed demographic: she described children from 'very elite' families, but also one who fell into total panic when a policeman arrived to do a Tufty the Squirrel road safety talk; the child's only experience with the force had been during terrifying raids at home. It was good, she said, to be able to give kids from all backgrounds what she described as 'a little bit of security' and to see them blossom.

My siblings and I would be brought along to playgroup if we were too sick for school. This was rare, because she was a nurse and, as those of you with healthcare professionals in the family will probably know, feeling 'a bit off' won't wash for those in daily contact with the seriously unwell. Consequently, I have only a few memories of lying in the corner on a fold-up bed while smaller kids whizzed down a plastic slide, made dinosaur shapes with own-brand Play-Doh or mixed up all the paints into one satisfyingly sludgy brown. Now, I realise this offered rare perspective, which is transferable to the teenage sphere this book is about: I was seeing something outside of my age group's usual vista. Usually, you're only in playgroup when you're at playgroup, or, in other words, too young for school and probably too young to remember much. Being a bit older than the playgroup kids, and watching from the sidelines, I could see that it looked like a lot of fun, and I now know how important it would have been for exhausted parents too.

When I was about eleven years old, I started something short-lived and youth club-esque for myself and a couple of friends. Fame Club was centred around the TV show *Fame*, which was itself set in the fictional New York City High School for the Performing Arts. Meeting weekly in the back garden of the three-bed semi-detached house I grew up in, we had a felt-tip-drawn sign, a very basic kind of boom box and *The Kids from Fame* album, which we would play repeatedly. We argued about who got to be which character, and made up new storylines and dances. On turning twelve, I joined the local youth club and went down every week, as did both of my siblings. Youth club was an important part of my life, expanding my friendship group and horizons until acid house propelled me into London's nightclubs. For a short while, the two worlds overlapped.

After spending most of my twenties writing about various iterations of the dancefloors I'd joined as an underage enthusiast, I started working at teen-run publication *Live Magazine* in Brixton as an editorial mentor. This was a new and industrious kind of youth club, where contributors attended after school to write articles, take photographs and to have as much of a laugh as possible while making a quarterly print publication, website and video channel. I learned a lot.

What I saw repeatedly at *Live* was the power of acceptance. An ex-partner, who was an experienced family support worker, introduced me to the phrase 'unconditional positive regard'. Those trained in psychology or social work will be familiar with the concept, but it was new to me, and it gave me a whole new way of understanding the benefits of such acceptance. Inculcating possibility, it contains a directed form of hope: that a youthful individual might become the best version of themselves that's available in the world they actually inhabit.

Professor and educational theorist Gert Biesta came up with a word for something similar: 'subjectification', or becoming the subject of your own life, not, as he put it, 'the object of what other people want from me'. *Live*, and the other places within walking distance – local authority clubs, youth music facility Raw Material and visual arts entity Photofusion – allowed a decoupling from local and social pressures to be Thing One, and to realise that it was also possible to be Thing Two, Thing Three or even Thing Eight Hundred and Eighty-Six.

Connections run into the next generation too. I have one child, now grown up, and in the early 2010s he'd sometimes be invited by friends to attend their youth club on the Ferrier estate in Kidbrooke, which was located between our flat and his school. It represented additional freedom, and, mostly, this group of friends played five-a-side or hung about outside, until the youth club and adjoining estate were demolished and replaced with unaffordable housing. When off school, or during half-term, he would come to work with me at *Live Magazine*.

Much younger than everyone else in the room, it offered him an unusual view of what was possible for young people, just as my mum's playgroup had for me. Later, he went into youth work. I'm saying all of this as a way of using the very local – my family – to show in a small way the existence of responsive, responsible street-level connection and co-operation; of experiencing it and passing it on; and of youth clubs as a physical, spatial expression of community.

Family also offers an opportunity to counter the narrative that youth clubs are a thing of the past. I have a connection through relatives with a thriving club in south-west London which has free activities and services for ten- to nineteen-year-olds, six days a week. Heatham House offers sport, dance, music production, gig nights and different themes each term that are selected by the young people – barber workshops or cooking, for example. There's a skatepark, a recording studio, pitches for football and basketball, and spacious rooms for pool, table tennis or just being. Additional space is carved out for those who identify as LGBTQ+ or neurodiverse. Heatham House made it through austerity for a combination of reasons, including that it has been open for over fifty years and that there was strong community push-back when closure was mooted in 2012.

Of course, not everyone benefited from a youth club. Not all young people wanted what was on offer, either because it maybe wasn't to their taste or perhaps due to being shy. Girls have always had to fight for their place. Parts of the nation also offered patchy provision and, for rural kids, the local youth club might have been miles away. Some families preferred to pay for teen leisure activities, and others wouldn't allow their children out, for reasons of either protection or control, or both. In other cases, parents sensed what Charlie Dark MBE described to me as a pipeline between the pool table and poor outcomes, and insisted on other options, like church. Youth club doesn't equate with utopia, but the concept, on the ground, is powered by an awareness of fairness, or the lack thereof. And it's worth saying out loud, at a time when everyone is used to socialising on screens, that the prominence and importance of the digital world doesn't negate the need for physical space. It's not either/or; both are required. Long-lasting, building-based places are essential for those members of society who are making the transition from child to adult, and I hope that these histories will help explain why.

*

Exploring the past, I was reminded again and again of the pointlessness of looking for single-origin stories or one definitive truth. Partly, this is because people's experiences are at the centre of this history, with the inevitable blurriness and uncertainty that come with individual memory. It's also because the official record tells its own story, sometimes evasive, other times aiming facts towards an end goal, or written by individuals in receipt of – or willing to share – only certain details.

Up the Youth Club, then, takes a more exploratory route around the subject. It asks questions, such as why youth clubs exist and why they're not well understood; or simply, 'Where have all our youth clubs gone?' Such enquiries have a momentum of their own and exploring these questions will, I hope, offer an architecture of understanding and a basis from which we can collectively argue the case for creating and sustaining the spaces young people need now. It is also worth saying that the absence of youth clubs has been filled very effectively by adults who make teenagers feel valued by sending them to county lines trap houses to produce, distribute and sell drugs.

With all that in mind, I've attempted to communicate interlocking evidence and experiences in a way that is recognisable to people who were there, and which allows safe entry into the space for those who weren't. I've tried my best to recreate aspects of the picture on the ground at various points in time and to give a sense of the national context. My version of the youth club story is urban, not rural, and has omitted far more than it contains. I selected these stories in the knowledge that they're partial. In any given year there would have been thousands of youth clubs across the country, and this book acts as a sampler, criss-crossing decades, countries and countless lives. Hopefully the inevitable gaps will be filled by writers, researchers, poets, documentary-makers, artists and other storytellers over the coming years.

The youth club is a rich part of the world. While in basement archives or chatting with interviewees in person or on calls, I burst out laughing more than once – there was so much teenage comedy – and I found myself tearful too. All youth clubs contain precious life material, and I have loved spending so much time with these histories, picking out echoes and repeating motifs that spiral through the years. My version of the youth club history comes through the double doors and is written from the floor up. It attempts to channel the grounded confidence of an experienced youth worker. Occasionally, it's quite high on the ubiquitous cheap squash and biscuits.

Writing this book sometimes felt like I was being harassed and exhausted by the teenagers of the past, and at other times the material seemed to turn its back on me, going off in a strop. Frequently, I was amazed at what had happened, and still happens, in these spaces, and I was humbled by the collective effort. I came away thinking that every youth club could generate a novel or a stand-up show, ideally ones directed by the kids themselves.

Inevitably, as communal public space has receded, youth clubs have become an increasingly frequent shorthand for forward-thinking positivity – their combined rarity and universality making their value somewhat more visible. My hope is that this book acts as a signal boost for everyone doing the work, whether on the ground or in well-appointed offices.

In short, youth clubs have always existed. They always will, because there will always be young people. How we care for our youth and what we owe them are questions for all of us.

PART ONE
THE ORIGIN STORY

1

1880: RUCTIONS AT THE MISSION HOUSE

The youth clubs of these islands are unique. Like pubs, comprehensive schools and the NHS, spaces for young people are a distinct product of history, economics and policy; social power and dynamics; the weather; beliefs about teenagers; and cultural ideas about community or volunteering. Similar spaces do exist elsewhere: for example, the Jugendzentren in Austria and Germany, or the Maisons des jeunes et de la culture in France, which began as a response to Nazism and, until the late 1960s, were for under-twenty-fives. Fascism, of course, preferred a youth wing to the youth club.

This specificity wasn't always clear to me. In 2019, I received an email from a Norwegian man, in which he described building a cultural centre in Oslo 'along the lines of the UK youth club'. At that point I didn't know that what we had was unusual or admired from afar. I'd assumed that our youth club dynamics, structures and culture were, broadly, replicated everywhere else. I was wrong. Most other countries don't appear to have the same freewheeling, culturally responsive style of youth club, which, for over a century, has been a defining rite of passage for large numbers of people.

'There are some international similarities, but are they culturally distinct here? Yes,' said Dr Tania de St Croix, when I contacted her to try to clarify this question. Having spent twenty years as a youth worker in Manchester, Tania is now a leading expert: she is the author of *Grassroots Youth Work:*

Policy, Passion and Resistance in Practice and countless academic papers, and is also a senior lecturer at King's College London. 'It's partly because youth work, at its best, is defined by the young people who take part, and that's mostly working-class and marginalised groups. There's a bottom-up creation of what the youth club is, by young people and youth workers and communities.'

A phrase that appears in one of her articles, co-authored with fellow youth worker–academic Louise Doherty, is evocative: 'youth work that refuses to disappear'. Why, I ask, have youth clubs hung on despite all the difficulties? 'Because young people want spaces where they can be themselves, express themselves and create their cultures,' she said. 'Even if they don't know the notion of a youth club, young people will say, if asked, that they want somewhere to go. "Couldn't there be a building where we could do things we enjoy, where we could do arts or drama or football, where it's informal and not like school?"' Tania pauses, and smiles. 'If youth clubs didn't exist, they'd be invented by young people, again and again.' This, it transpires, is precisely what has happened.

There is no Year Zero, a point in time when UK youth clubs arrived, fully formed. However, there is a family tree of sorts that helps us understand where they came from. The period known as the Industrial Revolution, roughly between 1760 and the mid-1800s, provides an unexpectedly early starting point as we try to understand how so many of us ended up living down the road from a space where teenagers could play ping-pong, make music or simply hang out with friends.

Within the burgeoning British Empire, cities including Manchester, London and Liverpool began to generate new forms of wealth disparity between factory workers and their bosses, and they did so with an extremity unmatched by our European neighbours. Children and young people paid the price, with the children of workers in the UK starting employment, on average, at the age of ten. Youth work academics generally tend to start their histories during this era, when colonial wealth powered industrialisation.

In 1980, Sidney Bunt and Ron Gargrave wrote one of the classic texts, *The Politics of Youth Clubs*, and described the 'squalor' of Victorian society. Industrialisation, they believed, had played out in specific ways here: 'in no other town in Europe did the extremes of human existence meet in so horrifying a way as in London . . . What was true of London was equally so of large towns and cities in the United Kingdom.' While rural people had long been poor, the sheer numbers in the cities must have made it easier for motivated individuals to engage in collective community action. Additionally, the struggles of large numbers of newly urbanised people were visible to the existing middle classes in a way they might not have been when families were starving in villages dotted across a county or whole country. The cities acted as a magnifying glass.

It was inevitable, during a period of great change, that some adults would consider what the next generation needed, and that motivated youths would organise entertainment, education and respite for themselves. After all, there's something very human about noticing what is required and attending to it. I believe that needs, whether they're practical or emotional, contain energy that can be harnessed, an idea best expressed in the phrase 'behaviour is communication'. Youth clubs exist on these islands because of mills, factories and mines, and the needs – and behaviours – these workplaces generated for children and young people, including the need for downtime with peers away from factory bosses.

Given that youth clubs are often considered an informal wing of education, let's take a look at the ways proto-classrooms emerged differently across the nations. Churches had been closely involved in early forms of education, with author Mark K. Smith writing that youth work 'emerged largely out of the activities of evangelical Christians during the first half of the nineteenth century'. The Society for Promoting Christian Knowledge in England was one such group, founded by lords and lawyers in 1698, who were concerned about the growth of what they saw as immorality in England and decided this was best addressed by encouraging Christian education at all levels. They built libraries in market towns and founded charity schools.

Similarly named but separate, the Society in Scotland for Propagating Christian Knowledge appeared in 1709, focusing on evangelising in the Scottish Highlands, insisting on the use of English, not Scots Gaelic, and resisting Catholicism. The existence of the Society in Scotland also helps explain why youth work evolved differently in that country. In England much of it has Anglican roots – with the 'Anglo' aspect of this offshoot of Protestantism meaning they did not concern themselves too much with life north of the border.

In Wales, educational entities known as Circulating Schools started in 1731, when converted Methodist Griffith Jones made it his business to create roving schools in churches, barns, farmhouses and cottages, with teachers staying in each location for three or four months at a time during autumn or winter. Children and adults were to acquire basic reading skills, but not writing or arithmetic, as this was considered unnecessary. All were expected to learn psalms, parables and prayers by rote, and the demonisation of Catholics was an explicit part of the curriculum.

Across Occupied Ireland, necessarily secret *scoileanna scairte*, or hedge schools, sprung up after 1695, when the Penal Laws made it illegal for Catholics or other non-conforming denominations to set up schools. As depicted in Brian Friel's famous play *Translations*, children learned poetry, history and home economics alongside Greek and Latin, all taught in the Irish language. Examples from Éire are instructive and can be summarised as follows: if state structures don't offer the necessary provision, leaving gaps, groups and individuals will very likely step in, to try to offer whatever is deemed relevant as recompense.

Sunday Schools, the first of which is recorded at St Mary's in Nottingham in 1751, appeared in the wake of the mass exodus to the city. Often free to attend, or at least affordable, these were mixed environments where boys and girls could learn and socialise together. And, for hundreds of years, before compulsory education began in England in the late 1800s, tradespeople and labourers could spend some of their wages sending their children to 'dame schools', which were often run by women, some widowed, others unmarried.

Emma Griffin's alternative history of the Industrial Revolution, *Liberty's Dawn*, draws from 350 autobiographies penned by working-class people. In one, she describes a notice, printed near Manchester in the early 1820s, which paints a very familiar picture. Addressed to 'poor people in Preston and the neighbourhood', it informs them of 'a Sunday school, for youth of both sexes, from fourteen to twenty-one years of age', which will be 'kept in a commodious room'. While ping-pong was some years off, the youth club was beginning to come into view.

Our sketchy family tree of youth clubs as we know them grows from this collective material: industrialisation, increasing literacy, church evangelism, plus a colonial mentality that extended, to some extent, to low-paid British people as well as those in far-off countries, along with intermittent government responses to the human cost of massive private profits. Legislation attempted to balance industrialisation with the rights of the youngest children. The Factory Act of 1833, to give just one example, stated a maximum working week of 48 hours for nine- to thirteen-year-olds across Great Britain, with two hours of schooling per day for under-thirteens. An Inspectorate of Factories was created, albeit with only four staff to cover 4,000 mills. At the same time, socially influential individuals began to organise spaces for adult factory workers. One example is the Brighton Working Men's Institute, established in 1849, which offered recreation and cultural education in order to divert 'energies and ambitions' away from 'social agitation and hostility to religion'. Working men's clubs and mechanics' institutes proliferated – a kind of youth club for grown folks.

In England, education became formalised and compulsory in 1870 with the Elementary Education Act, which ensured schooling for children aged five to thirteen, and then, in 1876, with compulsory education for most eleven- to thirteen-year-olds. The type of person in charge at a dame school or hedge school probably went on to teacher training. Some of their temperamental ancestors, however, would have entered the informal wing that provides the subject of this book.

Unemployment was another important driver, as it would be throughout the youth club story. For example, during the

American Civil War (1861–5) cotton couldn't be shipped to the mills and factories of England's north. In the UK, this caused unemployment. Local clergy set up daytime sewing classes for nearly 3,000 girls, who would receive aid if they attended. This example of youth work as a response to unemployment, and of the use of incentives, was echoed more than a century later in the 1980s' Youth Training Schemes (YTS), whose primary role was arguably to delete young people from the headline unemployment figures.

When many of us think of the YMCA, we'll think of the dance inspired by the Village People song. The organisation, of course, goes back much further than the disco hit. Formed in London in 1844, initially as a prayer and Bible study group designed to address the spiritual welfare of young men working in drapery, it quickly grew to address other issues affecting those moving from the countryside to the city.

In the early days of the organisation, the YMCA set up local associations, running public lectures, education classes, reading rooms and refreshment areas for young working men. By 1852, the organisation was to be found in Wales too, and had spread internationally, with over a thousand YMCA secretaries worldwide by the end of the decade. Fast-forward to the mid-2020s, and they're still working with and for the youth, running over two hundred free youth clubs each week in seventy-eight of their centres across England and Wales.

As I researched, a thought began percolating at the back of my mind: what was so dangerous about drapery? After all, fears about this particular trade had kick-started an international organisation that is still alive and well today. Deborah Wynne, a professor of nineteenth-century literature, offered an answer in her 2015 essay 'The "Despised Trade" in Textiles'. 'The draper was viewed as an anomaly among men,' she wrote, 'despised for his association with a largely female world of fashion.' Her fascinating work, delving into shop life beyond memory, helps me understand why these workers attracted the attentions of saviour evangelists. Aside from the undercurrent conflation of effeminacy and homosexuality, the 'live-in' system required young male shop assistants to live communally on or near their employers' premises. On top of that, wages and conditions were poor and the hours long. Drapery attracted men who loved style and wanted to work with fabric, despite the marginalisation and stigma, and perhaps because, in ways that might have been hard to articulate at the time, they'd find kindred spirits in the trade. Suddenly, the Village People's hit seems prescient.

In autumn 1863, the Reverend Arthur Sweatman presented a paper to the Social Science Association in Edinburgh. He outlined a new entity that had emerged to cater for those too young for the working men's clubs and mechanics' institutes, with the first example opening in Dover in 1857 and reaching London three years later. He argued with some passion for an urgent national roll-out of such interventions, which, he said, 'have acquired the distinctive title of Youths' Clubs or Institutes'.

Defining the class 'contemplated' by these associations, he outlined the ideal demographic: boys and young men aged thirteen to nineteen who had left school and were working in junior positions – for example, as a clerk in an office or warehouse, as errand boys or apprentices. Describing these lads as capable of 'appreciating a superior kind of recreation', presumably unlike those undertaking manual labour, he explained what he believed they needed: recreation, companionship, reading and instruction, 'all of a pure and healthy kind'. Using the Islington Youths' Institute as an example, he described a warm and well-lit room that was open on weekday evenings until 9.30 p.m. during the winter months, offering a large central table spread with newspapers and magazines, and smaller tables covered in red baize offering games including chess and draughts. Members were required to attend classes too, picking from a less fun-sounding list that included book-keeping and elocution. Attracting a steady membership of around a hundred, with nightly attendances ranging from fifty to seventy-five, the club had a cricket team over the summer and offered an energetic set of excursions, inter-club visits and tournaments, and social meetings at Christmas or Easter.

We can't know how Reverend Sweatman's words went down at the time. Maybe those in the audience nodded in agreement or shook their heads, or just carried on smoking their pipes. However, we do know that the words travelled, because five years later the text of his speech was included in a book by Henry Solly, entitled *Working Men's Clubs and Educational Institutes*. It is now considered the earliest known call for a national network of youth clubs. Youths' institutes were taken up by a range of voluntary organisations, including the ragged schools. An illustration from one of their clubs, on Latymer Road in west London, and drawn in 1880, shows a happy hubbub: young men reading at a long table, others playing chess and dominos, and a small group engaged in woodwork and painting. An instructional sign hangs on the back wall in large, capitalised text, an early example of enduring youth club signage. It reads: 'Hats Off'.

The Reverend Arthur Sweatman said something else, a couple of lines that transcend the unknowable social context of the mid-1800s, and which bring a big smile to my face. 'It will be quite understood that any attempt to prescribe a scheme of universal applicability must be hopeless,' he said. 'Local circumstances must greatly guide any plans undertaken for the purpose in question.' The words could have been written today, at least by anyone who understands how youth clubs operate on the ground, and these words, from over a century ago, offer a timeless riposte to policy-makers and their enduring preference for centralised solutions.

An important and adjacent line in our family tree is comprised of those connected through 'old boys' networks to prestigious universities. Here, wealthy men were motivated by one or more of the following: social or religious conscience; a desire to impart the values of the wealthy to those without such values (or wealth) in their family networks; intrigue about those outside their own demographic; or fear of the social changes that might be wrought by young and increasingly literate workers. Institutions including the Church of England, public schools and the universities of Oxford and Cambridge feature heavily in this lineage.

As alluded to earlier, the concept of sending missionaries around England, instead of just to the colonies, had been gaining ground in the latter part of the 1800s, as concern about widening inequality began to take hold. New railway lines made it easier for vicars and academics to travel around and spread the word about a new idea: missions. One aspect of this involved clergymen, often from a socially radical Christian tradition, generating undergraduate sympathy and nudging them into action: setting up a committee, collecting promises of subscriptions and opening a space, usually for boys.

Uppingham was the first, followed by Winchester, which established an East End Mission in London Docks in 1876. Eton followed in 1880. Ernest Pilkington was one of the early volunteers, joining his friend who'd set up a boys' club at the Eton Mission House at 27 Gainsborough Road in Hackney Wick. His memoir, *An Eton Playing-Field: A Reminiscence of Happy Days Spent at the Eton Mission*, was published a decade later and contains a famous refusal. 'I am not going to give any harrowing detail of the lives of the very poor,' he stated flatly. 'It would not do anybody any good.' Instead, his reminiscences describe the mission's focus on sports and fitness.

Pilkington and friends taught swimming in the filthy Hackney Cut and set up nine football pitches in Victoria Park after tiring of uneven ground and the need to use a hat and an umbrella for goalposts. Shinpads were disallowed as 'unsporting', despite the real-life penalties faced by injured boys who couldn't work. In an early example of youth work's long arc, and the idiocy of short-term evaluation, it's worth saying that the Victoria Park football pitches remain in use, as do those the mission built in nearby Hackney Marshes when the original pitches became over-subscribed. The Eton Mission Rowing Club survived the Blitz, but not the 2012 Olympics, when a substantial part of the building suffered compulsory purchase so a 'legacy bridge' could be built that would take journalists, and later Hackney Wick residents, across the water.

Alongside descriptions of dances, concerts, lectures and sing-songs, lively enough to attract drunken men whom volunteers would have to keep out, there are admissions of difficulty at the mission. 'We had a good many "ructions" of one kind of another,' wrote Pilkington. On one occasion, the boys had blown the gas pipes out ('that never-failing source of amusement') and 'all sorts of missiles – boxing-gloves, bagatelle-balls, draughts and chessmen – flew about the room'. Large patches of plaster had fallen from the walls and the place 'looked like becoming a total wreck'.

Reading their reminiscences now, the old boys seemed relatively unfazed by the violence, but perhaps it was familiar to them. After all, the Bullingdon Club, historically popular with Old Etonians, in which members were required to be riotous, was already a hundred years old at this point. Either way, the missionaries tried different ways of turning the young people's interests towards less destructive activities. In an appendix to Pilkington's book, C. G. Kekewick described how mission leaders came up with the idea of night runs, which took the ragged crew across the marsh, through the streets of Bow and occasionally as far as Epping Forest. 'When the fellows came back from a run they were quite incapable of doing any mischief that night.' The scheme worked, and would be replicated in unexpected ways by future youth leaders.

Mission work laid a foundation upon which a corner of UK athletics could be built. In John Few's history of Eton Manor, he explained that it emerged from a split with the mission and, in 1913, set up a purpose-built sports complex in Hackney Wick, where public school tutors and top-flight sports instructors offered everything from table tennis to running. Olympic boxer Harry Mallin was an early success story, a middleweight who won gold in 1920 and 1924. By the early 1920s, Eton Manor and three Old Etonians bought three acres on Hackney Marsh, tidying up the original mission football pitches and adding, among other things, rugby and cricket pitches, courts for tennis, netball and squash, and a full-size running track. The latter was floodlit in 1951 – the first in England to be illuminated in this way – and had been laid with track used during the Summer Olympics that had taken place three years earlier. One of the runners to benefit from the track at Eton Manor was Roger Bannister, who in 1954 became the first British man to be recorded running a mile in under four minutes.

In the early days of what would become the Settlement Movement, in the late 1800s, this long view was unavailable, and within a few years the missions were considered insufficient. In *Practicable Socialism*, Reverend Samuel Barnett and his wife asked their readers to imagine a visit to the Mission District of their college, where one might expect to see the positive effects of 'loving supervision'. Instead, the authors said, one would find 'an Ireland in England'. It's a comparison that explicitly links in-country work to the colonial missionaries, albeit ones who'd take trains or buses, not boats. The pair went on to describe 'people paying 3s. or 4s. a week for rooms smaller than Irish cabins, without the pure air of the Irish hillside, and with vice which adds depth to squalor'. It's one particular phrase, though, that evokes the human tendency to notice the needs of the young: 'Even the children,' they wrote, 'are not joyful.'

Reverend Barnett was one of the individuals who appeared repeatedly, attempting to apply their structural power to communities made poor by systems that enriched their peers. He attended Oxford University, became a vicar and took work at St Jude's in Whitechapel, east London. By 1875, he was returning to his old college, spreading news of poverty and seeking funds. The college missions, he said, had achieved some of their aims but were, by their nature, limited. He proposed a new scheme to supersede the missions: university Settlements, funded by colleges and alumni. Settlements should be purpose-built in an impoverished quarter, and, unsurprisingly, given his workplace's location, he suggested east London. Buildings should contain 'habitable chambers and large reception rooms' and 'common ground for all classes' through lectures, music and play in conversation rooms, and through weekly receptions for 'all sorts and conditions of men' where the settlers – the university students and graduates – 'would mingle freely in the crowd'. The idea was that the rich would come and live among the low-paid, and from this position of apparent togetherness, dispense blessings.

Committees were formed, subscriptions were raised, and in 1884 the first Settlement House, Toynbee Hall, opened in Whitechapel. The universities of Oxford and Cambridge essentially divided London up, with the former focusing on the famously poverty-stricken East End and Cambridge taking south London. Within these areas, they'd run what we'd now describe as youth provision. By 1887, there were enough boys' clubs to require an umbrella association: the Federation of London Working Boys' Clubs.

In the same year, female students at Cambridge's Girton and Newnham colleges played catch-up for the girls, founding Blackfriars Settlement. New College Settlement in Edinburgh (1893) and Bristol University Settlement (1911) followed. The idea would spread nationally and beyond: by 1911, there were forty-nine Settlements across the UK, 400 in the USA, and Settlement houses in Austria, Finland, Russia, Germany, Canada, Japan and Palestine. Settlements are acknowledged as central to the emergence of social work practice and research, in the UK and globally.

Bricks and mortar housed a variety of beliefs relating to the interests of founders and settlers. Sometimes the foundational focus related to social activism, other times evangelism or gender. Patchwork beginnings, and the lack of a national framework or direction, ensured local flavour in each Settlement. Such variance would be replicated in the youth clubs that followed. Part of this is to do with the energy and determination often present in the young; as youth clubs have found throughout history, if users don't like an offering, they won't attend. If they are in the building, then there's a reasonable chance that they'll bend the offering to better fit what they want or need, regardless of the founder's intention.

There are long-lasting cultural and sporting legacies from the Mission Houses, Settlements, Boys' Brigades and clubs, often in the shape of buildings that remain broadly oriented towards the poorly paid. For example, poverty-reduction centre Toynbee Hall, creative community space Blackfriars Settlement and community arts hub Oxford House fit this category and are all still operational as charities in east London. Barton Hill in Bristol now operates as Wellspring Settlement, and Manchester Settlement is still going in Openshaw.

New spaces, including those imagined and paid for by members of the 'officer class' in the spirit of control and containment, created pipelines for sporting talent. They generated local resources and created spacious environments where culture could be expressed collectively. In a small way, members could shape the activities, offering a rare opportunity to exert power, and occasionally to turn a request – say, for free cocoa or more football – into a reality. Power – or the possibility of influence – was planted here too.

Perhaps, by offering respite and an opportunity for sport, art or education, these early youth spaces created a new type of person. Majority-worker communities were joined by small numbers of economically cushioned people who didn't need to work long hours for low pay, and who may themselves have learned new ways of thinking and being in these environments. Youth clubs would have schooled those who volunteered in them too.

———

Reverend Jonathan Roberts is a cultural descendant of the clerics and social workers who created the Settlements. He's also one of the many youth work experts who combine their knowledge with on-the-ground action – in his case, as an Anglican minister. I'd been chatting to the headteacher of a comprehensive school I'd been involved with for years, and she mentioned that I should talk to him, and so off I went to the vicarage, just off the Walworth Road in Camberwell, south London.

Reverend Roberts was a charming host, able to punctuate a hundred-miles-an-hour conversation with furious googling in order to fill in the gaps regarding one sidestream or another. He's a lifelong youth worker as well as a senior lecturer on the subject, who picked up his love of music from Saturday nights dancing to Motown, reggae and pop at youth club discos in Birmingham. He's also the author of the highly readable *Youth Work Ethics*, written to support students on youth and community work degrees. When we met, he was also chair of the church youth club.

'Youth work was one of the things that came out of the Settlements,' he explained over a cup of tea. 'Another thing they [the settlers] all found was that there was much more they wanted to understand about the nature of poverty.

'It – youth work – comes when there's lots of young people. In the nineteenth century, everyone rushes into the industrial cities; there are masses of young people, they're all having sex with each other and producing children, and their children are all dying because the sanitation is so bloody awful.' He then identified an unexpected strand in the youth club lineage: the Broadwick Street water pump in Soho.

Cholera, he said, was a big motivating factor in the mid-1800s. By the end of 1840, Dr John Snow and his friend, the Reverend Henry Whitehead, had worked out that the disease wasn't airborne, as most people thought. It was the result of clean water being contaminated with waste, and it was being transmitted through water pumps. 'The moment the water companies started separating sewage, people stopped dying,' explained Reverend Roberts. 'Everyone's still producing twelve children, but, now, more than two will survive.' He paused and turned away from his computer screen. 'It's one of the reasons youth work starts,' he said. 'Because you've got an enormous amount of young people. You've got to do something with them.'

Walking back to the bus stop on the Walworth Road, at kicking-out time for the local schools, I think back over our lively and informative conversation and wonder about the widely held assumption that youth clubs are for getting kids off the street. This assumes that pavements are bad places; a culturally specific assertion even, once you remove the tendency to move inside as a reasonable response to the frequently wet and often chilly British weather. Streets are neither good nor bad. Young people are not inherently likely to cause trouble. The street is part of public life, forming an essential aspect of the civic space that democracy requires. Ideally, young people would be as welcome on high streets, in parks and on low walls as any other demographic, but in a world that fetishises youth while not liking actual young people very much, we're some distance from this kind of equal access. And if we do want young people 'off the streets', I think, watching a high-energy bundle of kids in blazers getting on the bus, then we'd better provide space for them.

In what you might consider a maternal line, trade unions also played their part, at least once they'd been legalised in 1867. The National Union of Women Workers evolved from several groups that came together for a series of conferences, and which coalesced nearly two decades later in Liverpool, in 1891. This was not a trade union as we might imagine it today, run by hard-knock men with megaphones. Instead, it was a non-political organisation of wealthy middle-class women who wanted to improve the daily lives of their working sisters. While far from an attempt at structural change, their beliefs, and actions, generated powerful subcommittees whose influence is still felt today. The National Association of Youth Clubs (NAYC), later rebranded as Youth Clubs UK and again to UK Youth, can be traced back to two of these: the Girls' Club Sectional Committee and the Rest Rooms Special Committee. Agenda items turned into physical spaces. Adults laid out chairs, cocoa and biscuits, and the girls came streaming through the doors.

The National Organisation of Girls' Clubs (NOGC) was founded in February 1911 by the coming together of unions of girls' clubs, in London, Liverpool, Manchester, Salford, Nottingham, Glasgow and York, with individual clubs joining from across England, Wales and Scotland. It was rooted in girls and their work. 'The original intention of the NOGC was to support clubs for girls and young women in factories, whose work in industry was long and hard,' reads the preamble to the NAYC archive, which is located underneath a tower block on the Birmingham University campus. 'Many of the clubs of the time were places of refuge for the girls and an essential means of support.' Activities listed included crafts, reading, drama, music, singing, lectures and discussions, and members were encouraged to take part in the running of their clubs. The organisation campaigned to improve working conditions, encouraged the development of new clubs, trained club leaders and produced publications and resources for leaders and members.

By the penultimate decade of the 1800s, foundational clubs for factory girls had become the subject of newspaper commentary. In April 1888, the *Manchester Times*' anonymous weekend columnist, 'A Lady Contributor', wrote of the growing number of clubs for these factory girls, explaining that the Factory Helpers' Union and the Recreative Evening Classes Association had helped establish several clubs. Luckily for future readers, she described the practicalities. A large comfortable room would be borrowed from sympathetic friends or rented from the school board and made 'as attractive as possible' with brightly coloured tablecloths, a 'good fire' and plenty of light. Girls paid a subscription and ladies decided among themselves what should take place. Sewing and singing classes, reading, writing and arithmetic lessons and picture-frame-making were on offer, along with games and a lending library. Girls would either buy or be given cost-price cocoa and two biscuits, with a prayer and a hymn before closing time at 10 p.m. Religious observance aside, it's not too different from the picture a century down the line.

Other threads connect youth clubs of the past to present scenarios. A report from a club our Lady Contributor covered describes catering to 'a very rough set' of thirteen- to seventeen-year-olds and contains lively colour. 'The door bursts open and four or five girls come tumbling in, one on top of another, after the manner of Newfoundland puppies,' she writes. Some went straight to the warmth of the fireplace, with others holding out 'a grimy paw for a friendly handshake'. In a telling phrase, the writer evokes the ageless ways in which society creates tiny spaces for the poorly paid and over-worked to take control: 'the spirit of Misrule is rampant'. In this telling, factory girls are akin to peasants. As with the Lord of Misrule, who'd preside over unruly annual parties in the Middle Ages, they're able to let off steam.

A few months later, the *Manchester Times* columnist reported again, this time from a conference held at the Soho Club in Greek Street, London, aimed at 'stimulating efforts for the establishment and encouragement of girls' clubs'. There were now so many such places in different parts of London that a guide to clubs, homes and refuges for girls and women was about to be issued. The impulse was also being felt across the Atlantic, with the conference reporting that there were now fifteen clubs in New York. The American context provided a novel idea: club leaders over there were encouraging young people to take control of club management, 'an arrangement which proved exceedingly beneficial'.

Reading from a distance of more than a century, I can sense the pleasing shock of this suggestion, which upturns some very basic ideas about who should be in charge in an

English situation, and how quickly this novel arrangement is reimagined in service of the status quo. 'If the girls are at all rough and disorderly – and in many clubs this is sure to be the case – the best check on their wildness is to make the members themselves the preservers of order,' she declared, thinking out loud. 'If rough girls or boys freely elect policemen from among their own number they will almost always obey them more readily than they will anyone else.'

The column ends with another observation that has resonance today, both in terms of young people and the criminal justice system, and the ways in which youth work fundamentally alters relationships, particularly for those who arrive from a position of material comfort. The writer, who I assume is a woman of means, is up in arms at the imprisonment of two fifteen-year-old girls for public drunkenness, and suggests that clubs might 'protect' youngsters who are brought into a police court for a first offence. The use of the word tells me that the writer has understood, perhaps through her own interactions with young people, variances in the way that citizens are criminalised. 'One is indignant to think of two children going to jail for taking a little too much drink,' she writes. Wild and rough animals with grimy paws have become human and, momentarily, even familial.

Youth clubs in the distant past overlapped with the criminal justice system. It remains so today, with government long conflating youth provision with crime prevention. Most adults who have worked in youth clubs, or adjacent environments, will have come into contact with the criminal justice system through young people they know and care about. It's also worth saying that we in the UK believe that young people are responsible for their actions at a very young age: criminal responsibility in England, Wales and Northern Ireland begins at the age of ten years old. This is anomalous by international standards, where the average is twelve, according to campaign group Penal Reform International.

When I was working at *Live Magazine*, this meant occasionally writing character references, or attending court cases, so that those within the judicial process could meet a defendant through their skills and interests: for example, as a committed member of the editorial team. Sometimes the young person probably had broken the law, and, often, they'd been groomed into criminality by older and more powerful adults. Other times I suspected they had been scooped up by the police for offence A because the police believed they'd committed offence B, or because of affiliation through neighbourhood or family to known criminals. Frequently, my whiteness and social mobility came into sharp relief as I observed differences in the degree to which people could – or couldn't – get away with breaking the law, and the differing ways criminality was assumed, or not, in a teenager. Or as the poet Yomi Ṣode asks in his collection *Manorism*: 'Who gets to get away with it?'

There was also a period when a few of us had ongoing correspondence between our youth-run magazine office and contributors with addresses that began 'HMP'. Many years, and a few further stretches in prison, later, one such young person came along to my first book launch. Another rings me up sometimes to ask about my family. In the low-judgement zone of a youth club situation, bonds can be deep and long-lasting.

2

1645: A SHORT REWIND

Before we move on, into the twentieth century, let's stop briefly and think about the word 'club'. We use it so easily, but what does it mean and where did it come from? The club, as a place of association for like-minded people with similar interests, is linked by some linguists to the use of etched sticks as a way of inviting people to ancient village meetings or drinks, in the same way that 'staff' once meant a piece of wood that indicated your job role – think Gandalf – and now means 'employee'.

The idea doesn't quite fit and it feels like suggesting that kindling is the same as fire. Discovering the Germanic root word *klumbon*, meaning 'clump', helps explain the name-roots of the kind of club a caveman might swing, but doesn't get me much further towards understanding how a word for a weapon came to signal togetherness.

So I get digging, back down the back of the internet's sofa, and come across an intriguing suggestion on a forum that the use of the word to suggest association dates back to the English Civil War, which took place in three waves between 1642 and 1651. History blogger and freelance photographer Haydn Wheeler, who wrote and published *Clubmen 1645*, describes Parliamentarian and Royalist armies alike rolling repeatedly through towns and villages across the country, stealing horses, weapons and food, and burning crops and houses in their wake. Thousands of townspeople and villagers were attacked and displaced. Sorrow, starvation and disease inevitably followed.

Farmers, craftsmen and a small number of local gentry, mostly in the south-west and Welsh borders, joined together in a refusal to pick sides. Local groups emerged and became known as 'Clubmen', emblazoning their intentions on a now-lost banner:

If you offer to plunder
or take our cattle
Be assured we will
bid you battle.

Clubbing together offered a powerful third way to protect everyday people against both armies. In 1645, over a thousand Clubmen gathered at Woodbury Hill in Worcestershire to present a petition to the local governor, Gilbert Gerard. The text announced that they considered club work their duty, and that they had been 'enforced to associate ourselves in a mutual league for each other's defence . . . protecting and safeguarding our persons and estates by the mutual aid and assistance of each other against all murders, rapines, plunder, robberies, or violences which shall be offered by the soldier or any oppressor whatsoever'.

It's a remarkably recognisable declaration, made timeless by writers three and a half centuries older than us who opted for collective action. It's an idea that exists in the natural world too, as low-growing plants clump together to preserve heat and protect one another from the wind and the cold. Across time and space, conflict has required like-minded people to work together as a buffer against external pressures. In doing so, they have formed clubs.

The word was absorbed into the world of the monied and structurally powerful, with the first gentleman's club, White's, opening in London in 1693. Such clubs were also a form of protection, arguably against wealth-sharing, and they grew in number over the ensuing decades. Eventually, the kind of gentlemen who might have taken membership of the Carlton Club, founded in 1832 and still going today, formed or supported Boys' Clubs, so that young folk on poor wages could also experience some benefits of mutuality. Women left at home while their men went to the club, meanwhile, set up spaces for factory girls.

Youth clubs exist, if only in the linguistic sense, because of Englishness as it relates to power.

3

1909: SCOUTS IN ENGLAND AND IRELAND

The era of youth club history that emerged out of Queen Victoria's divided and industrialised society was comprised of a patchwork of provision. Boys' and girls' clubs catering to teenage workers in factories and mills would be joined by Scouts and various Brigades, alongside the existing layer of youth provision at Sunday Schools and in Settlement Houses.

Uniformed youth organisations sit on a particular branch of the youth club family tree. They proliferated in the early twentieth century, all across Europe, in some cases strategically metastasized by fascist leaders. Uniformed organisations also spread with empire. While some young people have benefited from the space and welcome offered by these groups, they're categorically different to the youth clubs of this book, mostly because of the unavoidable hierarchy built into organisations with military roots.

Zooming in on the most famous of these – the Scouts – helps explain the differences, and offers additional clarity around the distinct shape of youth club spaces in the UK. The founder of the Boy Scouts was Robert Baden-Powell, who had been a young army officer stationed in India under the British Empire and then in South Africa during the Boer War. He developed new and unorthodox techniques for wartime reconnaissance and map-making, techniques known as 'scouting', and wrote a short military handbook on the subject.

By 1903, when he returned to England, his booklet had escaped from the Army library and was being used by youth leaders and teachers in England to teach observation and woodcraft. Invitations to talk at meetings and rallies followed, including one run by an existing uniformed organisation, the Boys' Brigade. The Brigade's founder, a Glaswegian named William Smith, set Baden-Powell a task: to develop a technique to inculcate good citizenship into boys. In response, Baden-Powell ran the first Scout Camp, for twenty boys from a range of backgrounds, in 1907, and rewrote his war manual for a young audience. *Scouting for Boys* was published the following year, with the subtitle: *A Handbook for Instruction in Good Citizenship Through Woodcraft*. It aimed to promote 'the vast reserve of loyal patriotism and Christian spirit lying dormant in our nation' and was written in the form of twenty-eight 'campfire yarns'. It went on to sell over 100 million copies worldwide and inspired the international movement that continues to this day.

Baden-Powell's Scouts and the Girl Guides, founded by his sister Agnes in 1910, were, from the start, strongly connected to the military, and not just through the founder's experience as an Army officer. Historian John Springhall quotes the organisation's first chief Scout commissioner, Sir Edmund Elles, in an instructive potted biography that outlines a military career and a role as colonial commander in Peshawar, India. Elles is quoted, tellingly, stating that his 'sole objective' in taking the role was 'for the purpose of getting recruits for the Territorials'.

The military aspect of Scouting created an immediate response in Ireland, itself still occupied by Britain. Louise Hurley's paper, 'The Historical Development of Irish Youth Work (1850–1985)', described the roots of modern youth work in England, emerging when individuals and groups, 'usually from the influential sector of society, motivated by anxiety about disorder, initiated provisions aimed at social improvement and control of working class young people'.

She also examined the influence of Irish politician, revolutionary, socialist and suffragist Countess Constance Markievicz, who responded to Robert Baden-Powell's Scouts by co-founding Irish nationalist youth organisation Na Fianna Éireann. Launched in 1909 in Dublin, it offered an alternative to the British Boys' Brigades and Boy Scout troops forming in Ireland.

Na Fianna Éireann would train young people in establishing an independent Ireland through military exercises, Irish history and language, and had its own version of Scout's Honour: 'I promise to work for the independence of Ireland, never to join England's armed forces, and to obey my superiors.' Troops were formed across Ireland. Historian Marnie Hay, in *Na Fianna Éireann and the Irish Revolution 1909–23: Scouting for Rebels*, described Fianna as 'military trailblazers of the Irish nationalist movement in the early twentieth century', tracking the role of members in the 1916 Easter Rising, the War of Independence and Irish Civil War. Rebel scouts, she wrote, would form 'the era's most significant Irish nationalist youth group in terms of size and impact on the Irish struggle for independence'. Continuing to exist as a dissident republican youth organisation during the Troubles, and beyond, Na Fianna Éireann remains a proscribed organisation in the UK.

Interwoven youth work histories would divert along the road to Irish independence, which arrived in 1921, when the Anglo-Irish Treaty retained British rule in the north-east of the island. In Northern Ireland, youth clubs developed that would be mutually recognisable, if localised, to peers in Cardiff, Middlesbrough or Bournemouth. In the new Free State, later the Republic of Ireland, the cultural soil was different. Clubs organised by the St Vincent de Paul Society or Brigades did appear, but they didn't take root and spread in the same way as they did in Britain or Northern Ireland. Some leaders in the new republic were setting their sights on the past as a route to the future, and, by the 1920s, the Gaelic Athletic Association (GAA) was flourishing, with the intention to 'pass on belief, values, attitudes which would ensure the continuation or revival of a traditional culture'. Local branches provided space, instruction and opportunities to take part in sport, music and dancing deemed sufficiently Irish.

Youth club stories are seen with fresh clarity when observed from across the water.

1939: LAYING THE FOUNDATIONS

Recovery from the First World War was very much a long haul, and local organisations, including youth clubs, played a vital part in pulling life back together on the ground. In 1916, the government drew on voluntary sector organisations, including the Boys' Brigade, in order to form the Central Juvenile Organisations Committee, 'to liaise with educational bodies and to co-ordinate the provision of recreational facilities for young people', according to youth club historian and youth worker Sue Robertson, a situation formalised in the 1918 and 1921 Education Acts, which allowed local authorities to spend taxpayer money on youth facilities.

By 1919, 203 clubs and twenty unions of clubs had signed up to the National Association of Girls' Clubs. Young Farmers' Clubs were formed in rural England and Wales, first in Hemyock, Devon, in 1921, after the United Dairies milk factory ran a calf-rearing competition for children in the area. Focusing on the Welsh language and culture, Urdd Gobaith Cymru (the Welsh League of Youth) was established in 1922, with early work taking place in the home of founder Sir Ifan ab Owen Edwards, in Llanuwchlyn, Gwynedd, north-west Wales. Provision in Wales was substantial: youth service historian Mark K. Smith found fifty-two clubs in industrial areas such as the Rhondda Valley in the 1920s, providing for 9,000 young people.

Training for leaders emerged, with the National Council of Girls' Clubs setting up the first professional training course for youth leaders in 1925. Following a similar-but-different train of thought, youth-hostelling arrived in 1930. In 1935, a grant from the King George V Jubilee Trust helped 'extend club work through the country'. A law passed in 1937, the Physical Training and Recreation Act, created an environment where some councils went beyond sports and fitness provision to provide the first local authority youth centres.

In September 1939, the Second World War broke out, causing a 'significant expansion of clubs, many of them for war workers who were often separated from family and friends'. In this way, youth clubs provided a home from home in a more literal way than elsewhere in this story. 'In June 1940 there were no youth clubs in one small rural area; three years later there were twenty-five,' wrote Sue Robertson, quoting the National Association of Girls' Clubs annual report of 1943, noting that this was probably due to the evacuation of large numbers of children from the cities and the billeting of troops in rural areas. Conflict, again, was affecting the size and shape of clubs across the nations.

Wartime once more prompted government action, including the publication of 'circulars' – written statements containing information and guidelines; a kind of official newsletter. One of these became iconic in youth work circles, and musically minded readers might like to think of it as a riddim or motif that would be referenced repeatedly through the decades. Circular 1486 was published in the first year of war, was titled 'The Service of Youth' and is considered the beginning of the state youth service in England and Wales. It stated that youth work had been a neglected aspect of education, that it was for boys and girls aged between fourteen and twenty who were no longer in full-time education, emphasised youth involvement in club management and encouraged partnership between state and voluntary organisations at a time of great constraints.

Seven months later, Circular 1516 set a 'general aim' that local authorities and voluntary organisations would provide 'social and physical training'. The title nodded to the ongoing way in which young people are seen as troublesome and was set out as follows: 'The Challenge of Youth'. Monies were made available for the voluntary organisations, in the form of grants from local education authorities and the central Board of Education.

In the post-war period, the welfare state was established, with youth clubs seen as 'a fourth province' of the education service. The Education Act of 1944 nominally created a state commitment to a youth service, but did so weakly, noting only that local authorities should offer 'leisure time occupation . . . for any person over compulsory school age' and failing to clarify what 'adequate' facilities looked like. Grammar schools, secondary moderns and technical schools were also created, but never really fulfilled the ideal of offering high-quality education for everyone.

Youth clubs, then, could be seen as a kind of safety net for the large numbers of young people failed by an education system that generated high-quality grammar schools for the few who passed the eleven-plus exam and under-funded secondary moderns for everyone else. Education that mirrored and entrenched class divides was central to the youth club context post-war, even when clubs were widespread and theoretically open to all, just as had been the case when public school 'old boys' were taking boys for night runs at the Settlement Houses.

A name change for the National Association of Girls' Clubs in 1944 reflected a new trend for youth clubs where boys and girls could attend together, the phrase 'and Mixed Clubs' tacked onto the original name. Three houses in Devonshire Street, central London, were purchased, with another rented, offering headquarters and a London house that was available to clubs nationwide. Avon Tyrell, a country house in Hampshire, became the NAYC residential centre in 1949, with two others opening over consecutive years in Scotland (Kilmory Castle) and Wales (Kilvrough Manor), thanks to a grant from the South African Aid to Britain Fund.

In 1946, white supremacist South African leader Jan Smuts, who had been part of the British war cabinet and who was a field marshal in the British Army, presented gold certificates and other monies to the UK government worth over a million pounds (more than £63m in today's money). The gift was described as being 'from the people of South Africa and the High Commission Territories' – now Lesotho, Botswana and Swaziland – 'as an expression of their deep sympathy and admiration for the people of Britain for their heroic war effort'.

Parliamentary record-keeping publication Hansard recorded the government's gratitude, noting that one half of this money, which flowed from South African mines towards the centre of the British Empire, should be dedicated to benefiting the young. 'To the givers of this gift we are profoundly grateful,' said Prime Minister Clement Attlee. 'Those who in the days to come reap the fruits of their generosity will not forget them.' I can't know what effect the gift had on the inner workings of British government. Perhaps none. It is true to say that successive British governments would repeatedly oppose international sanctions against South Africa, until the fall of the apartheid state in 1994 – a 'unique stance', according to Sam Matthews Boehmer in *The International History Review*.

I'm not sure the young people attending NAYC residential houses in England, Scotland or Wales knew who'd paid for their buildings.

By the end of the 1940s, there were training courses and an estimated 1,800 full-time youth workers in post, along with at least 900 new centres opened by local authorities. Thanks to the usual see-saw of funding instability that has plagued youth work, cuts inevitably followed this period of growth. Complaints aired at the National Association of Youth Leaders conference of 1948 and quoted by author Bernard Davies could have come from almost any moment in the youth club timeline: 'local education authorities have made drastic cuts in youth service estimates to such an extent that the maintenance of essential facilities has been impaired'. The need for state-funded youth work wasn't – and isn't – written into law as it is for the NHS and schools. Without a statutory base, it's eternally vulnerable, a little like young people.

Bernard Davies, now an elder statesman of youth work theory and practice, came up through Jewish youth clubs in Manchester in the late 1940s. A former youth work practitioner, he is an influential thinker whose three-volume *History of the Youth Service* remains an essential cornerstone of the literature. He very kindly agreed to an in-person conversation, and met me armed with a big umbrella, just in case it rained, at the railway station in Leamington Spa on a spring afternoon. It was only a ten-minute walk back to his home, but in this short time I was gifted an illuminating socio-demographic exploration of the area's changing streets and a careful description of the local community centre, where he's a trustee.

Bright pinks and greens flowed from flowerpots dotted around his patio, thanks to Sally, Bernard's wife. While Bernard grew up in Manchester, Sally's parents had run a Jewish youth club in east London, a period documented in her mother Celia Rose's fascinating book, *Touching Lives: A Personal History of the Clapton Jewish Youth Centre 1946–1976*. Bernard and Sally first met at a Manchester youth club, and, between them, they have decades of experience and insight, despite wearing their work and successes extremely lightly.

As well as protection from post-war anti-Semitism, the youth clubs Bernard attended offered culture and conversation. For him specifically, this happened because of a person who was to become famous in youth work circles. Stanley Rowe was appointed as the first full-time youth worker at Bernard Davies's local club, after stints at the Kingley Hall Settlement in the East End of London and in Belfast, before his move to Manchester. Stanley's extensive youth work archive is now kept at Birmingham University and he had, said Bernard, 'a huge influence', directly encouraging a number of lads and girls to go into youth work themselves. Additionally, Rowe opened his home to members, in ways that expanded their minds. 'Every Saturday he'd run a discussion group in his cellar, and anyone could turn up,' recalled Bernard. 'He wasn't preaching at us. Suddenly you realised there was permission to ask questions.'

Some of these clubs really stretched the experience and expectations of all the young people, he explained. 'People got huge support to move on in their careers and aspirations.' Crucially, young attendees also absorbed the idea that they could and maybe should contribute to the ecosystem of supporting the next generation. Many young people who encountered Stanley Rowe later worked in the helping professions, said Bernard. 'Many who went on to successful careers did see themselves as having to give something back as well.'

What this told me is that the community instruction to fold benefit back in isn't automatic. It's learned, and it's best learned when you have experienced it yourself. It's one thing to be told that something is important, but it's an entirely different thing to know it first-hand. It is learned in the community, rather than on an individual level. The impulse to contribute comes, I think, when you see it happening from multiple angles. Perhaps this is why so few people in power appear to understand this basic principle of hands-on contribution: they haven't experienced it themselves.

As well as tea and knowledge that day, there was a flow of archive boxes that contained Bernard's university essays and field reports from the middle of the last century. He's one of the personality types that appear infrequently but repeatedly through the youth club story, turning very high levels of education to communal benefit instead of personal profit. In his case, this meant using a degree from Cambridge to undertake a youth leaders qualifying course in Swansea – one of the very few available in the UK in the 1950s.

Inside one of these dove-grey boxes are notes from one of his first placements, in 1958, when he spent two weeks in a then-new youth club in Belfast, where both Catholics and Protestants attended. 'Gosh, what an eye-opener that was,' he said, opening up another way of seeing how youth clubs can operate across lines of faith and conflict. 'Talk about learning through experience. Someone thought it was important enough to set up a youth club which crossed the communities.' He hadn't been aware of the situation across the Irish

Sea, he added, and if he had been, it was only in an incredibly distant way. 'Seeing these Protestant and Catholic kids mixing and talking with each other was a way of introducing me to the realities.' Once more, the effects of youth club spaces, the reasons for their existence and an actual sense of what they could achieve was visible only on the ground.

5

1943: IN SEARCH OF JOSEPHINE MACALISTER BREW

One particularly iconic figure became closely aligned with youth clubs in the 1940s and into the '50s. Her name was Josephine Macalister Brew. She had risen to prominence with her book *In the Service of Youth*, which became a classic of the genre. Compiled from a series of popular talks delivered at meetings and gatherings, it gave me an instant feeling of connection, of having met a kindred spirit across time and space. Her observations rang true, reminding me of my experiences of youth work many decades later: 'We all know the girl in the mackintosh or the boy in the white muffler, who is with difficulty parted from his cap, who comes to the club and never does anything, or indeed seldom speaks to anyone, for whom nevertheless the club must fulfil some need or he would never come at all.' On the criticism that young people just want to 'dance and listen to that horrible jazz and go to the pictures', she makes a couple of cheerful and down-to-earth observations. Firstly, that maligned and scoffed-at popular dance, the Lambeth Walk, was 'a great folk dance of the day'; and, secondly, this gem: 'True culture is the appreciation of everything, from a plate of fish and chips to a Van Gogh.' These sample lines will doubtless resonate with readers who have their own youth club recollections.

Over a period of fifteen years, Josephine Macalister Brew would write three classic books and regularly contribute to national newspapers. *In the Service of Youth* referenced the sector-famous government circular of the same name and was published with an initial print run of 2,000 copies, manufactured using ultra-thin economy paper due to the ongoing war. Demand was high. It was reprinted two months later, and another four times before the following summer. In September 1944, she wrote to her publisher with a recognisable single-mindedness: 'I would be so grateful if you could do something about hurrying up the reprint of my book,' she wrote, in her almost unreadable hieroglyphic handwriting, which was then typed up by a patient secretary–translator. 'It is a book which is so frequently referred to by lecturers in youth service that students themselves are becoming a little frustrated when they find that they simply cannot get hold of a copy either on a bookstall or in a library,' she added. 'As I think I mentioned before, I am so tired of being attacked for it!' The Young Communist League had written to her directly about a bulk order, as it was 'difficult in our Districts to be able to get supplies of the book'.

Jo, as we'll take the liberty of calling her, is someone I would love to have met; big-brained, no-nonsense and funny, totally committed to youth work and unrelenting in her work ethic. She threw herself at life, a tactic that left a lasting footprint on the world and, when combined with a diet consisting largely of strong tea and cigarettes, possibly contributed to her sudden death from stomach cancer in 1957, at the age of fifty-three. While in hospital, she finished her final book, although she did not have time for revisions. Awarded a CBE posthumously, her *Times* obituary stated that 'she understood young people and they knew she did'. Brew comes across vividly in her writing, and in media coverage of her work, as fiercely kind and idiosyncratic, an eminently quotable 'national treasure' type who'd grown up in Newport, Wales, on High Street, where her father was the manager of a shoe shop. Not that anyone would have known this detail about her beginnings. She was extremely private and, it seems, able to shape-shift, to fit in anywhere.

Much of the detail about Brew's home life and background comes from detective work undertaken by youth work expert Mark K. Smith. He'd grown up in youth clubs around Hemel Hempstead, with volunteer youth worker parents, and went on to do the work himself, initially offering time for free during the punk era, then as a youth and community worker in Amersham. Next was a stint at the NAYC, followed by articles, pamphlets and books, including the iconic *Creators Not Consumers* and multiple titles with his regular collaborator Tony Jeffs. In the years before he moved up to Orkney – where, unsurprisingly, he's become a trustee of a village hall – he created a gem-filled digital encyclopaedia of youth work, the endlessly informative Infed.org.

Coming across Jo's work in the NAYC library, he started the long process of discovering the nearly forgotten information, talking to older colleagues who'd worked with her and seeking out contemporaries. Opening the closed doors of time became easier, however, when he contacted Gladys Gildersleve Powell, who had lived with Brew for many years. 'She must have been eighty years old. She had Brew's desk and various bits and bobs in there as well. I went down, had a cup of tea and interviewed her.' In an act of great generosity, Mark sent me the audio file, which he recorded in Gladys's front room circa 1997.

It's a fascinating listen, full of layers and the kind of glitches that the passage of time will deposit on an analogue recording, and which also exist in the complexities of people's lives. The sounds of coffee cups punctuate the pleasantries. Questions are asked and answers are given, initially with some reticence. 'What I do want to know is that what you write is accurate,' said Gladys to her interviewer. 'When you get a character like Jo, who was really, in some ways, a national figure, you get all sorts of legends come up around it.'

Reassured, facts began to flow. Gladys had been teaching PE at Shaftesbury High School in the early 1930s when she met Jo – born Mary Winifred Brew – who joined the school as a history teacher, before moving to Cardiff to pursue journalism and further study. 'She became very involved with work with the adolescents in Tiger Bay and the Valleys,' said Gladys. 'That was the time of the dreadful depression. [There were] Settlements in the Valleys and she got involved in that – and that's how she started.'

It is unclear when Jo added the Ulster-flecked Macalister to her surname, although it seems to have been while she was in Cardiff. What is easier to ascertain is that doing so undoubtedly contained meaning. Names are signals, and new ones, especially, contain messages, even if the meaning is indecipherable from the outside. Three years before war broke out, Jo moved to Lincoln to become youth officer there – one of the first local authority-funded youth work posts in the whole country – and took on the committee-based task of secretary of the Lincoln Federation of Girls' Clubs, before joining the National Association. 'She was a realist,' said Gladys, who had her own youth work life, working for the local authority in Waltham Forest. 'I went up to Lincoln once or twice, and I went to the youth club she set up for the children of the canal barges. She had a good idea in that club. Her principle was, if you break a window, it stays broken until you mend it. If you muck up the wall, it stays like that until you paint it.

'She always started from the young person, not from our idea of what young people ought to be doing. There's no point getting upset with people misbehaving at football matches. The question is always: why do they do it? You can't do anything until you know why. Jo was very much a realist,' said Gladys. 'She looked at young people and saw all their faults, but liked them all the same.' Josephine Macalister Brew, said Gladys, with great authority and radiating pride, 'had *thousands* of ideas'.

By now, an hour or so in, Gladys and her interviewer are chatting like old friends. Did she have a soft spot for young people? asks Mark. 'Very much for young people,' answers Gladys, with a strong emphasis on the 'very'. 'She used to say they're like babies. They fall about, they want help. She was not much use for priggish people or snobbish people or people with cast-iron minds, but she did like fun.' Gladys pauses, perhaps recalling Jo as she was, young and alive. 'I think she thought the worst sin was to not enjoy life. She wanted young people to have the opportunities to *enjoy* it.'

By her forties, Jo had become chief outside consultant on youth for the BBC, according to Melanie Tebbutt of Manchester Metropolitan University, who wrote about the broadcaster's war-era youth programming for the *History Workshop Journal*. She'd realised that Jo worked on the ground-breaking programme *To Start You Talking*, which was designed to be played in youth clubs to generate discussion. Aimed at teenagers, the programme went out on Thursday evenings between 1943 and 1944.

It began with a short drama on a topic – for example, sexual promiscuity or scrounging – with scripts based on round-table conversations with teenagers. The show attracted four million listeners. Melanie dug into the BBC's archives in Caversham and came across a BBC internal circulating memo from October 1942. It announces with relief that Dr Macalister Brew had 'stepped into the breach' to help out. 'She is very definitely a personality,' reads the memo, 'freakish in appearance, but with great gifts. There will, I believe, be no difficulty in establishing her merits, as she is already well known in the Youth Movement and greatly respected . . . She has a very good head, lots of imagination, writes well, and knows the audience thoroughly.' The phrase 'knows the audience' is underlined.

There's only one black-and-white photograph of Jo online, so I look at it again for signs of the BBC's 'freakish' appearance. She is sitting for an official portrait at an out-of-shot desk, pen in hand, as if interrupted mid-flow. The background is plain, suggesting a photographic studio, not a busy office, and she looks out of the frame, facing the camera. She transmits capability and thoughtfulness; strongly grounded. Her hair – platinum blonde, according to Gladys – is tied back and she has a thick fringe. Behind her ears a hairband emerges, a thin strip of ribbon or other dark material, and a small knot or bow sits atop her head. She wears thick-framed, roundish spectacles and a dark blazer, with a buttoned-up white shirt or blouse just visible underneath. It's not possible to tell if the adornment below her throat is a brooch or a tiny bow tie.

Later that year, she travelled to Australia and New Zealand. In Perth, she gave a talk entitled 'Youth and Tomorrow', and in Sydney was 'besieged' by boys and girls at the YMCA. 'National youth work has to compete against the cinema, the commercial dance hall, and the radio and must offer young people something ever more exciting and progressive than these amusements,' she said. The *Sydney Morning Herald* added that Dr Brew could see no reason why Australia shouldn't follow the English example, as 'everyone she had met had told her they were more than 90 per cent British and all Australians seemed to have a Scottish grandmother.' Back home, by 1955 she was fronting a campaign for 1,000 voluntary leaders to join the existing 2,000 youth clubs catering to 130,000 boys and girls. Leaders would be trained courtesy of a grant from King George VI – paid for by that South African gold.

Two years later, she attended a youth clubs event at Queen's University, Belfast. Immediately afterwards, she went into hospital and died soon after emergency surgery for stomach cancer, symptoms of which she had been ignoring. A new blurb was hastily rewritten for her book, *Youth and Youth Groups*, which doubled up as an obituary. The two versions sit next to each other in the archive, like sorrowful sliding doors. Death had prevented her from seeing the book published, but Dr Josephine Macalister Brew had helped generate a strong signal. Youth leaders and their clubs were changing – and society was about to catch up.

6

1958: WELCOME TO THE HARMONY CLUB

Mid-twentieth-century clubs across Britain and Northern Ireland continued to be built upon a patchwork of benevolence and volunteering. In England especially, these often replicated public school values and beliefs. A 1954 short film, *Youth Club*, appears to show what it describes as 'the youth club movement' in the context of self-improvement for young workers. Aspirational apprentice Jerry is shown spending his evenings at physics classes, unlike his mechanic friend Peter, who prefers the pinball tables at the amusement arcades. Jerry's hair is neat. Peter's is slicked with Brylcreem and suggests a Teddy Boy quiff. Jerry, holding books, shepherds his wayward friend down to the youth club.

Inside the village hall, there's a drum kit, table tennis and a pool table. A chalked list includes boxing, drama, carpentry, cycling, painting, modelling, gymnastics and music, alongside weekend rambles in the country. Additionally, there's the first aid group, and a rota to cover club cleaning and repairs, as well as a self-governing club committee. 'No single club can provide for everyone, and so there has grown up in Britain a wide variety of different types of club,' says the voiceover, which is performed by an actor using received pronunciation, the preferred accent of the landed and wealthy. Club life, explains the film, is designed to socialise young people: 'They all endeavour, through their leaders, to help the youngsters develop desirable qualities, such as self-reliance, self-discipline and willingness to serve the community.' In the middle of the twentieth century, youth clubs were being described as useful for everyone, especially if 'everyone' came from a low-income background.

The film is not exactly what it seems, however. Produced by Verity Films for the Central Office of Communication, which was the successor entity to the wartime Ministry of Information, it was dubbed into languages including Indonesian and Urdu, and UK distribution was forbidden. Youth clubs were a potent way to communicate Britishness.

Away from the cameras, most youth organisations in Britain operated on an independent and voluntary basis, albeit with a growing number organised by local authorities. An NAYC leaflet from the era shows a wholesome-looking girl in a headscarf and a bonny teenage boy somewhere windswept, both looking off into the distance. The cover claims there are 122,612 boys and girls attending 2,140 clubs, and leads with a bold and very recognisable statement: 'It is vital that this country should have more clubs and more club leaders – NOW!' The stated aims of the NAYC help us understand what people thought youth clubs were for in the immediate post-war period: 'to help young people through leisure time activities to develop their physical, mental and spiritual capacities so that they may grow to full maturity as individuals and members of society'. Definitions of youth work, youth services and clubs themselves ebb and flow with societal changes, and, in this moment, the overarching impression is that it was about knitting society back together again. Togetherness, in the face of divisive forces, is a recurring theme in the youth club story, one that remains relevant today.

Newspaper cuttings compiled by the NAYC show changes as they were happening. Glued into a huge maroon-and-black book, there's a particularly full section covering autumn 1955. Pages are crammed with articles that relate to the demonised teenagers of the day, the Teddy Boys. Editorials attempt to explain the appeal of draped Edwardian suits and dramatic hairstyles, with headlines such as 'Young Gangsters' and 'Do Girls Really Like Teddy Boys?'

Teenagers' post-war love of music and dancing generated panic from above. Working youth had more money than their parents and some of them channelled it into clothing that drew from both Edwardian dandies and American rock 'n' roll. Youth culture pushed a new phase of the youth club into existence – by, once again, creating the feeling in adults that the kids needed to be contained, and by offering spaces that young people actually wanted to hang out in. Societal anxieties about contemporary life wrapped themselves around Teddy Boys. The film *Rock Around the Clock*, featuring Bill Haley and His Comets and the multimillion-selling song of the same name, came out in 1956, and was famously controversial.

Youth-oriented spaces have long fed and nourished undercurrents of music, art and sport, in the same way that public schools feed politics and captaincy culture. Teddy Boys were shaping youth culture and they would also remake the youth club. Karl Reinz's documentary *We Are the Lambeth Boys* was filmed in the summer of 1958 at Kennington's Alford House, which was open throughout the week and remains open today. The voiceover gives a sense of the overall picture: 'Alford House is not a typical London youth club. It is a very good one – friendly and alive and enjoyed by 350 members. More like it are needed.' Most of the Alford House youth club members were working, with only a couple still at school. One teenager has an admin job in the Post Office, another is a butcher, while others are dressmakers or secretaries. Beryl, who says very little but expresses herself with great seriousness on the youth club dancefloor, works on a factory production line putting pastry lids on pies. The Alford House crew represented the majority: most youth club attendees in the 1950s were in full-time employment. The school-leaving age had been raised to fifteen in 1947 and wouldn't be raised again until 1972. These teenagers were also workers, coming to the club for communal down time at the end of a shift.

At Alford House there's cricket, drawing, discussion and, of course, dancing. Trips to the chippie after the club ends at 10 p.m. look like a right laugh. A club visit for the annual cricket match against private boarding school Mill Hill in north London, which had been supporting Alford House since 1923, feels less cosy. The Kennington cricketers need borrowed whites to take part in the match and, afterwards, they lounge about, smoking, not saying much and looking either surly or stressed, depending on your perspective. They chant, cheer and catcall on the journey home through central London, including a very lairy moment inspired by a stationary policeman: 'I'll sing you a song, it's not very long, all coppers are bastards,' followed by a new version for the next constable, in which the insult was swapped out for 'handsome'. The voiceover gives some sideways context a few beats later. 'When the boys pass through the West End, the West End remembers for a while that they have passed through. And that's how the boys want it.' As soon as their open-backed Army-style jeep crosses the river, over Westminster Bridge and away from Big Ben, they break out into the titular song, the bare bones of which can still be heard on football terraces across England and Scotland to this day.

We Are the Lambeth Boys was sponsored by Ford Motor Company as part of their *Look at Britain* series, which feels like a useful antecedent for any youth workers currently pondering the ethics of taking corporate money. The soundtrack was written by British jazz instrumentalist and composer Johnny Dankworth, whose orchestra was the first British band to be invited to the Newport Jazz Festival, and who played with certified greats including the Duke Ellington Orchestra and Louis Armstrong. Top Rank records recognised the potential appeal, and released the *Lambeth Boys* soundtrack.

Dankworth's involvement with youth clubs would continue. Over the August bank holiday in 1958, white mobs in Notting Dale and Notting Hill violently attacked newly arrived British citizens and their homes. Teddy Boys were prominently involved. In response, Dankworth became a founding member of the Stars Campaign for Interracial Friendship (SCIF), using music and culture to combat racism and the 'colour bar', which created legal space for segregation in the UK until the introduction of the Race Relations Act in 1965. Actor Laurence Olivier became chairman, with members including multimillion-selling British–Trinidadian pianist Winifred Atwell, who had multiple Top Ten hits in the 1950s, *Absolute Beginners* author Colin MacInnes and jazz musician and critic George Melly. Rick Blackman's history of SCIF, *Forty Miles of Bad Road*, describes fundraising gigs in Soho cellars with guest appearances from national celebrities, and a SCIF Christmas party for over 250 children 'of all races' from three west London schools. The event was televised by the BBC.

In January 1959, the group opened a youth club at St Mark's Church Hall in Notting Hill. 'SCIF's first permanent initiative was to found a club to promote interracial mixing and openly oppose the colour bar,' wrote Blackman, describing a 'young people's youth club' with a jukebox and live music from artists including Dankworth and his wife, the singer Cleo Laine. Club chairman, actor Harvey Hall, told the *Kensington Post* that there would be weekly meetings, adding a detail that puts this underage club night firmly into the youth club lineage. 'The youngsters will have a say in the running of the club,' said Hall. 'And they will be asked to bring their friends in. But this will not be a select club, we do want to bring the rougher element in. Teddy boys will be welcomed.' The Harmony Club was situated on Blenheim Crescent, where extreme street-level violence had taken place only six months earlier.

SCIF's intention for a 'chain of Harmony Clubs' did not materialise. In fact, the celebrity-organised youth club lasted only six weeks, before closing after an acrimonious split between two organisers, *Six-Five Special* BBC TV presenter Josephine 'Jo' Douglas and blues musician Alexis Korner. The latter cited the pressures of success: the club had space for only fifty or so members and yet attracted hundreds. The SCIF youth club would be a flash in the pan, albeit alongside other powerful sparks.

Notting Hill Carnival founder Claudia Jones was working in west London at the time, setting up the *West Indian Gazette and Afro-Asian Caribbean News* (*WIG*) and joining SCIF. At the end of January 1959, she organised the first Notting Hill Carnival, which took place in St Pancras Town Hall and was a huge success. It is now, of course, the largest free event in Europe.

Later in life, Johnny Dankworth would write a score, *Tom Sawyer's Saturday*, which was designed for young musicians and could be played by 'most reasonably competent youth orchestras'. From 1970 onwards, he and Cleo Laine ran a jazz education summer school in their back garden near Milton Keynes. A venue evolved – The Stables – which continues to host concerts and National Youth Music Camps to this day.

7

1960: ARCHITECT-DESIGNED YOUTH CLUBS ARE ROLLED OUT

Black-and-white photographs from a youth service fundraiser offer a useful perspective on the post-war past, particularly the way youth clubs existed as a charitable receptacle for those with inherited wealth. Le Bal Masque took place in February 1954. Society photographs, such as those you see in certain Sunday newspapers, show aristocrats in glamorous masks who would be almost unrecognisable if the picture captions did not name them: Countess Beatty, Lady Irene Astor, the Right Honourable This, Major That. Such society fundraisers were on their way out as an income source, though, and would soon be as hard to imagine as Old Etonians running rowing clubs for East End boys. UK youth provision was shifting again, and this time it changed because of a woman who could have been in those society photographs: Lady Diana Albemarle.

Albemarle gave her name to the most influential report ever written about youth clubs. She was a wealthy woman with a social conscience. Commissioned by a Conservative government and published in 1960, with in-depth and expensive recommendations around building and revamping youth clubs and training youth workers, the Albemarle Report was accepted by ministers within hours of publication and £28m was allocated over the next eight years. Mark K. Smith's suggestion that the committee was a means to legitimise an agreed expansion of local authority youth provision takes some of the romance out of the story but removes nothing of the impact.

Behind the report was a heavyweight committee, including sociologist and girls' club organiser Pearl Jephcott. Its co-author Richard Hoggart grew up knowing poverty and championed the arts and low-income families for the rest of his life. He also wrote about Teddy Boys in his book *The Uses of Literacy*. Fellow co-author Leslie Paul was the founder of the Scouts' socialist little brother, the Woodcraft Folk, and brought the phrase 'angry young man' into the lexicon through his 1951 autobiography of the same name. Another committee member, Denis Howell, went on to become a Labour minister for youth.

Lady Albemarle's connections and pre-publication discussions with senior ministers, and an existing desire within government to invest in the youth, meant that something was done, and anyone who ever spent time in an old-style youth club will understand the impact of the committee's work in a literal, facts-on-the-ground type of way. Architect-designed youth clubs were rolled out nationwide, with wooden dance-floors and coffee bars. Some 3,000 buildings went up, alongside 160 sports projects aimed directly at young people attending secondary modern schools or who had left school, and to fill the gap left by the end of National Service in the year the report was published. Historian Sue Robertson aired an idea that helps explain the context at the time, or at least the interlinked assumption that grammar school children didn't need what the youth club had to offer, and the idea of the youth club as a space that mops up social unfairness. Youth clubs generated by Albemarle, she wrote, 'aimed to give young people who had left school an equivalent setting to those who had gone to university, and were part of students' unions'. Albemarle had planted physical space across the UK, an act that would have a long echo.

Molly Lefebure was an active part of the management committee of a youth club that opened the year before Albemarle's report. Another of the lively women who populate the youth club story, she was the daughter of a high-ranking civil servant and grew up in a well-connected north London family. During the Second World War, Molly became private secretary to the Home Office pathologist and was, according to her *Telegraph* obituary, a regular sight at Scotland Yard, mortuaries and murder sites throughout England. Proximity to death made her hard to shock, which, once she'd married, moved to south-west London and had two children, made her well placed to help run the Cambridge Club, a youth club designed specifically to cater for the descendants of Irish costermongers and the Teddy Boys of Kingston-upon-Thames. Such adolescents attracted a telling name during this era: 'unclubbables'. The phrase was common in the 1950s and linked more to exclusive gentleman's clubs than those attempting to avoid being murdered by Roundheads or Cavaliers in the English Civil War. It suggested someone socially unappealing, not suitable for membership. Also, at least to me, it suggests defiance and a refusal to be clubbed into shape.

Molly's account of helping to run a club for unclubbables, *Razor Edge: The Story of a Youth Club*, was published in 1967 under the pseudonym Mary Blandy. Taking its title from a line in the Albemarle Report, which described youth work as 'a tense day-to-day walking on a razor-edge between sympathy and submission', it contains distinct admiration for refuseniks encouraged through the doors.

Razor Edge provides a sight-line into this southern English club. Damp, leaky and often 'refrigerator cold', it began life in a disused back-street furniture storage facility, opened the year before Albemarle, moving to new premises in a specially converted school, with a new, contemporary interior, five years later. Molly got stuck into the thankless grind of club work, and we meet the clubs' teenage members as she observes them, from her vantage point serving coffees in the canteen, or being roped into refereeing an ad hoc boxing bout in a ring fashioned from decrepit pianos, or collecting jumble during an unruly fundraising drive. Written in brisk and entertaining style, it simultaneously maintains a slight remove that was perhaps honed at the mortuary slab.

As well as offering a fascinating sideways view on Mods and Rockers fighting on the south coast of England, alongside brilliantly detailed descriptions of the music, fashion and make-up choices of unclubbable teens in the early 1960s, Molly's story also offers an insight into the inner workings of clubs during this period. Provision for kids, many of whom had been designated failures at the end of primary school by failing to gain access to a grammar school, would be overseen by volunteers from sectors of society specialising in control. Molly's fellow management committee members included a senior probation officer, a police inspector, a judge from juvenile court, a female welfare officer, a worker among deprived children, three or four local businessmen and two parents.

Management's presence in day-to-day youth club life, at least through the pages of her book, seems detached from club realities. It's almost as if a layer of adult 'clubbables' were required, even if they were mostly for show. In one telling exchange between Molly and another volunteer, the disconnect is made explicit. The women are discussing one incident out of many, where the young members had bent the rules, or the law, in service of the club or themselves. 'We call this social work,' says the lady described as Mrs Z. 'But sometimes, you know, I really do feel it's more like we do anti-social work.'

Stories of the youth club being robbed appear repeatedly throughout the decades. Describing a break-in after the Christmas Fair, Molly gives a sense of the bigger picture. 'Youth-clubs are, of course, always being broken into,' she writes, adding that it was surprising they hadn't been burgled before, and that suspects included club members. Incidents like this could paint youth workers into a tight corner. 'It was strongly suspected that the miscreant, or miscreants, belonged to the Club,' she adds. 'Indeed, I was later told the names of the guilty parties, who were, sure enough, Club members.' Tight corners could be breezily navigated, at least by some.

Another remarkable takeaway about community relations pops up in Molly's chronicle of club life. Petitions were raised in an attempt to stop it opening at all, and the group's move to the new purpose-built centre was 'seriously delayed' by the objections of those living nearby. However, it's an anecdote relayed about a door-to-door collection of donations for a jumble sale that gives the strongest sense of the mood on the street. She describes an encounter with a 'vitriolic old man' who slammed the door in her face on hearing about the recipients of her fundraising drive, but not before making his views clear: 'Madam, I'd rather eat my jumble than give it to a youth club!' While their importance was lauded by politicians – even when they weren't offering actual funding – youth clubs were contentious and unpopular, at least with neighbours.

Lovely as they were, the Albemarle buildings quickly proved troublesome, and not just for nearby residents. Within a few years, local authorities were having trouble affording the upkeep and there were grumbles about young people ruining premises that had so generously been gifted to them. The youth clubs where writer Mark K. Smith worked, in Amersham, offer another case in point. 'It was a local authority building, an Albemarle centre, with a committee and canteen run by young people,' he explained. 'When I came it'd been open seven or eight years and most of the doors had been bashed in. There were some part-timers running it. They had a bouncer and a dog in order to control things at discos.' 'That sounds a bit strong,' I said. 'What did you replace the bouncer and the dog with?' 'Saying "hello" at the door,' he replied wryly. 'We had women on the door, several local part-time workers. It was obvious what to do.'

It was the committee's first recommendation that perhaps had the deepest impact, shepherding in changes that would shift the demographic of the adults who worked in youth clubs. Recommending an expansion in the numbers of, and training for, professional leaders, it outlined the need for an emergency training programme and a negotiating committee for salaries and working conditions. The number of full-time workers doubled in the decade after the report was published, with about half of them attending the National College for the Training of Youth Leaders in Leicester. In the first year, 148 students enrolled, seventeen of them women.

Our esteemed youth work author and expert Bernard Davies met Lady Albemarle in his late twenties, while working at the aforementioned National College. 'At some point in my first year she did a visit,' he told me. 'Given that it was the product of her report, she might have wanted to.' It was a brief meeting – 'we were in the same room and she probably shook my hand' – but it strikes me as a poetic moment that knits together aspects of the youth club timeline that might otherwise seem separate, a bit like the famous night in 1951 when Charlie Parker played at Birdland in New York, with Stravinsky in the audience. 'She presented a very accessible figure,' remembered Bernard. 'Looking back, I could understand how she'd managed to get responses from the range of people that contributed. She certainly wasn't above herself, as my stereotype of lords and ladies was.'

Bernard had been appointed to the National College in the early days of its existence. He replied to my follow-up email about cohort demographics with characteristic thoughtfulness. 'These questions touch on a very important learning period in my life and professional development because the students I met and worked with at the National College taught me as much as I could ever teach them (if not more), and not just about youth work.'

Aged twenty-seven, he was younger than most of his students. 'Almost certainly, there was a wider class representation than in post-eighteen (or even post-sixteen) education at that time as many had been in "manual" or clerical-type jobs,' he wrote. 'Many were married, many had children – and all had, often substantial, youth work experience, part-time and/or voluntary.' Trained youth workers were changing, becoming demographically more akin to the young people they served, and increasingly came from within the youth club ranks. It strikes me as relevant that training was taken seriously, or even insisted upon, only at this point, when there was a shift in the background of the people doing the work; the assumption being, perhaps, that the well-off or privately educated could be trusted simply because of their social credentials.

Training came at a cost for some of these first-wave youth workers. 'As "mature" students, they were now being asked to learn, read, write, analyse, discuss in ways which initially they could find very challenging,' said Bernard in his reply to me, 'especially as many had been deeply alienated from school and had left ASAP, when they were fifteen or perhaps even younger. Indeed, one of the great joys of the job for me was to watch them discover with fellow students that they had a brain and that they could learn.' Taking the course also put some trainees under pressure, though, and added strain to their personal lives, 'including helping to break marriages, as, living away from home for most of the year in a residential setting, they, in effect, left partners behind'. At this point, youth work was the subject of national debate and had the media shining a light on it. The creation of new youth clubs also meant that, for the moment at least, there would be jobs for the new graduates.

Terminology began to shift, reflecting the changing class demographic of those who worked in youth clubs: youth leaders became youth *workers*. The balance had tipped and this change in terminology marked a shift in power dynamics. Young people who attended youth clubs were more likely to meet adults who understood the need for and believed in the possibility of social change than those who saw youth clubs as a way of ensuring an unchanging status quo.

8

1965: TABLE TENNIS ROUND THE OPEN FIRE

Boxing and football have clear connections to youth clubs, although it's been some time since primary-age kids were allowed to punch each other in the face before grabbing a snack from the tuck shop. The history of table tennis, too, owes a particular debt to youth clubs.

The game is synonymous with these spaces, and has been for decades. In 1963, the government produced the second of its Building Circulars, designed to help local authorities spend that Albemarle money. The circular focused on Withywood in Bristol, which had been built as a 'model club' a year earlier on a large and then-new estate in the south of the city. The two-storey club, used by other community groups in the day-time, was open six days a week, and included spaces for 400 members to 'dance, put on plays or concerts, drink coffee, hold meetings large or small, read or talk, watch television, listen to records, pursue any number of hobbies or crafts, play active games, and change or take a shower', according to the *Times Educational Supplement*. The Bristol city architect's drawing of the central area showed members crammed around the edges of the main club space, in the centre of which were, inevitably, two girls playing table tennis.

Paul Stimpson is a journalist-turned-communications officer at Table Tennis England. 'There's no doubt that youth clubs were fertile ground for talented players, particularly in the decades after the Second World War and through to the

1980s,' he told me, adding that the National Association of Youth Clubs held annual championships between 1976 and 1986, attracting competitors from all over the country. Several players who played the sport in that setting, he said, went on to have success at national, and in some cases international, level.

Table Tennis England continues to work with youth clubs, particularly in London and Essex, in partnership with the Jack Petchey Foundation. 'There's evidence from teachers and youth workers that the sport is associated with better behaviour and greater self-esteem,' said Paul, 'as well as having positive impacts on mental and physical health and on developing social skills.' It's an affordable and accessible sport, he pointed out. 'Long may that continue. And, of course, the more people who learn to play at a younger age, the greater the chance of unearthing more talented players who can excel nationally and internationally.'

One such talent is David Bowles, now aged seventy-four and living in Essex, who plays for England Veterans. Attending Forest Gate youth club in the 1960s with Chester Barnes, who was England champion aged fifteen, and national squad member Stuart Gibbs, he learned to play in constrained and often cold circumstances. 'We played dustbin cricket, with an actual dustbin, and table tennis in a building where the rain came through the ceiling.' Mad for the sport and keen to play as much as possible, he also attended Fairman House, in a church hall. 'It was like a youth club, but you had to go to church if you wanted to play ping-pong,' he says, describing a hall with six tables in it and a big fire in the middle of the room. 'The fire had a guard around it, but you had to be careful where you put your backside.'

Spotted by the youth club organisers as having talent, he was invited to join Fellowes club in Plaistow, where he describes thirty boys and girls running round the table tennis table, taking turns to pick up a bat, because there weren't enough to go around. 'So many of us progressed from there,' he says, before adding an intriguing detail: 'We played in church halls that were very cold. We came from the grassroots, and it changed people's style. There wasn't much room. That's why a lot of people used to stand up to the table, because they couldn't go anywhere else.' Youth club table tennis, he believes, had an effect on the British style itself through the very act of playing in small spaces.

'If we didn't have it [the club], we'd have been walking round the street, just singing songs or something like that.' Youth club was a launchpad, he says, allowing him to travel the world.

9

1967: RENEGADE KIDS RESHAPE THE YOUTH CLUB

In the mid-1960s, a new kind of youth club began to appear, facilitated by the UK-specific mix of voluntary work, faith structures, the physical space opened by Albemarle and the changes soundtracked by rock 'n' roll. Threads of denim and leather began weaving into the youth club fabric in 1962, when Reverend Bill Shergold opened a biker section of the 59 Club in east London. Church of England curate David Collyer made his own leap of faith when he opened a youth club for Hells Angels at St Basil's in Deritend, Birmingham, in 1965. Double Zero, as the club was known, became famous outside of its home city, covered in newspapers both national and local. Collyer wrote a book about his time at the club, its title borrowed from the name of the club, and it paints an intentionally striking picture. The opening line reads: 'Enter seven youths with shotguns.' This is gleefully frontline work, where the vicar made space for young men and women who were otherwise vilified. In another example of the youth club as a centre of redistribution, his car was frequently drained of petrol by club members, who'd siphon it off. 'Oh well,' he would shrug, subsequently keeping the tank as close to empty as possible.

Rockers weren't the only young people towards whom youth work bent. A pamphlet from 1965 illustrates the Weekenders project, with a photograph of Mods in button-down shirts and parkas crowded around a lamp-lit table. Weekenders was launched by the National Association of Youth Clubs in response to the bank holiday disturbances immortalised in films like *Quadrophenia* and was funded by the Carnegie Trust. Existing youth club members were sponsored to bring their 'unattached contemporaries' into the fold. The project offered facilities at seaside resorts, making shelter, refreshments and information available 'to cope with the sort of problems which arise when young people are far from home'.

Weekender projects included discotheques on a Midlands housing estate, rehabilitating a cottage in a village for use as a weekend venue and organising a late-night club in a Home Counties centre. A shelter in Soho was available from Saturday night into Sunday morning.

By 1967, there were 3,271 clubs affiliated to the NAYC, with a further 500 pending affiliation or otherwise connected. Approximately 1,800 full- and part-time leaders, plus 11,300 voluntary leaders and helpers, created space for over a quarter of a million young people. On top of this, there would have been unaffiliated church youth clubs and those too informal for official associations. It was a boom time for youth clubs, as Albemarle money worked its way into brickwork, with activities developed by trained youth workers who increasingly believed that young people should be central to decision-making.

Meanwhile, a particular tension was appearing. Successful youth clubs were retaining teenagers as they grew up, while continuing to absorb and cater for a constant flow of younger ones. 'Leaders report that older members are put off by being organised and want to decide for themselves what they should do.' One development, described in the 1967 NAYC annual report as 'widespread', was the provision of club rooms for the exclusive use of older members. In another moment that allows you to understand how wildly different the past was, these are described as 'rather like a sixth form common room in a large school, which staff enter only by invitation'. One London club had a licensed bar for its over-eighteens. A south-coast club issued keys to senior members so they could use the premises freely. It is worth recalling that the school-leaving age wasn't raised to sixteen until 1972, and that many of these senior members had bosses and were two or three years into employment. For others, leaving school would take them in a different direction, towards the dole office. Joblessness in the recession of the early 1970s was amplified by changes to the school-leaving age, at a time when school-leavers were less likely than ever to find work. Over the coming decades, unemployment would continue to shape the UK youth club.

PART TWO
CLASSIC YOUTH CLUBS, THE EARLY YEARS

10

1970: 2-TONE, THE SPECIALS AND THE HOLYHEAD

Some youth clubs weren't just reflecting popular culture; they were generating it. Nailed to the wall of a large Victorian building in central Coventry there is a black-and-white plaque. Unveiled in 2009 as part of the city's 2-Tone Trail, it names the location, the Holyhead Youth Club, and explains that reggae and blues jam sessions took place in the basement, alongside a sound system run by The Specials' Neville Staple. 'The music created here was fundamental,' it reads, 'in the development of the 2-Tone sound that would follow.'

Like a Midlands version of CBGB in New York or Bob Marley's house on Hope Road in Kingston, the Holyhead offers a digestible version of events by centralising the story. However, there is never a ground zero; everything emerges from everything else, and this is especially true of an environment populated by teenagers, themselves emerging into adulthood.

It is accurate to say that, for two decades, this youth club offered rare space for local teenagers to hang out, get involved in activities and express themselves. It opened at a time when British citizens of Caribbean descent were poorly accommodated, or outright unwelcome, in white youth clubs, and was carved into existence in non-standard fashion by young people themselves, actions that later supported the emergence of world-famous musicians and a whole genre of music.

However, this was not the only output: the club also counts among its former members a high-profile barrister in original

Holyhead co-founder Courtenay Griffiths KC; TV presenter and original member of the *Loose Women* line-up Trish Adudu; academics, artists and dancers, including cult hip hop dance group Future Shock and at least one ballet school alumnus; and numerous adults engaged in art, music, teaching and youth work. Not all of this, of course, could be squashed onto a 2-Tone Trail plaque, but it's important from the get-go to acknowledge the breadth and depth of this very special place.

A baseline explanation of how this came to be might begin with the basics: that the youth club took place within a Quaker Friends Meeting House, constructed in 1898 and later transferred to local authority ownership. Gradually becoming semi-derelict, it was brought back to life in the very early 1970s by a group of around twenty young people, many of whom had connections to reggae sound systems and soul clubs. Charley Anderson, who co-founded The Selecter, Neville Staple and a supportive adult, renowned singer Ray King, were among those contributing in a central way to this alternative, grassroots example of youth clubs' long history of volunteering.

Within a few years, various processes brought it under the control of the Community Relations Council, and then the local authority itself. In 1992, the club was forced to relocate to YMCA premises at the rear of the Methodist Central Hall, after members were told that the building was structurally unsound. Education Committee minutes from the time recorded that it was 'surplus to requirements' and in poor repair, with ownership transferred to the city's Property Management Committee. The building remained in use, though, and is currently home to Coventry Artspace Limited, who offer affordable fine-art and print-making studios.

Between the beginnings and staggered endings are decades of activity, with thousands of young people walking up the steps and through the building, or being supported by the youth workers who themselves came through the Holyhead, before spreading out into the city's other youth clubs and music projects. Such depth, and the connection to individuals who became pop stars, ensures that the Holyhead story is, at the very least, complicated. Personal testimony does not always chime with journalistic accounts (then and now) or with official council reports from the time. Between individuals, there are different perspectives. Discord emerged across a range of fault lines, voices not always in unison. Holding this universe together, though, were young people and their allies, sharing a centre of gravity – albeit sometimes in different orbits.

The Herbert Museum contains a gallery and an archive, hosting exhibitions that explore Coventry's history from the 1500s onwards. The city's youth clubs offer a similarly rich window onto society, culture, sport, politics and art, with the effects especially visible in Coventry because it is a small city.

In a back room, through a door that required pass-card entry, a group of musical and youth work legends had gathered. Founding Holyhead member and academic Louis Hassan had arrived first, asking me, very reasonably, about my politics and intentions. Others followed, including musician Chris Christie, who initiated the club's influential Music Workshop in the 1980s. Next was Milton Harvey, who had arrived in Coventry after eight years in the British Army. DJing at clubs around the city and keeping an eye on the then-underage Specials, he became the founding editor of the club's newspaper, the *Holyhead Mercury*, which launched in the mid-1970s.

Next-generation youth workers had joined us too, giving an age range that spanned from one young man in his mid-twenties to gentlemen in their sixties and seventies.

It was a rare gathering, convened by Emmanuelle Henry-Cottrell, a youth worker, lecturer and artist. I'd met Emmanuelle through his daughter, who runs youth project Fyah Kamp with her brother, and I offer this additional context both to state the facts, that people came because Emmanuelle asked them to, and as a reminder. The human lifespan is often too short to learn from history, but we can pass on methods that we've experienced first-hand. Family and neighbourhood connections are often the catalysts in this passing-on, in this case between father and children. Such transmission is woven through the fabric of the Holyhead youth club.

As we sat on chairs around the edges of the Herbert back room, an origin story began to emerge. 'It was the first youth club I had involvement in,' said Louis Hassan, 'because we set it up. I'll tell you a little bit about how,' he said, describing how young people would hang out in the city centre, and that the Holyhead had previously been used by the fire service for training recruits in emergency situations. 'That old building, we gained access and then went into the Community Relations Council. We made it legitimate,' he said.

At this point, Chris Christie interjected, offering his own version of events. 'Actually he's smoothing over; it was commandeered by young people,' he said. 'It was an empty building, and the youth didn't have anywhere else to go. They took it over and then went into the process of legitimising it through the Community Relations Council.'

Memories created mental images of Louis and friends bringing an empty building to life and beginning a process of stabilising their under-the-radar situation by engaging with officialdom. But the apparently straightforward story I'd arrived with – that The Specials came out of the Holyhead – was unravelling in front of me, along with my hope for a better understanding of what happened when. A wall of detail was emerging, spanning many years. Over the course of a few hours I went from knowing very little about Coventry youth clubs to absorbing large amounts of behind-the-scenes detail. It was as if I'd tried to comprehend the entirety of the pyramids by reading the hieroglyphics in logbook reports or graffiti left behind by workers. Towards the end of the morning, Milton Harvey made explicit this disconnect. 'There's no short story here,' he said, with devastating clarity. 'There's no soundbite in our lives.'

I gave up trying to untangle the timeline and instead accepted what was coming towards me: a story of creative resistance, of individuals working with institutions for the betterment of young people and also being undermined by the same institutions, and of the schisms that inevitably occur when communities take control of organising responsibilities that the state has discarded.

Afterwards, I left the Herbert Museum and walked past the cathedral and around the boundaries of Holy Trinity church. Sat on the stone step of a side building, I felt a sense of youth work done through bold necessity, and the cost of carving out space. Everyone I'd met had done remarkable things – even if I still wasn't sure what had happened when.

Connecting with guitarist and vocalist Lynval Golding, a founding member of The Specials and Holyhead regular in the early days, came through my own ongoing forays into youth work. For a few years, I'd been running a journalism group within a free weekly music club for nine- to sixteen-year-olds in south-east London. Members of Woolwich Creative Club would come after school on a Tuesday, hang out and eat crisps and sandwiches, before learning trumpet with UK jazz don Byron Wallen or drums with Kenrick Rowe. The latter has played with PJ Harvey, Aswad and Annie Lennox, and had been touring with The Specials since just before the Covid pandemic. Talking to Kenrick on the bus home one day, he suggested I talk to the man direct, and he put us in touch.

Lynval was a warm and friendly conversationalist, happy to take me back in time to the early days, when the youth club shared space with the Jah Baddis sound system. 'What the Black youth was going through . . . it was wonderful that we could run our own youth club,' he said. 'And Holyhead youth club was right in the city centre,' he added. 'The city centre, it wasn't pretty. Coventry was quite a violent city. We needed a little premises where our Black youth could congregate and gather and share ideas. We couldn't get into the white youth clubs, you know? We weren't allowed. The Holyhead youth club gave us the opportunity to have a little Friday-evening, Saturday-evening dance. That's where we could congregate as a Black community.' It offered necessary space, he said, albeit one that was 'a shell . . . in a right state'. Running the club, he said, was a huge challenge for Ray King. 'The first bit of Holyhead was like giving it to a bunch of wild kids,' he explained. 'Youths were energetic and aggressive. He had to stand firm with them. At the same time, he had to deal with the police. Ray King showed very good leadership. He had to lead the youth and talk to people in authority. We were going through a stage of survival, and he could represent us.' While he dismissed the story that The Specials came out of Holyhead with a short and definite 'nope', stating emphatically that the band never rehearsed there, he agreed that the youth club did play an important role.

'What effect did the Holyhead have on you as a musician?' I asked. 'The coming together,' he replied. 'We had somewhere we could all meet up, whether good, bad or ugly. We were all under one roof. We would fight for each other. We have disagreements, everyone does, but the youth club united all of us.' Togetherness was a source of pride. 'That's the one-sidedness of racism,' he added. 'We were the positive ones. We stretch out our hand to the whites to come and join us at our club.'

Holyhead's members had created a controversial fact on the ground, which existed because of social conditions relating overtly to racism, unemployment, housing and attitudes towards young people. In a deeper way, to me at least, it also signalled Britain's unwillingness to reckon with its colonial realities, acting as welcome respite or unwelcome reminder, depending on your perspective. Like the monochrome chequerboard of the 2-Tone aesthetic, Holyhead would be seen as inspirational or concerning, powerful or dangerous, necessarily lively or way too loud. What follows is my attempt at explaining what happened when, bringing together disparate perspectives to give a sense of how young people created their own space, how it evolved, and to celebrate what happened along the way.

Coventry Youth Service's annual report 1971/2 makes mention of the Holyhead, in ways that make clear how different it was to other youth clubs in the city. The report describes approximately 700 youth organisations affiliated to the council, including church clubs and those for sports or special groups: for example, young deaf people. Scouts and Guides were counted separately, numbering 297 units. Over 30,000 young people were catered to, with around 4,000 attending 'cultural organisations', mostly for Asian girls and young women.

Surveyors from the Department of Architecture and Planning visited each of the twenty-six buildings owned by the authority's youth service, including converted farm buildings and schools, and huts built of wood and concrete. Purpose-built community centres provided in 1945 by American War Relief and centres constructed during the Albemarle Report's funding spree also appear. Provision comes across as plentiful; there are a lot of buildings, especially by today's standards. However, the overriding impression is of spaces that are scrappy and unkempt, in need of the kind of maintenance that would more routinely be applied to schools or hospitals. Vandalism is referenced repeatedly.

Holyhead received a significantly shorter entry than any other in the list. A 'large scale two-storey building on a small site' is described, constructed from red brick, with timber floors and sash windows, bound by six-foot-high brick walls. Backing away from the additional detail present in the other entries, the authors employ two curiously passive phrases: 'this building was not inspected internally' and 'services were not assessed'.

The missing details suggest a compromise. The building belonged to the council, and it was being used by young people who had not initially asked for permission through the usual channels. The Holyhead was included in the survey despite not being properly surveyed. In the background, off the page, negotiations were taking place.

In August 1972, the Holyhead entered a second phase. The Community Relations Council (CRC) got involved, and agreed to act as an organisational bridge between Holyhead's young pioneers and the council. The West Indian Youth Club was granted one day a week, with another added to the schedule by the end of the following year. Sound-system dances run by Jah Baddis continued on the weekend. Visitors, including researchers from the NAYC's Youth and Race project, described the club's founders as 'a collection of politically aware and very able individuals'.

Others followed the founders into the building. In an example of the way gentrification works, someone needed to make the space habitable for the artists who'll come after them, in this case the Belgrade Theatre Company, which was sharing the space by 1973. Later that year, Coventry's CRC awarded Holyhead a £200 grant 'to purchase disco equipment'. The next phrase tip-toes around the realities with style, capitalising on the mainstream popularity of such activity. The grant would allow the group to run 'fundraising discos every Saturday night'.

The Jah Baddis sound system was a few planetary systems away from the world of the disco, providing intense, high-quality musical offerings. Within a few years, this strand of the Holyhead multiverse was accompanied by free kicks and slide tackles from the Jah Baddis football club. Ad hoc games would eventually turn into a tournament where sound systems from across the country would compete. Teams for netball and basketball were also formed.

By early 1974, there was formal, albeit self-built, organisation on the youth club side. The members committee put together a constitution and a list of objectives, the first being to 'promote the social, physical, intellectual, cultural, and spiritual wellbeing of West Indian youths in Coventry and to articulate their needs'. Further objectives outlined a desire to promote human rights and justice: 'with the support of Law, be active in the promotion of human rights and human justice and to work towards the eradication of all forms of prejudice or discrimination'. The final aim was 'to foster mutual respect and community harmony'. It's notable to me, reading from this distance, this foregrounding of mutual respect before attempts at harmony.

An NAYC-sponsored report on the Holyhead described a programme of activities, including sports fixtures, supplementary education, a series of discussions and training in martial arts. Upkeep of the club rules would be borne by the members committee, and the regulations give a sense of the young leadership's intentions. The group, aware that they were viewed as 'unrespectable', and that their Rasta hairstyles amplified this view, were particularly concerned that 'they should be seen to be conducting themselves as an organised group in a manner which would inspire confidence in them'. The report continued: 'They also felt that despite their youth, they could achieve some degree of respect from the Black community as a whole, and bring about a feeling of unity, and saw this also as a way of encouraging West Indian mothers to allow their daughters to attend the club, being fully aware that the plight of girls was probably more acute than theirs.'

Things were about to go further underground, a process that would deepen the creative and cultural activities at the Holyhead and simultaneously signal the arrival of new constraints. At some point in 1974, someone discovered a trap door that led to a basement full of rubbish. A whole new world, almost literally, opened up. Members began clearing it out, but soon realised it was a task that required funds. Gaining the grants necessary to replicate the rejuvenation they'd already enacted in another part of the building would signal beginnings and endings, as the arrival of official money brought officialdom closer.

A series of photographs from the Holyhead allows sightlines into the basement and beyond. The images were taken in 1975 by Warwick University student Jake Bernard. He'd been working for the student newspaper, *The Boar*, documenting sit-ins and protests, including an early incident where police riot shields were used outside of Northern Ireland. The student union wanted a series of images to show the diversity of the city and sent Jake over to the Community Relations Council, which, he said, when we chatted on the phone after being introduced by my friend, who is his cousin, 'pushed me in the right direction'.

Walking around the Foleshill Road, telling people that he'd been sent by the CRC, the nineteen-year-old pointed his lens at a variety of scenes: a young Sikh boy proudly holding a tower of Lego bricks that rises higher than his neatly tied patka; the wall of an English class for South Asian women, adorned with a fabric banner reading 'Sound City: Down Beat'; a halal butchers; the Hindu Mandir; and the Shree Krishna Temple. Thirteen images were exhibited during the university's Freshers' Week, including one of the Holyhead.

Jake had walked into the youth club off the street, found a dozen or so young people inside and shot the one roll of film he'd brought along, using the available light and a single fixed-focus lens. Most of the shots are cropped close to the subjects, who include future members of The Specials and Selecter, along with Ray King at the piano, emanating palpable charisma. Young men about the same age as the photographer gather around the hand-painted Jah Baddis sound system or gaze out from beside the wooden case, which contains two turntables, looking variously stylish, serious, grounded, contemplative and, in at least one case, a bit worried.

I can attempt to tune in to the undercurrents, but, from my vantage point, separated from the Holyhead by factors including time and location, I'll only be guessing. But still, I think about the dynamics, before and after the shutter closed and reopened. Which of the people in the room would have gravitated towards Jake and his camera, and who would have shied away? I wonder also about the value for teenagers of being photographed at the centre of their own self-built universe, even though these individuals didn't see the results until they were exhibited at Coventry Music Museum over forty years later. 'I think it would be presumptuous of me to think it changed anything,' said Jake, when I asked him for his perspective. 'Possibly the attention enhanced or increased their confidence, but I think it was unlikely. Did it give them validation or were they just confused that this nineteen-year-old student had walked in off the street and asked if he could take photographs?' You have to remember, he added, that in 1975 there was no internet or social media. What we call 'youth culture' was in its infancy, and music newspapers like *Sounds* and *NME* were still very traditional in their coverage.

One of Jake's remarkable images shows an empty space. The Holyhead's basement is lit by a single lightbulb. Everything is askew, including chairs, which are pulled away from a table; audio effects units balance precariously on speaker stacks, while the contents of a toolbox are lying on the floor. Names are daubed on the wall in blocky white paint alongside portraits painted onto the brickwork, or taped onto it, gallery style. It captures a moment of calm; perhaps the after-effects of compressed air, powering out of the multiple speakers visible in the image.

There have been countless documentaries and exhibitions exploring 2-Tone, the music that followed the silence suggested by Jake's photograph, including at the independent Coventry Music Museum, which was set up by Pete Chambers and his wife, Julie, who run it with an army of volunteers. The young people who heaved Holyhead, and other clubs like it, into life contributed a new node to the matrix of pubs, clubs and record shops that are more easily recognised as contributors to creative cities in this era. Cultural activity resonated outwards.

Local residents were unimpressed by their proximity to such a future-legendary location. Activity at the Holyhead was an irritant to some neighbours, who, like householders before and since, didn't recognise the compromises that had already been made or appreciate the effort required to create a safe place for young people. Two neighbours led complaints about excessive noise, including 'rowdyism' after the closing of the centre at nights, and 'dangerous behaviour in the streets'. Once again, the Holyhead was being experienced in very different ways by those within the gravitational pull of the place.

It's easy for me to feel aggrieved from a distance, especially as I've come to see persistent noise complaints by individuals against communal spaces as vexatious and literally anti-social, as unfairly weighted power dynamics that can cause significant social damage. However, the role of the neighbours in the

Holyhead youth club story also highlights the everyday ways that state failings show up on the ground; a reckoning here played out through reverberant basslines. Music and noise more generally are facts of both urban and teenage life, and yet adults often expect young people to be quiet in cities. This power play can still be seen when people contact the council, or even the police, to demand action against teenagers being teenagers.

Back at the Holyhead, pressure was increasing, and it was coming from different directions: from official bodies, sometimes generated by internal politics, the promise of grant money and the subsequent need to respond to the funder's requirements; and a desire, from some quarters within the Holyhead, to create a more stable and safe environment for young people.

In October 1975, a tectonic shift took place when a new management committee was imposed on the club, replacing the members-run group. It comprised three ward councillors, two residents who had organised the petition to get the club closed, a police inspector, one representative of the Coventry Education Committee, two members of the CRC and three representatives of the original members committee. It was common at the time for youth clubs to have management committees that were similarly constituted. This shift was perhaps inevitable. But in this unique environment, the transition from membership-run to management-run would have been, at the very least, complicated. Louis Hassan, part of the original group, offered more context when we spoke again. 'After that [first period] we started getting things moving in the right direction,' he said. 'The first concern was to create a place where young people could pick up the baton and pass it on.'

Local newspapers reported the opening of this new phase. 'A youth club with a difference will be officially opened next month,' wrote the *Coventry Evening Telegraph* breezily in summer 1976. 'The Holyhead Road Youth Centre has risen from the ruins of an old Quaker meeting place, thanks entirely to the work of around twenty jobless youth.' Actor Norman Beaton, who would later take the lead in TV show *Desmond's*, attended the opening in August. New positions were advertised for youth workers, and existing Holyhead committee members were not appointed to paid roles.

Babs Christie remembered the reopening from a very particular perspective: that of a child. Her dad, Hugh Wright Hay, was a community leader who'd later receive an MBE, and she attended with him. Her memory allowed us inside the building: the basement with rooms off it, the ground-floor office, the coffee bar and a huge hall with lots of windows and tons of space, walls freshly painted in magnolia. Upstairs, dance and keep fit, in a huge room with mirrors.

It's so grounding to feel like I'm being taken through the doors, I told her, given the shifting perspectives on what was happening behind the scenes. 'That reopening, there were some issues,' she said. 'There was a bit of rub. Generational. People my dad's age have come in and taken over. The flipside was: what experience and qualifications – not academic – did these young people have to run an organisation? I can see it from both sides. Also, again, the politics. Do you think the council was going to let a load of young Black people run a centre? It's never gonna happen in the '70s and '80s.'

The conversation was wide-ranging, Babs offering a long view and her perspective on the social context: that Holyhead first opened at a time when membership of the National Front was rising, and when children would hear racial slurs from their teachers. She also noted the role of one particular group. 'The

Rastas of the time were key players in getting us a building,' she said. 'That's an important thing to recognise. We wouldn't have had Holyhead if they hadn't done that.' It was the same, she observed, with the Osaba Women's Centre, which she would later run. 'That was got up and running by Rasta women. I'd hazard a guess that if you went anywhere in the country, it would be similar. The Rastafari movement bound us together through the political turmoil of being Black in Britain.'

In 1977, Holyhead youth club was closed again. Proposing that it should not reopen for use by the original group, the CRC decided it should become a standardised youth club for fourteen- to twenty-year-olds, with a focus on Black youth and employability at a time of high unemployment. 'Job-oriented projects' were envisioned and Holyhead changed again, into a place where young people could learn carpentry or electrics. Holyhead original Milton Harvey, who founded and edited the *Holyhead Mercury* magazine, remembered this period with disdain. 'The last thing we needed,' he said, 'was a job centre in a country with no jobs.'

In 1979, the local authority advertised a role at the Holyhead. It stated that the club was open five days a week, with a senior officer, two assistants and a projects officer. A range of activities were taking place within the building, catering to 600 members aged sixteen to nineteen. The transition from commandeered space to legitimised youth club was complete, and the club would operate throughout the following decade, providing steady support to many hundreds of young people from all backgrounds.

The Holyhead's Music Workshop provided a heartbeat through the 1980s, operating from the basement where Jah

Baddis had run reggae dances. The daubed paint in Jake Bernard's photographs of the Holyhead had been replaced with multicoloured, graffiti-style text, which signalled the Workshop space and which remains on the walls to this day. The Music Workshop is another of the storied and yet undersung entities within the Coventry music scene, where Chris Christie would encourage young people to pick up an instrument and play together, with a focus on the ways musicians communicate with each other. As well as occasionally recording sessions and organising established musicians to act as Workshop teachers, Chris shared his interest in electronics with the group, acquiring a ZX Spectrum and building an early sampler.

A decade after attending the reopening with her dad, Babs Christie started hanging out at the Holyhead in her very early twenties, and within eighteen months had made the shift from older young person to young youth worker. She remembered a range of musical styles represented at the Music Workshop in the early 1980s. 'I'd never listened to rock music before,' she said. 'I didn't mix with Asian men or young white men with long hair and biker jackets. Before you knew it, I'm jamming with these people.' She laughed. 'We're all in a room making music. That was the thing about Holyhead. I don't think it could have happened anywhere else. It was central, it was big, and as long as you were well behaved, anyone could come in.' With a pause and a laugh, she connected the past to the present, by making an observation that will be familiar to anyone regularly using public transport: 'I see it now, with young girls on the bus being really loud.'

After a while, the conversation with Babs shifted from explanatory, helping me understand a past I didn't inhabit, to reminiscence. 'Fridays used to be crazy! End of the week, forty or fifty people in there, you'd be watching all these young people interacting. Sometimes you'd feel like a little mother,' she said, 'all twenty-three-years-old of me.' The club was successful, she said, sustaining numbers and keeping young people out of trouble, including very few – 'zero, I think' – teenage pregnancies among members.

'Young women wanted somewhere to go where they were safe, meet their friends, somewhere they could have a laugh, somewhere they could talk to us youth workers,' recalled Babs. 'What I think they were searching for, most of all, was somebody to show them how to be young women. They were children transitioning into young people. They didn't always understand the rules of engagement.' Space, opportunities and a focus on girls made good on the intentions set by the members committee a decade earlier.

In 1987, Her Majesty's Inspectorate reported on youth work in Coventry. It found twenty-two youth clubs based in schools and colleges, fifteen council-owned community centres and seventeen voluntary groups, ranging from Scouts and Guides to the Coventry CRC and the YMCA. Inspectors also spent time in fourteen 'other projects', including the Holyhead, the only youth club in this category. Other groups listed in this miscellany were an adventure playground, a girls' group in Willenhall and Osaba Women's Group. It must still have been considered notable.

'It was special,' said Coral Poyser-Lindo, who attended the club as a young teenager in the mid-to-late 1980s, with Babs as one of her youth workers. 'Holyhead was a safe place to go, share creative ideas, find alternative education and empowerment,' she told me. 'From my viewpoint, as a child, these individuals were heroic, revolutionary. They established a building and carved a foundation for a generation to make informed decisions.' In unsurprising fashion, Coral passed on the flame, with a stint working in youth justice.

'The legacy for Holyhead is positive,' said Louis Hassan, in our final call. 'It may have been to our detriment, because they took away the building, but we did it so that young people would get positive experiences. During the school holidays we were able to run events, use the minibuses to go to Wales. People still come up to me and they say, "I used to come to your youth club. My kids need what I had!"' He paused. 'Right now, up and down the country, people are concerned about their kids. The young people we brought through Holyhead went on to bigger, better things.'

We doubled back to the conversation that began outside the doors of the Herbert Museum in Coventry. 'This is why I was saying to you, in the entrance: what are you hoping for? What's the outcome of this work? It's the ears of the decision-makers you need, for them to take this seriously. Get them to reinvest in a youth service, which they've depleted. My vision of it is this: you have two poles, the social and the economic. The decision-makers will always give preference to the economic. So no matter how you weigh up and show the importance of the social, it will always play second fiddle, even though they're inextricably linked.' Youth clubs, we agreed, offer both.

The economic benefits can be seen. Sounds that can be traced back to the Holyhead, as suggested by that 2-Tone plaque, were central to Coventry's tenure as UK City of Culture in 2021, with £44.5m received to bid for, win and deliver the festival, and a £150m boost in tourism and £183.1m of investment flowing into the city, 'secured at least in part' as a result of the activity, according to an evaluation by the universities of Coventry and Warwick.

On a national level there's impact too. Lionbeat describes itself as 'a bass culture development agency' which, among other things, works with south London youth clubs. Sound systems are attached to cargo bikes and taken out by their riders to community events in Newport, Luton and across London. Founder Jean-Claude – he goes by his first name only – has been identifying datasets to better understand the economic contribution of music that relates to reggae sound systems. The current estimate, he believes, is between £859m and £1.3bn per year. Youth clubs played a part in generating this wealth.

Really, we shouldn't be asking the Holyhead to be anything more than what it was: a place where many young people were able to make the transition to adulthood with joy, humour and everyday teenage drama, the effects of which became spectacularly visible when Coventry bands hit the charts. But if we were to ask the Holyhead to perform another task, to act as a kind of looking glass, then we may be able to perceive something else: an emerging future, constructed by teenagers whose parents were born elsewhere, from which multiple benefits would flow, in many different directions.

11

1971: TV CAMERAS TOUR SCOTTISH CLUBS

In Easterhouse, just outside Glasgow, a club existed that illuminates the relationship between hardship and the need for youth spaces, as well as the historically constant swing between feast and famine when it comes to funding. The story of how it came about, briefly succeeded in ways that were impossible for outsiders to appreciate, and then fell apart – or was nudged into failure – is instructive.

Easterhouse's infamy spread after popular 1960s singer Frankie Vaughan decided to try to address youth violence on the sprawling estate, which had been built with great speed and zero amenities a decade earlier. The fact that he felt the need to organise an arms amnesty gives a sense of the situation. He also corralled funds to create a youth club. The army built two long corrugated-iron domes, resembling metal polytunnels, and a name was painted over the front door: the Easterhouse Project.

A particular type of social context is offered, in 1970, by a BBC news reporter whom we hear but do not see in a report from the time, delivering detail through a voiceover in a studiously English accent. Easterhouse had 40,000 residents living in a place with no public toilets, banks, theatres or cinemas, no dance hall, no restaurant or community centre and 'nowhere to collect the dole'. There is one pub, the Casbah. The camera pans over masses of graffiti, disapprovingly. Young people in Easterhouse painted, scrawled and otherwise made their mark on the area in a way that is visually reminiscent of the early graffiti writer TAKI 183, who'd started writing his name on New York City walls around the same time.

Easterhouse's club, explained the BBC reporter, was the 'most ambitious youth scheme in Britain'. It was run by ex-teacher Graham Noble, who, according to the voiceover, was 'a lifelong socialist . . . an idealist with little administrative experience who thought he should run his club in a way no one had ever tried before'. The radical idea? To not expel troublemakers. While this was widely reported as meaning that the club had no rules, I find it hard to believe that was precisely the case. I imagine that a report made by the young people would present a different set of facts and perspectives. Noble looks beaten down – gutted, frankly – as he explains the idea behind the club, which had been closed by the time he appeared on camera, which was to cater to boys who were excluded elsewhere.

Scenes showed a happier time, six successful months into the project. On a lively dancefloor, teenagers – or 'up to 200 ex-gang members', if you prefer the reporter's opinion – were dressed up and dancing hard to a rock 'n' roll band. The camera takes us to another part of the city, where a pipe band is marching and where James Anderson, who was chairman of the police committee, 'knew virtually every police officer, as well as each police horse and dog, by name', according to an appreciative *Glasgow Herald* obituary. Unsurprisingly, he was not a fan of the youth club's methodology or practices, despite having been a trustee, before resigning when he discovered that club funds had been used to put up a member's bail money.

'The iron hand of the law is the answer to the problem of gangs,' he said to camera, wearing a pair of thick-rimmed black glasses and describing with barely contained anger young soldiers of the Royal Engineers constructing the prefabricated club while 'up to their knees in November mud'. Using the derogatory local slang for 'hooligan', he described local kids as 'Neds . . . stood around in their fancy clothes' while the soldiers grafted, stating that Easterhouse teens were allowed to do whatever they liked: play football within the project; vandalise the place.

Club leader Noble explained the policy of not ejecting troublemakers so that youth workers could discuss behaviour with those causing a disturbance. 'We would have lost them,' he said, with a mindset way ahead of his time. 'It was a therapeutic thing.'

In ways that would be recognisable to those who followed the story of Camila Batmanghelidjh's south London Kids Company a half-century later, prominent and previously supportive citizens stepped back and the 'establishment began to unite against the project'. Within a year the club itself was lost.

A metaphorical dance between unemployment and the youth club at a national level would drive institutional change. In 1971, the NAYC launched Community Industry (CI). Funded by the Department of Employment in response to ultra-high unemployment the previous winter, it was designed for young people 'facing particular difficulties' in finding work, although, of course, the difficulty was mostly to do with a lack of jobs. Involving work experience of up to a year in supervised teams on community projects, it started small before growing substantially. By 1981, it offered 6,000–7,000 placements nationally, with an article in the NAYC annual report explaining the rationale: 'Since its inception CI has seen its role as providing help to the least able and unqualified young people, to enable them to adjust to life in society, and has been particularly concerned with those young people who were likely to have employment problems even in times of full employment.' Likely participants were described by the Department of Employment Careers Service Branch, in the same report, as having the following characteristics: histories of truancy or frequent job changing, behavioural problems, lack of motivation, poor literacy and numeracy, difficult home backgrounds, mental and physical handicaps and, in the report's words, 'being known to the police'.

In what strikes me as cognitive dissonance, given high levels of unemployment and no doubt the expectations of the CI participants, the report went on to state that the scheme was more about self-improvement than a system for ensuring the recruitment and retention of young people who had additional barriers to finding and holding down a job. 'CI does not see solutions purely in terms of work creation, nor of skill training, but rather in terms of a broad approach to development of the individual in a disciplined yet non-authoritarian work environment.' Through this lens, CI looks more like social control dressed up as a job club. As the precursor to the Youth Training Schemes that plagued areas of high unemployment in the 1980s, the youth club was, in ways that were hard to see at the time, affecting the national picture.

Another clip, from 1972, shows a black-and-white BBC news report from Clydebank, on the other side of Glasgow. It begins with a statement that offers context: 'Youth clubs used to take place in draughty drill halls and some no doubt still are. But this is what an up-to-date youth club looks like.' Alice Cooper's 'School's Out' is on one of the two turntables. Boys in jackets and girls with thick false eyelashes are bopping confidently. The voiceover is being read by another Englishman with a received pronunciation accent, who explains that youth clubs in Scotland are plentiful, and who then presents the mining village of Fallin, near Stirling, as an example. The village lacks a café, cinema or dancehall, but it does have a busy youth centre, open throughout the week and attracting an estimated 75 per cent of the local teens.

Footage shows kids wearing the heavy Judogi jacket that comprises the top half of the judo uniform over PE knickers and bare legs, chucking each other about in a municipal Dojo. Elsewhere, others play dominos. Teenage members display a strong awareness of the need to keep funds trickling in: the cooking group sell the results of their labour to fundraise for the club, while another group of serious-minded girls come up with further ideas. One suggests a twenty-four-hour bed push, which sounds very exciting, until her more practical friend asks the question: 'Yes, but where are we going to get a bed from?'

Structures that dictated how adults should behave towards young people, and vice versa, were loosening, and the youth club provides a way to see this. Scooter maintenance at a youth club in Kirkcaldy had begun at the request of members, prompting a useful observation from the reporter: 'This is a new approach – those leading clubs believe they should listen to what their members want instead of laying down the law of what they should do . . . What these youth centres are trying to do is to give people a chance to find out what they're good at, so they can enjoy life a bit more.'

Scotland recognised the overlap between youth and community work. A report, 'Community of Interest', had emerged from the Scottish Education Department in the late 1960s and encouraged a community-based approach to both adult education and youth work. In 1975, the Alexander Report built on the idea that all areas of informal education are linked, and proposed the creation of a Community Education Service. The authors believed there would be 'much advantage from still closer association'. One line from the report stands out, despite the passing of many decades: 'It is becoming obvious that adults must in future accept young people as social equals and no longer as children expected to play adult roles only in those areas where it is convenient.' This future, it seems to me, is still to arrive.

12

1972: YOUTH CLUBS IN NORTHERN IRELAND

The power, influence and paradoxical invisibility of youth clubs across the UK zoom into view when you see how they existed, and operated, in war-zone conditions. However, the Troubles in Northern Ireland were not a conflict I experienced first-hand, instead receiving news and context through childhood and into adulthood via carefully managed British media coverage. And so, before heading any further into this complicated part of the youth club terrain, a brief look at a useful concept. Artist Tara Fatehi was born in Tehran in 1987 and lives in London. In 2020, she published *Mishandled Archive*, in which she grapples with her rights and responsibilities when it comes to telling stories about Iran. She decided to navigate the complexities by collecting over 2,000 family photographs and assorted paperwork, cutting them into new shapes and leaving them in a café or by the waterfront. Pictures of these new scenarios appeared in her book, and they're reproduced along with a record of the temperature: a reference to the controlled environments of official archives, which are often inaccessible. Like Tara, I recognise the risks that come with handling the past. I've never lived in Northern Ireland; however, I believe that the following stories are worth handling, albeit with maximum care and respect.

The ferry to Belfast skated flat across the Irish Sea. I was heading to Cushendall, in the Glens of Antrim, fifty miles north of the capital. I'd been invited to stay at the village's Curfew Tower for a month, as part of something that could be explained as a rotating artist residency, but would be better described as staying at a uniquely storied squat that had dropped into a pocket of time, circa 1996, and stayed there. Built with East India Company profits in 1817, the original owner, Francis Turnley, imagined the four-storey edifice as both a unit of oppression, with a cell to imprison riotous villagers, and, according to his writings, the heart of an 'ideal world government' where people could live in harmony. All of which explains why it might have been attractive to artist and KLF co-founder Bill Drummond, who became the tower's custodian.

It was my first time in Northern Ireland, and I arrived a few weeks before the twenty-fifth anniversary of the Good Friday Agreement, meaning that the past was more clearly on display than usual – for example, in performances of *Agreement* at the Lyric Theatre, in media commentary and in cornershop conversations. I was planning to use the time to decompress after a busy and stressful period, and to talk to people about youth clubs.

Quickly, a few things struck me. Resourcefulness and layers of community connection were notable and a high degree of self-sufficiency was apparent in business and entertainment: music and storytelling in the back room of the pub, or a strong commitment to sports – hurling and camogie – expressed through support for celebrated local team Ruairí Óg. Over the weeks I was there, I began noticing local kids, sat on benches or blasting trance versions of pop songs out of wireless speakers in the twelfth-century church ruins at Layd. I began to recognise a few, partly because Cushendall is a small place, but also because I had arranged to volunteer with a couple of youth groups.

Around fifteen young people were lounging around on soft chairs, chatting, laughing and eating pizza before their session started within the Glens Youth Club, in rooms that had once been part of St Aloysius Secondary School. Voluntary youth worker Gerry McClafferty, alongside other local people, kept the club going part-time, securing money from the Community Foundation fund to reopen the club after its Covid-era closure. Gerry had gone through this self-built system himself: he'd attended the local youth club and then volunteered there in the early 1990s, supervising football. A community leadership programme followed, part of which offered three months working in a youth club in Denmark. Fast-forward a few decades, and members of the group now took part in music production workshops, made videos, went on trips and ran fundraising jumble sales. The Glens Boxing Club shares space in this superficially straightforward and low-resource youth club, its happy ordinariness at odds with the difficulty of keeping it open, or even the fact that it was open at all. Only time will reveal what it will have done for those who attend: maybe nothing, maybe something life-shaping. Much like parenting, youth club results emerge with a time lag.

As with so many people, Gerry ended up with youth work responsibilities without having chased them. 'I was never meant to be there at all,' he told me, 'but agreed to work on securing funding and keep things ticking over until a new worker was in place. I'm still there, albeit down to thirteen hours a week, so I'm really only involved in admin and Boxing Club, and some cleaning if I can. I'm hoping our new youth worker can take control in the very near future, and my plan is only to be involved with the Boxing Club and perhaps support the club at management committee level.'

Education Authority youth service area worker Tara McHugh Logan helped keep things going in multiple ways, not least by hiring the Glens Youth Club space to run a leadership programme called Horizons, set up to tackle educational underachievement and funded by the Department of Education. It's her Horizons group that was meeting in the space when I dropped by. The programme is designed to produce well-skilled, qualified and experienced youth work volunteers. She told me: 'These volunteers start at the age of fifteen and, over time, they'll act as role models to the young people they work with, inspiring a new generation of young people into volunteering in their own communities.' The work that goes on behind the scenes to build and sustain such groups can't be underestimated. Equally invisible – and inevitable – are the effects.

Another part of her work was to offer youth provision in three rural areas, dotted up and down the coast: Cushendall, Glenariff and Cushendun. The latter had lost its youth space. I was able to see how Tara navigated the absence when I joined her for a youth club session in the village. Instead of giving up and closing down, she'd erected a gazebo around a picnic table between the chip van, the car park and the sea and welcomed a small handful of teenagers. Handing out fleeces like sweets – this was chilly springtime in Northern Ireland – she got them making videos with iPads, creating a functional and fun youth club around a trestle table. I watched a girl circle off and catch a joke in the teenage way, which meant literally dropping to the floor with the hilarity of it all. This is another thing that needs to happen when you're growing up, I think to myself: to perform falling, or to fall and be picked up again. 'We, both Gerry and I,' she said, when we spoke after I'd returned home, 'are local people with only the best interests of the local youth at heart. We are both trying to do our best, in our own way.'

Later during my stay, I organised a drop-in session in the Café Cova back room, inviting people to share their own youth club stories, with scones and pre-bagged jelly babies from the corner sweetshop as refreshments. A handful of people generously dropped by, bringing with them cross-generational stories of Portakabins with pool tables and Pacman, or a tuck shop stocked with local fizzy drinks brand Smak Cola and Tayto's playground-popular Banshee Bones crisps. There was flirting – 'getting your cousin to get your cousin's friend to ask someone out', as someone put it – and the odd fight, mostly over bullying. In a way that I suspect would be familiar across the nations, there was a local 'scary house' providing chaperone-free space outside of youth club hours. Two stories in particular illustrate the experience of people who were young at the same time as me, over here, not over there.

One young person, at the hurling pitch, went to retrieve the sliotar, or ball, which had gone over the high nets and down a short incline towards the beach. He tripped over a British soldier who was hiding in the bushes, surveilling the caravan park. Another recalled a camping trip with a friend. There had been a car bomb down the road and the place was swarming with soldiers. It might not have been the wisest time to camp in the woods, but kids aren't always wise, and he certainly did not expect to wake in the night to someone walking around the tent. He knew it must be a soldier, and the knowledge froze him. He couldn't move, couldn't wake his friend, just had to wait it out. The experience imprinted itself on him and, decades later, was still causing occasional nightmares.

We'll stay in the village of Cushendall for a while longer, dropping back into earlier decades to try to understand the layered history of youth-led provision in this part of Northern Ireland. I met Paul McAlister, now retired from life as a teacher and senior member of the ETI, Northern Ireland's equivalent to Ofsted, because I'd been told he started a youth club as a teenager in the village in the early 1970s. Over cups of coffee, he told me the story.

Aged nine or ten, he'd attend a youth session upstairs in the Men's Club, where he was taught how to catch a ball properly, above the head. In 1972, aged fifteen, he and a group of friends decided they wanted a youth club of their own, to reflect the changing times. 'Boys were starting to grow their hair long, congregating around transistor radios and listening to pop music,' he said. 'Adults were almost scared of you – these youths were starting to have opinions.' The group put a notice in the parish newsletter, asking for someone to help them get started. Supportive adult acquired, the group was allowed use of St Aloysius school, and pooled their emerging skills to make what they felt was needed for the necessary fundraising discos.

One thirteen-year-old made lights by wiring the starter from a strip of fluorescent lighting into a putty drum that contained three primary-coloured bulbs. Unsurprisingly, the proto-sparky went on to become a consultant electrical engineer. A girl, Caitríona, who was good at art, copied Disney characters from a colouring book onto the wall, which glowed in the dark once they discovered that someone's big brother in

Belfast had an ultraviolet light for sale. The school's woodwork class was put to work making a case for the record turntables. 'It was really very creative for a crowd of teenagers,' he said, with a smile. 'This occupied us Saturday after Saturday.' Cushendall's youth-run scenario was now established and had become self-financing, adding an extra digit to the number of voluntary clubs in existence at the time.

Raising funds for a basketball – just the one – was their first aim, and the discos made this possible. 'We had a team,' said Paul. 'Games against youth clubs in Ballymena. The early 1970s was a terrible time in Northern Ireland, and for a group of young people to be venturing to Ballymena to play basketball was . . .' He trailed off and sighed, with an exhalation that signalled the difficulty of being young during the Troubles, when travelling outside your immediate area was, at the very least, complicated. 'It was something parents were concerned about, but it was never any difficulty in terms of the sectarian violence that was going on. In fact, it was very beneficial that young people had something to put their energy into.'

Youth provision was built from the ground up, at least partly because of the politics. Paul has a long view. 'In this area, one of the things I learned from a young age was, don't expect the authorities to do anything for this area,' he said. 'I had that background: don't wait for somebody else to do something for you. The way the political situation was in Northern Ireland, this area was not going to get any favours.'

All of this took place, of course, while the Troubles played out. Cycles of conflict had been reignited in the late 1960s, after civil-rights-inspired demands for an end to gerrymandering and discrimination against Catholics in housing and employment were met with extreme violence, most notoriously in January

1972, on Bloody Sunday. While youngsters from that demographic had to deal with specific issues, all young people were exposed to the long haul of trauma caused by conflict, which bent every aspect of life out of shape. Segregation and sectarianism led to whole-society harm, in a country with higher than average numbers of young people, and which also suffered from disproportionate levels of poverty and unemployment.

Many attempts to describe the Troubles lean into basic, binary simplifications, leaving out the similarities between working-class people, or those whose families contained both Protestants and Catholics, or the reality that many people were sucked into everyday peril by individuals with structural power, including politicians, chief constables, army captains and paramilitary leaders. Inconvenient nuance is easily overlooked, such as the existence of pro-Irish Protestants, Catholics not keen on reunification, atheists (Catholic and Protestant, as the joke goes) and those of other faiths or none. Some areas were often free of violence, even as they absorbed shockwaves emanating from elsewhere; not everywhere was Belfast, not even Belfast. It is fair to say, though, that youth clubs across Northern Ireland were to varying degrees all coloured by events, with youth workers attempting to provide something approximating normality.

Nothing here can be separated from the British occupation of Ireland, which lasted for centuries, until the War of Independence (1919–21). Eleven months of Civil War then followed (1922–3), culminating in partition and the unequal society that followed. And so, when I say that youth work evolved in specific ways across the border, this is because of what might politely be described as 'reasons'.

Youth club histories in Northern Ireland would, then, develop in the British style, in terms of not only formal clubs affiliated to the UK-wide NAYC, but also grassroots, DIY alternatives, both relying, at least to some extent, on volunteers. By the onset of the Troubles, there was a range of youth groups. Young Farmers' Clubs, adventure playgrounds and the uniformed organisations – the various Brigades, Scouts and Guides – were well established, alongside the YMCA and an umbrella organisation, the Northern Irish Association of Youth Clubs. In 1972, the Westminster government passed the Education and Libraries (Northern Ireland) Order. Requiring the provision of facilities for 'recreational, social, physical, cultural and youth service activities', the Order made Northern Ireland anomalous in this way too, as the only part of the UK with a strong legal basis for youth work.

Between the establishment of the youth service and 1981, when Thatcherite cuts began to bite, Northern Ireland experienced a funding boom comparable to that unleashed by Lady Albemarle's report. The upswing was huge: in 1972, the annual allocation to the youth service was £125,500. Between 1974 and 1979, funding increased from £2.5m to over £6m per annum and the number of youth workers doubled. There were 143 purpose-built youth facilities completed, including youth centres, residential centres, premises for Brigades, Guides and Scouts, and school-based youth wings. Churches could apply to government for funds to open youth clubs, although these needed to be, technically at least, non-faith-specific. Full-time youth work posts were created, including new 'detached' youth workers deployed on the streets and estates instead of within youth club halls, and professional training was developed.

Derry-born Dr Desmond Bell, known as Des, is an award-winning film-maker and academic, digging into the worlds of film, photography and media for universities across Britain and Ireland. In his study of youth culture and sectarianism, *Acts of Union*, he outlined the changes the Troubles brought to Ulster's youth provision. For example, before 1975, less than one in ten clubs were state-provided, and 65 per cent of all leaders came from the uniformed organisations. The colonial DNA of Scouts and Brigades would limit their reach in specific ways. Uniformed organisations were, he wrote, 'unequal to the challenge posed by civil conflict', adding wryly that they 'had little purchase on the activities of working class youth, particularly Catholic teenagers from the most riot-prone areas of Belfast and Derry'.

When we chatted, I asked Des if he'd attended youth club himself, in the era just before the Troubles reignited. No, he said, although his younger brother did. 'The creation of the youth service in Northern Ireland happened because of the Troubles,' he said. 'Before, if it existed at all, it was voluntary and largely attached to church membership. If you weren't into church membership, you wouldn't have wanted to go to those youth clubs.' Instead of drilling with the Brigades, Des instead joined bands, playing rhythm and blues, jazz and rock in dive bars and on the American naval base in Derry – 'which is why I would not regard these places as terribly cool'.

Conflict, then, generated clubs for the young. The youth service, reiterated Des, 'was a response to young people throwing bricks in the street, as was the provision of sports facilities. They were all "get them off the streets" tactics paid for by the Labour government that was in power for a period of time during the Troubles.' A predictable series of processes would be set in motion: government diktat would open doors into newly constructed buildings, and once inside, the youth workers would do what was *actually* necessary.

'Government policy was that this was a way of drawing young people out of conflict situations. I think a lot of the clubs saw their role much more seriously,' he told me, describing efforts to address the problems young people were experiencing: sectarian division, territorialisation, depression, suicide, marginalisation and 'a terribly divided education system'. Youth workers, he said, 'with some training and some awareness of the broader social framework in which this system had evolved, were pushing at the boundaries and doing interesting work – courageous work – with these young people, because despite the bravado, the reality was that many of these young people's lives were shattered.' Youth clubs in this era, he asserted, played a central role in allowing young people to talk to an adult they trusted.

Even with cash flowing, the voluntary sector outstripped the newly grown state provision. In 1975, the Education and Library Boards identified 130 clubs operated by the Boards, alongside 1,300 voluntary clubs, including Paul McAlister's in Cushendall. Community-run clubs were the majority by some distance. Then and now, 'community' was a shape-shifting word that did a lot of heavy lifting in a society being trained in the indirect. It could mean 'of the people' or 'village', or it might be shorthand for working class or an alternative to words including 'Catholic' or 'Protestant'. The meaning depended on the telling, and the teller.

To claim state funds, youth clubs needed a constitution and a management committee. Those that wanted a less formal set-up had to look elsewhere. The Open Door youth club in east Belfast was set up in 1977 with grants from the Prince's

Trust, which the young people themselves applied for. BBC news footage from two years later captures boys and girls playing table tennis and snooker, while a group of girls are shown their way around a sewing machine. A nervous young man wearing two jackets over his shirt and jumper answers a reporter's questions while saying as little as possible: 'It's very important, keeps them off the streets. It keeps them out of trouble. There's people here can look after them, no worries.'

Club organiser Winnie Jordan offered a no-nonsense adult perspective: there were a lot of young people standing around on street corners with nothing to do and nowhere to go. 'They don't conform to the traditional youth club scene or the church unfortunately. We don't try to sweep them under the carpet. They're there, so we must help them.' She looks the reporter clear in the eye. 'I can see a vast difference in the young people since two years ago when we first started,' she says, with something approaching a smile. 'I can see them blossoming out . . . I think there should be Open Doors all over Northern Ireland, and that the local mums and dads should make the management committees for them, and look after them with the young people. I think it would break down the generation gap an awful lot.'

Young people at the sharp end of the political chaos must have required a multiplicity of spaces. Some would have had tiny amounts of room to decide where they went or who they met, with many of these decisions being laid down by the realities of family or community life. Even those growing up some distance from bombs or riots, in theoretically quieter parts of the country, or coming to visit family in the holidays, must have been on high alert compared to their peers in many other parts of the UK.

Northern Ireland was represented when the NAYC met in Sheffield for its annual conference, eight years after violence broke out. George Johnston was the director of the Northern Ireland branch, and he brought a message to his contemporaries across the water. 'Youth clubs in England could find themselves in competition with the youth sections of agencies which see violence as a means to an end if the country is not prepared to learn from the lessons of Northern Ireland,' he said, adding that ordinary young people, 'just like many of you here', played a significant part in paramilitary organisations, planting bombs, carrying out assassinations and forming torture and punishment squads.

Ending his speech on a positive note, Johnston told the NAYC conference that things were improving in Northern Ireland. 'More volunteers are emerging and up to 500 community associations have been established,' he concluded. 'Many self-help ideas have been introduced.'

This response, of 'self-help ideas', can be seen throughout the youth club story. The effect, of course, is especially clear here.

———

Investing in Lives is Ulster University's unparalleled two-volume history of the youth service in Northern Ireland. Volume One covers 1844 to 1973 and was written by leading lights of NI youth work Professor Sam McCready and Richard Loudon, whose death in 2022 was marked with a fundraising musical celebration at Belfast's art venue the Black Box, with proceeds going to peace and reconciliation organisation Corrymeela.

Volume Two was edited by the pair and contains chapters from key voices in the field, covering 1973 to 2017. Both are hefty contributions to our collective knowledge and offer structural context, precise factual detail and street-level intel. There are many remarkable moments: the arrival of evangelical preacher Billy Graham in Belfast in 1946 with international outfit Youth for Christ, which would later run a youth club and one of Northern Ireland's first coffee bars on the Ormeau Road; or mind-bending tales of CIA officers masquerading as youth workers.

Another section tells the story of nun and secondary school teacher Sister Mairéad, who started the Ichthus Youth Club in Short Strand, in inner-city Belfast, in the very early days of the conflict. In the wake of a major gun battle that took place on the streets, Sister Mairéad began taking Saturday-evening walks around the area with her colleague, Sister Geraldine, to get to know the young people better. This resulted in the pair asking the local priest and the Army for permission to use a Portakabin in the grounds of the local boys' primary school to run discos, with two nineteen-year-old women helping run things. In a carefully oblivious phrase that typifies alternative economies and grassroots youth work across time and space, *Investing in Lives* tells us that the nuns 'borrowed a turntable from somewhere'.

Dances followed, along with the need to develop youth leaders from among the girls, who were less likely than the boys to be recruited by the paramilitaries. Quickly, the group outgrew the Portakabin and moved into an empty two-up, two-down terraced house on Thompson Street, refurbished and redecorated by youth club members, because, at this point, neither the nuns nor the kids even knew that funding existed. Activities included weekly dances, five-a-side football, with occasional cross-community matches, and a tug-of-war, with rope borrowed from the Army. Other testimonies in McCready and Loudon's book describe incredible manoeuvring around very tight spaces: for example, ensuring paramilitaries didn't infiltrate youth club committees and governance, or church youth clubs that were robbed 'very many times'.

Some youth workers paid with their lives. Memorialised in McCready and Loudon's book is Sean Armstrong, who had been organising international holidays for cross-community groups of young people when he was shot dead at home by Loyalist paramilitaries in 1973. Nicholas White was killed by the IRA in 1976 while unlocking the gates of the youth club, and teacher and voluntary youth worker Michael Brennan was shot the following year outside St Mary's Youth Club in Belfast by an offshoot of the Ulster Volunteer Force.

Despite the risks, the work continued. Youth workers created and preserved tiny spaces in which attendees could do ordinary things during extraordinary times. These experiences allowed for the widening of their worldview, through trips out of locked-in areas or via limited cross-community activities. The fact that youth workers were able to do this at all suggests that even paramilitaries, the RUC and the British Army understood that the youth needed a break once a week or so.

Investing in Lives author Professor Sam McCready was on the other side of my laptop screen. The co-founder of the Centre for Young Men's Studies at Ulster University opened the conversation with a very reasonable question: 'So, why are you writing about Northern Ireland?' He paused and laughed. 'I think you might find it's slightly different – but maybe that's the appeal.'

I accounted for myself as follows: that it would be wrong not to include Northern Ireland if I was also including England,

Scotland and Wales, and that doing so would amplify my message that making space for young people is an essential part of a functioning society.

He nodded, if not in agreement, then in acceptance. 'One of the key things about Northern Ireland is how intrinsically our provision is tied in with the Troubles. In a simplistic way, whenever the Troubles occurred, people were trapped in their own communities and had to look inward for their social outlets,' he said, describing the way men and women took to building their own shebeens or social clubs. 'The community I came from was part of a very broad movement in working-class areas where you so-called had to defend your community against others. We had our own vigilante groups.' In short, he said, the men in his area of south Belfast had decided they'd open a social club, and this process raised another question about space for the next generation.

'Somebody rapped on my door and said, "Sam, you go to university, would you look after the young people?" They commandeered a hall and they gave me the keys at nineteen years of age. My introduction to youth work was not forced, but my contribution to my community's defence of itself was to run a youth club. For others of my friends, they had other choices to make. My choice was made for me, and I was able to escape, if you like, any combatant duty.' He paused and recapped, like any good educator. 'So that, in a nutshell, is my story of how I became a youth worker. Someone put their hand on my shoulder and said, "You do this." My mate down the road, he was given a gun, and I was given the keys to a youth club.'

The clubs Sam grew up in and ran from the late 1960s onwards were unavoidably political. 'Many of our youth workers and youth clubs came from that indigenous, instinctive way of providing your own provision,' he said. All of the above meant that running youth clubs in Northern Ireland at this time wasn't simply a matter of finding a space and inviting people in. 'Half of the time it was about the row going on outside. It was about locking doors, sometimes, not opening doors. It's carried through thematically: peace and reconciliation, the role of a youth club in a community.'

Music did allow for doors to be opened, however. By September 1973, he had completed a degree at Queen's University, Belfast, and had gained a postgraduate qualification in youth work at Birmingham University. Now married, he returned to live and work in east Belfast, and took his first full-time job. Operating from the house he shared with his wife, he ran youth provision and mobile discos. 'It allowed the young people to go into different communities – the safety of bringing music. It didn't matter which community you were from. We were clearly from a Protestant community, but we were able to go into Catholic communities.' Travelling across the city with a box of Top Twenty pop hits allowed for somewhat safer passage.

Political realities had quickly transformed every aspect of teenage social life, but the teenage DJs from his youth club knew that music could bring people together, and they made the most of the opportunity. 'It was mostly the young men that did all the work around the twin decks,' observed Sam. 'They'd go into another community, start playing the music, and other young men would come up and ask them about the music and the decks and how you played them.' After a while, he said, they'd swap places, giving young Catholics a chance to select and play the tunes, while the Protestants got to dance with young women from across the faith divide – offering a rare opportunity for these girls to come into contact with non-Catholic young men. This was the youth club disco at its most powerful.

Moving together to music is bonding, and while conditions did not allow these dancefloor connections to flourish, they provided an example that would later be built on in the 1990s, in coastal rave arenas like Kelly's in Portrush, where faith affiliations could be temporarily left at the door, or, at least, made less important than the next tune and the slippery rush that might accompany it. A memorable phrase from McCready and Loudon's history of youth work seems appropriate here and in so many other places in this story. 'Good people,' they wrote, 'have a multiplier effect.'

———

Youth-run activities emerged in generational waves, some of which I was able to catch during my time in Cushendall. I'd been introduced to storyteller, musician and elder care specialist Feargal Lynn before I'd arrived because he knew so much about the history of the place. He became a great guide, lending me books, introducing me to people and generously fielding my endless questions about how youth clubs had worked in the area across the decades. His story is personal, but it leans towards the universal, at least in explaining how attending youth club can kick-start a lifelong process.

At St Aloysius, during his first year at secondary school, he picked up the baton. 'It was a gathering place,' he told me, 'like school without the lessons.' Woodwork and sports were on offer, but it was the music that really captured his attention. An old-fashioned box record player, beige, with a grey lid, came with a collection of singles. The girls had majority control of the turntable, putting on smash hit songs from *Grease*, like 'You're the One That I Want' or 'Summer Nights', and Feargal remembered seeing his mates acting out the dance scenes from the film, briefly inhabiting a character or an emotion. Others were learning traditional Irish music, some of whom went on to be influential in the local Comhaltas – an organisation established in 1951 and now promoting the music, song, dance and language of Ireland worldwide. Youth club concerts entertained the parents.

Down the coast in Glenariff, a punky underage disco uplift beckoned and allowed Feargal to amplify what he'd encountered at St Aloysius. DJ Mulch played music in the parish hall: 'Le Freak' by Chic, alongside the Sex Pistols' 'God Save the Queen', The Clash's 'London Calling' and Sham 69's 'If the Kids Are United', with youth club volunteers overseeing events. The experience gave him access to subculture, and a place to create shared psychic space with music lovers over an hour away in Belfast or across the water in London, Glasgow or Leeds.

'We decided we were punks,' he grinned, animated by the comedy of youthful experiences that were able to emerge because of having spaces and places in which to practise being himself. 'To be a punk you had to dye your hair, but you couldn't dye your hair and go to school. We used yellow food colourant instead, and I remember walking in the door with this Toyah Willcox look, colour in my hair – the Pistols have arrived at the disco! We walked home in the rain, and it completely stained our skin. I remember having a shower and trying to get it off, and it kept going forever. It was like *Psycho*, but yellow.'

By 1983, sixteen-year-old Feargal and his friend Brian Kearney had got together the money to buy their own mobile disco. The proprietor at Kelly's, which could be described as a sibling to the Hippodrome and the Haçienda, sold turntables, speakers, lights, amps and various cables and controllers to Feargal and Brian for £260, a significant sum. The pair took the kit straight into the parish hall for their inaugural teenage disco, under a new name: Cloud 9. Once more, the metaphorical youth club trampoline was in full effect, bouncing Feargal and his friends from being participants to organisers.

Opportunities were being generated for slightly older young people to also pass on knowledge and opportunities to those a few years below them at school. By midnight, once Cloud 9 was over, Feargal and Brian would head up the hill to the Thornlea Hotel, where locally famous DJ and volunteer lifeguard Paddy McLaughlin was resident at the busy disco. One night, Feargal was standing next to Paddy, on the stage, in front of a curtain. Behind the curtain was a window, and it was being banged on by Paddy's brother. The lifeboat crew had been called out. Paddy went out through the window, leaving Feargal on stage to decide how the hell to follow Gary Numan's 'Cars', which was rotating on the turntable, threatening to finish before he made his next selection.

'Youth club gave me the confidence to have a life that wasn't oriented towards sport,' Feargal said. 'We live in a very sport-oriented community here. It's an adhesive in the village, whether you play hurling or GAA. I was not into sport at all. Youth clubs gave me confidence to make friends and to aspire, maybe, to music and the arts. To develop the social skills of how to be a friend.' Learning how to be friendly is an important skill for any young person, I think, but particularly so in environments marked by conflict.

These days, on a summer evening in Cushendall, local men of a certain age will probably start gathering in Duck's Sweetshop on the crossroads at the centre of the village. Eating crisps and chatting, they sift through communal comings and goings in familiar code, shared jokes and references forming multi-layered conversational netting.

Dominic 'Duck' McAlister runs the shop, so he'll already be there, behind the counter, from which he sells confectionery, candy vapes and colourful water pistols. Feargal Lynn will be there too, hanging out with his friends, happily gassing. 'I feel sorry for the tourists that walk in and think they're in the middle of a heist,' said Feargal. 'All these men, standing there. It's just class, it really is.' Only half jokingly, they call these informal regular meet-ups 'the Auld Boys' Youth Club'.

It is indeed a youth club of sorts, thrown forward. 'We probably talk about the same stuff, just forty-four years later,' he added, perhaps inhabiting both time zones at once. '"I fell off my bike." "Why is your dog called Rusty when it's white?"' The craic is freeform and local, amusing themselves with recent comings and goings, the car that went over the ditch out on the road last week or the recent storm that re-routed the river across the beach. 'It's a great release for me in terms of the way I think,' said Feargal. 'All the ludicrous goings-on. Dominic talks about his pigeons. A whole flock of pigeons will be going down Shore Street, and he'll say, "That five at the end, they're mine." It's amusing for my juvenile mind. It allows me to be thirteen or fourteen again, at youth club, talking crap.'

During the pandemic, they began live streaming on Face-book so that friends who'd moved abroad could join in. 'My generation are all over the world,' said Feargal. 'All the Cloud 9ers with their families in South Africa, America, China. Now we do it whenever there's news to be shared. They tarmacked the coast road last month, and we had a special broadcast.'

It's a kind of public service, I think. The Auld Boys' Youth Club is transmitting connection, for the middle-aged friends squashed into Duck's Sweetshop and for those attending remotely. In addition, a process is taking place of laying down what Feargal described as 'the very basic stories of the area, the habits and customs, the shenanigans'. It's a fundamentally human thing to do, something we've been doing collectively since caveman times, when prehistoric Feargals and Ducks scratched wavy lines and oxen onto the walls. All of which gives me a funny thought about teenage cave kids hanging out together and the inevitable comedy of Stone Age life, and the kind of collective togetherness they'd no doubt have generated for themselves.

I am surer than ever that the youth club has always existed.

13

1973: PHAB CAMPS BRING PEOPLE TOGETHER

Grassroots energies and mainstream concerns about discrimination had also begun to animate central structures. Awareness was growing that something had to be done for the estimated 11 per cent of young people with a disability of one form or another. In Birmingham, teenager Simon Wadsworth turned awareness into action after attending a summer camp in New York that aimed to bring together children from across the ability spectrum, and decided to replicate this experimental situation in the Midlands. In 1967, after two years of fund-raising and planning, he took forty children away on holiday to Hampshire, with the express purpose of integrating disabled and non-disabled youth, groups referred to at the time as 'physically handicapped' and 'able-bodied' respectively. Twenty-five of the holiday crew had varying forms of physical disability; their fifteen non-disabled peers mostly came from large families in the Balsall Heath or Sparkbrook areas of Birmingham, and, according to Andrew Miles's celebratory history, *50 Years of Birmingham PHAB Camps*, wouldn't otherwise have had a holiday.

The NAYC had created a group, the Physically Handicapped and Able Bodied (PHAB), in 1957, said Andrew when we caught up. 'The origins of Birmingham PHAB Camps and National PHAB – now Phab England – are quite distinct,' he told me. 'The Birmingham Camps were conceived of entirely separately, and in no relation to NAYC, but one of our founders, Jane Markham, heard of their work and used the acronym for our charity.'

Elizabeth McCann was twelve years old when she attended this first camp, along with two younger brothers. The siblings, whose parents ran a pub in Birmingham, had been referred by a local adventure playground leader. A half-century later, as part of the fiftieth-anniversary celebrations, Elizabeth recalled the circumstances of her involvement: her face had been burned in an accident a few years previously, other children had been unkind about the scars, and she'd been held back a year at school. 'To cut a long story short, I was having some problems and I think [the adventure playground leader] thought the holiday would help me.'

The interview with her, which is included in Andrew's history, is a delightful read, in which a woman in her early sixties is transported back to her pre-teen self. Reading it, you can feel both versions of this person peeking through, with detail and memory flooding through the lines afresh. Elizabeth recalled delicious cooked breakfasts, new friends, a 'beautiful' girl whose walking was impaired, and falling in puppy love with a 'gorgeous' boy who also happened to be in a wheelchair. The adults were young, or young at heart, and this she remembered too. 'People aren't being horrible to me or telling me I'm naughty or whatever. This was people telling me I could do things.'

Interestingly, Elizabeth also recalled aspects of interpersonal kid-level drama that might not have been visible to the adults, remembering punching a boy who'd probably be described as disabled because she thought he was bullying her brother. To me, this brutal but equalising logic cuts across the power dynamic that infantilises those whose bodies work differently:

if you're a bully, you can expect to be punched, regardless of how your body looks.

Fifty years later, Elizabeth has children, grandchildren and a nephew with cerebral palsy. Much of her working life was spent with the trade union UNISON, liaising with the city councils and other organisations. 'Standing up for others had always been important to me and disability's come into that. Looking back, I think the Camp could have been the start of that – for the good. Money couldn't buy that experience.'

Towards the end of the commemorative interview, the interviewer brings out a set of photographs from the 1967 camp that capture many of the memories she's already dug up. Her response leaps off the page. 'My heart is pounding here and the welling up inside me is like . . .' She then continues: 'That is the most wonderful gift to give a child: friends . . . people they can relate to. I suppose that was their aim, wasn't it, those that set it up – shared experiences?' The bringing together of young people across the perceived ability divide dealt in what you might call a profound economy: spending effort on relationships, connection and understanding, and continuing to draw interest from the experience many decades later.

The camp, deemed a success by both participants and funders, was repeated the next year and led to the formation of Birmingham PHAB Camps as an independent registered charity. To this day, it runs numerous holidays each summer for children of all abilities and backgrounds. Back in August 1969, however, volunteer Tony Gray kept a diary of his time on a Birmingham PHAB Camp, and it acts as a colourful counterpoint to an official report.

Operating what Andrew Miles described as a 'two-volunteer' rule, well before mandatory safeguarding, to ensure that individual adults were never alone with a child, the camp included a 'magical mystery tour', which started at the petrol station and ended at the cinema. Kids kept the grown-ups awake in classic school-trip style, and adult volunteers decamped to the pub most nights. Activities included art, singing and dressmaking, and sports such as archery and rifle shooting, while a celebratory mid-camp BBQ for 'friends, guests, relations and yobs' is detailed with humour. References to sing-songs in the 'Phabmobile' lead me to photographs of a mud-brown minibus, decorated on the outside with home-made artwork. The thoughts of the young people who attended are not recorded, but it looks like a right laugh, inclusive, liberal and truly memorable.

By 1980, the NAYC's Annual Youth Conference was reiterating that the organisation's PHAB youth clubs were meant to be for everyone: 'It is a club set up for handicapped and able-bodied members to help one another understand problems of both groups, in the form of a voluntary club organising social evenings and events.'

The unnamed report writer positioned other youth groups as extractive, specifically naming the Girl Guides, Scouts and people involved in the Duke of Edinburgh's Award, who 'use the disabled for their own achievement . . . Some of these people get involved, but when they have completed the given time, they sometimes do not return. Most people don't realise that involvement with handicapped children can bring enjoyment to both parties.' The underlying reasons for hostility towards those with additional needs were discussed, with the suggestion that 'other able-bodied people didn't know enough about them to show an interest'.

It occurs to me that everyone misses out when the able-bodied separate themselves from peers who find it more difficult to move through the world. Age will eventually cause almost everyone to understand what it's like when the body can't do everything the mind or spirit requires. And these early holiday camps initiated by Birmingham PHAB Camps back in the '60s strike me as the kind of practical exercise in togetherness and equalisation that is still necessary now. I see it happening in a long-lasting and brilliant youth club called Do Your Own Thing, as documented in Richard Phoenix's book of the same name, but it's rare. Embedding – or embodying – anti-ableist togetherness in this way would be good for everyone.

———

The radiating positivity that comes across in first-hand reports about integrated youth clubs makes it even more unpleasant to have to raise what comes next. Predatory adults have lurked on the edges of this story since the beginning, but it came as a shock when I came across references to Jimmy Savile in the archive, and having done so, I could not pretend I had not. These are the facts: in 1974, Savile became honorary president of PHAB. He had been awarded an OBE three years earlier for his charitable works and was a household name, famous through his Radio 1 show and his hosting stints on *Top of the Pops*. He handed over the presidency of PHAB to Rolf Harris in 1988. 'What seems like only a year or two ago,' wrote Harris, nonchalantly, in *Nursing Standard* in 2000, 'Jimmy Savile asked me if I would be president of PHAB.' By 2002, Harris had stepped down, joining instead the list of vice presidents. Fundraising pages created by individuals running the London Marathon described him as PHAB vice president as late as

2010. In June 2014, Harris was found guilty of indecent assault under the Sexual Offences Act, with eleven of the twelve charges upheld by the Court of Appeal in 2017.

I was sitting on a bench in Deptford when Mik Scarlet, co-CEO of the successor organisation – now styled Phab – called. Behind me was a colourful mural made by arts organisation Heart 'n' Soul, which is led by people both with and without learning disabilities and autism. Mik had taken the role a year earlier and was shocked but not surprised to read about Harris and Savile. He wanted to reassure me that the organisation had changed, adding for context that the role of president within charities is nominal, mostly ceremonial, and offered to send me their current safeguarding policies. 'We've moved from being a paternal disability charity to one that's inclusive and self-led, a co-production model,' he said, quoting the slogan that disabled activists made famous: 'Nothing about us without us.'

A year before taking the honorary presidency of PHAB, Savile had joined the long list of vice presidents of the NAYC. His photograph is hard to avoid in NAYC records from this era. One example appears on material relating to the 'Tea-Rific Fun and Happiness week with Jimmy Savile, OBE, Vice-President', which took place in April 1974. Sponsored by the Tea Council, forty-two young people from clubs across the country attended the week-long event, which was based at NAYC's London HQ on Devonshire Street. The itinerary began with 'tea and "pep talk"' from Savile and included visits to the Post Office's underground railway and the Tower of London, supper and a disco every night bar the Monday. The event was repeated, across a weekend and a 'mini-week', the following year. Savile remained on the list of vice presidents at the National Association – renamed Youth Clubs UK, and now UK Youth – until 1996.

Adults with bad intentions attempted to make their way into other aspects of national youth club life too. In 1978, the NAYC's Annual Youth Conference took place at Sheffield University. Operating under the title 'When Are We Old Enough?', resolutions dealt with the use of alcohol – a motion proposing that brewers give a percentage of their profits to the NAYC was carried unanimously – with others relating to crime and punishment. The conference agreed that police brutality was increasing and that a national investigation of membership experiences was required as a priority.

Also on the list of resolutions was a motion dealing with the age of consent. Intended as a request for parity at a time when the age of consent was sixteen for heterosexual couples and twenty-one for homosexual men, it was effectively hijacked by Tom O'Carroll, chairman of the Paedophile Information Exchange (PIE). The organisation's existence seems inconceivable now, but it existed as a campaigning group between 1974 and 1984, when the group disbanded. Three years after speaking at the NAYC conference, O'Carroll was sent to prison for conspiring to corrupt public morals, in a case centred around the PIE magazine.

A press statement included in the NAYC conference report makes clear that O'Carroll's presence was highly contentious. It explains that his involvement had been originally considered as part of the conference topic – the age of consent – stating that young people wanted to hear from PIE about just what the organisation stood for. The National Conference Committee intervened, writing to O'Carroll to inform him that his invitation had been withdrawn. The statement continues: 'Mr O'Carroll claimed not to have received the letter withdrawing the invitation and turned up at Sheffield University. After further consideration the Committee again asked Mr O'Carroll not to make any public statement to the Conference and the Committee hoped that Mr O'Carroll would respect their wishes and not involve himself any further in the conference.'

Involved he was. Author Mark K. Smith was also at the conference through his club work in Amersham. He was about to join the NAYC as the co-ordinator of a new political education project, which itself was part of an initiative by the Department of Education and Science. 'No one would take on chairing the meeting,' he told me. 'Being stupid, I said, "I'll do it."' The meeting, which I only experienced at a remove, through archive material, suddenly comes to life. It's like being swept from one time zone to another. The shock of seeing a historic detail from the archive come to life hits me like a wave. 'I think it is important to highlight that the thinking was *that* astray,' he said. 'I had a number of gay and lesbian friends, partly through NAYC, who were questioning this, for obvious reasons. I don't know why I said I'd do it – cocky bastard, really.' He paused again. 'It was an interesting meeting to try and contain. Great anger in the room. Complete bullshit from this whateverhisnamewas.'

In response, a motion was proposed by NAYC members: 'Having listened to a member of the Paedophilia Information Exchange (PIE) and being concerned for the welfare of children in our society, we condemn and wholeheartedly disagree with its teachings and practices. We have sympathy with and concern for those who share, or may be drawn to the attitudes of the PIE. People should be made more aware of paedophilia and given the chance to express their views and opinions, so that we have a much better understanding of each other.' The motion was carried, with three against and twenty-five abstentions.

The typed pages of the conference report contain a two-and-a-half-page statement written by Tom O'Carroll outlining his organisation's beliefs. I felt compelled to wash my hands after reading it.

14

1974: ALL ABOARD THE BARGE CLUB

Another example takes us through the doors of grassroots-generated youth clubs in the early 1970s, where workers created spaces for neighbourhood youth. Except, this time, we're not going through a door. We're stepping off the Thames quayside near the Isle of Dogs, onto one of four barges run by riverman John Westfallen. The forty-year-old ex-Thames lighterman was a real character, briefly elected one of two prime ministers of the Isle of Dogs, after Labour councillor Ted Johns and supporters barricaded Westferry Road and the road bridge over the entrance to West India Docks and declared independence in spring 1970. This real-life version of the Ealing comedy *Passport to Pimlico* was an attempt to force Tower Hamlets council to address some of the many problems facing the area, including the absence of a secondary school, poor health care facilities and only one bus route to get you into and out of the peninsula. Meetings with the Home Secretary followed, which, according to Westfallen's son, Tony, led to the earliest conversations about the development that would become Canary Wharf.

John Westfallen's floating youth club would soon make waves. Their first barge, *The Linwood*, was bought by Westfallen and renovated with the help of a group of local youngsters, who did it up with bunks, a galley and 18ft oars. In the summer of 1971, the group rowed across to France to raise enough money to buy a motor barge, which the young people named

The Westfallen J. By 1974, the club was thriving, with 118 members who sailed, scrubbed the deck and learned the ways of the water under their leader's no-messing command. On board there was a snooker table and sleeping accommodation for nearly thirty. After one trip away, the Isle of Dogs kids clubbed together to buy Westfallen a gift: an expensive lighter, which they presented with a handwritten note. It read: 'Thanks once again for a great time and for putting up with us all for four days. Sorry if we mucked you about a bit and we hope this present will account for it.'

Westfallen was petitioning the council to pay him to do the work full-time. It seems like a small ask, given what he'd already achieved through what a BBC *Nationwide* reporter described in 1974 as 'diabolically skilled scrounging'; donations included radar and a depth sounder to make the boats safe. 'Most work in working-class areas is done by unpaid, part-time youth leaders,' Westfallen told the BBC reporter at the time. 'To start youth work, you've got to start from the heart.' He explained that he couldn't afford to keep it going on a part-time wage. A local councillor popped up to say that, well, times are tight and everyone has to make cuts, and couldn't they just keep going anyway?

John Westfallen died suddenly in 1975, a year after the BBC stepped on board his floating youth club. His son, Tony, responded when I posted a request on an Isle of Dogs local history page and offered me additional context. 'Dad took his redundancy money from the docks in '73, after his first heart attack, and Mum worked in a sweatshop in Whitechapel,' he said, adding that the boats were bought and paid for by his father, and that the club survived on subscriptions and fund-raising, plus various donations of equipment and tools.

'My father very much controlled the club, and when he died, no one was available with the necessary boat or river skills to keep it going,' Tony said. 'A few members and my uncle tried to keep the club going with the canal barge. However, it didn't last long because the outings became less attractive and much tamer – just occasional trips up and down the River Lea.'

While it's important to avoid singularising collective effort, the story of the barge club clearly shows that these spaces also rely on extraordinary individuals. Keeping things going without them, in the absence of funding or structural support, can be almost impossible. Youth workers, I think, are unsung heroes.

———

Times were tight, but the UK did have a functioning youth service, albeit one feeding on scraps: for every pound spent on education, only one penny went to the youth service. MPs tried twice, in 1974 and 1975, to address the shortcomings of the 1944 Education Act, which called for 'adequate provision', but in vague terms. A patchy situation followed as some local authorities prioritised their young people and others didn't. And in the words of Conservative MP for Middleton and Prestwich Alan Haselhurst, 'when cuts have come it has been all too easy to make the youth service the first victim'. Before bringing a Private Member's Bill to parliament in 1974, Haselhurst spent over a year touring the country, asking youth officers, youth workers and many youngsters what should be included.

The passage of his Youth and Community Bill through the House of Commons was interrupted by the general election, although the winning Labour Party had stated that it would 're-introduce' it. Another MP, Cyril Townsend, of Bexleyheath, attempted to bring the bill back the following year, describing it as an attempt to offer overdue 'legislative underpinning'. MPs packed the house for the second reading, repeatedly describing the youth service as 'the Cinderella' of social services.

Calling for the duty of local authorities to 'compose a scheme for services in their areas', clearer co-ordination between state and voluntary organisations, better use of existing facilities, youth assemblies, adventure playgrounds, and provision that brought together disabled and able-bodied young people, the bill also described services that a good local authority should provide, noting that the majority of young people who used such services were 'disadvantaged'. Based on the belief that young people had specific needs that required special attention, the bill attracted cross-party support. 'Say it a hundred times, it still remains true,' said Townsend, in his speech to Parliament. 'A better society tomorrow starts with a better deal for youth today.'

Despite cross-party support, the bill was 'talked out' by a government minister, a tactic that meant it failed to progress. The debate had not concluded before the set time limit expired, and so it was shelved.

15

1975: THE YOUTH AND RACE PROJECT

In any organisation, attitudes to pressing social problems will vary. Individual perspectives are shaped by the interplay of education and experience, as well as personality. On occasion, these differences allow us to see more than the everyday drama of office life. An extended moment, when youth clubs at a national level began seriously addressing racism, is such an example.

In 1973, the NAYC created the Multi-Racial Project (MRP) with a grant from the Department of Education and Science. The rationale was explained in a paper prepared for the newly convened steering group. 'Disturbances between black teenagers and the police in London and elsewhere have heavily underlined two things. First, the youth service clearly has a crucial role to play in promoting racial harmony. Secondly, the warning which was contained in the last paragraph of the Hunt Report (1969) must be taken very seriously. It said "if England is not to be scene of race riots, the time for action is now".' Action was proposed in the shape of a committee with a set of integrationist aims and objectives designed with the NAYC's 4,006 member clubs in mind, and Grenada-born Oxford theology graduate and youth worker Gus John was hired as project director. At the second committee meeting, the ex-Dominican friar, founder of the supplementary schools movement and author of the prize-winning *Because They're Black* presented an eviscerating twelve-page paper outlining the logical, ethical and practical problems with the proposed approach.

'It is altogether praiseworthy for the Youth Service to accept its role in promoting racial harmony,' he wrote. 'For this reason, it is essential that it concerns itself not simply with the cause of this disharmony, but more importantly, of the social, cultural, emotional impoverishment of the Black youth population of Britain . . . what is the relevance of "integration", ill-defined as that is, to the everyday experience of Black youth in areas like Brixton, Dalston, Handsworth or Chapel Town?'

Arguing that the youth service had not awoken to the increasing numbers of young people moving away from it, Gus articulated a shift that had not yet been recognised by the mainstream. More and more youth and community workers were, he wrote, seeking to establish alternative forms of work 'arising out of a particular understanding of where they and the young people with whom they identify are placed in relation to society'. Such pioneering work existed 'amid hindrances posed by their Youth Service employers and by other colleagues in the field'.

Subsequent committee minutes show the slow-motion shockwaves of his bombshell perspective. Responses that would now be described as 'whataboutery' abound, along with the parachuting-in of senior Home Office staff to argue against the change in direction. It looked to me as if Gus was being blocked left, right and centre. Away from agenda-based machinations, though, the Multi-Racial Project provided him with the means to travel up and down the country, meeting with youth workers, visiting youth clubs and creating networks. It must have been very encouraging to have him visit and to know that others were mining similarly tough ground in, say, Bristol or Sheffield.

By 1975, the MRP had a new name, the Youth and Race Project, and an intention that came directly from Gus's attempts to bend the organisation's preference for 'integration' towards structural change. The project would examine the situation of young Black and Asian people in twelve towns and cities in England. Three development officers had been appointed to cover the North-West, the Midlands and the South, each collaborating with 'four youth or community situations in each region'. A research officer had been hired, and work would be ongoing, with agencies dealing with careers, probation, further education and housing. Project staff would assist colleges of education, especially those training youth and community workers, with support towards developing course content and training for those already working in the youth service.

By shifting the focus of the project from multiracial youth work, Gus told me, when we discussed the project, he sought to validate the ground-breaking efforts of youth workers and cultural activists involved with music, including reggae sound systems, as well as those dealing with the performing arts, football and netball. It was vital, he said, to 'engage with Black young people's own forms of youth organisation and youth work practice'. Additionally, he was signalling to youth workers, and those who trained them, that 'it was legitimate to acknowledge those forms of youth organisation as valid in their own right . . . building communities of resistance to marginalisation and minoritising'.

Gus's summation of the five-year study, which covered sixteen English cities and towns, was published two years later. 'NAYC only published a very limited number of the report, 500 copies I believe, although at the time they were publishing books on all manner of things associated with youth work,' he told me. 'They felt the report was "too political" and too challenging of the state and its attitudes to young Black people. Consequently, they were concerned about their reputation and, commensurately, their funding.' Just for a little context, it's worth remembering that the NAYC was still heavily connected to the aristocracy and landed gentry, with the Queen Mother as its patron and eminent titled people, including a princess, among the list of vice presidents at the time the Multi-Racial Project launched.

This era of Gus's work was coming to an end, and a new phase was beginning. In 1981, he synthesised his thinking in a book that referenced the classic text by Josephine Macalister Brew and the original government circular. *In the Service of Black Youth* came out weeks after thirteen teenagers died in a suspected racist arson attack during a birthday party in New Cross, and six months before nationwide uprisings against repressive policing. Prescient in ways undimmed by time, it was used extensively in community and youth work training in the decades that followed, a period during which Gus became director of education in Hackney (1989), declined a CBE from Tony Blair in 1999 and sat for a portrait displayed in the National Portrait Gallery. Now, aged seventy-nine, he has been invited to update *In the Service of Black Youth* for republication.

It's a work with ongoing relevance, and, even now, it inspires in Professor John ongoing fury. 'The more I reread that stuff, the more angry I get at the spineless people who ran NAYC at the time,' he told me. 'They did everything to impose their vacuous, integrationist and ideologically conservative agenda on the entire African and Asian diaspora and their young people across the country.' By doing so, he said, they prevented the nation from having to engage with itself. 'They clearly saw no need for Britain to ask searching questions about itself, given its own imperialist, colonialist and racist history.'

One of the youth clubs studied and supported during Gus John's time with the Youth and Race Project was the Moonshot Youth Club in Lewisham, south-east London, which had been founded by community leader and Methodist Sybil Phoenix. We have to leave the storied Moonshot for another day, however, because, instead, we're heading up the road to Lewisham Way Youth and Community Centre.

Opened in 1973, it provided a safe place to gather. For over forty years, generations of young people, many of whom were likely to have experienced systemic racism, took part in choirs, music production, classes in numeracy, literacy and Black history, martial arts, mentoring, photography, drama, film-making and dances on Friday evenings, which in 1970s Lewisham meant reggae sound systems. The youth club was a node in the constellation of spaces that helped build the genre of lovers rock, not least because the label of the same name was based just around the corner on Upper Brockley Road. Lewisham Way Youth and Community Centre was sucked out of communal ownership in 2022, when the council confirmed a change of use, redefining the building as Commercial, Class E.

One aspect of the multiple stories this place contained remains alive in the pages of a beautiful black-and-white photography book titled *Lovers Rock*. In 1977, the year of the Queen's Silver Jubilee and the Battle of Lewisham, where anti-fascist protestors battled the National Front and the Met Police, photographer John Goto was working at Lewisham Way Youth Club. The northerner had been teaching evening classes for two years to what he described in the informative introduction as a 'mixed group of working-class kids', using a few East German Praktica cameras. Classes were designed around members' interests, which mostly involved photographing each other.

As his time at the club drew to an end, Goto decided to create some artwork of his own. He had tried to photograph the regular back-room sound system dance, but found it too dark. Additionally, judging by the way one of his subjects is glaring out of the single dancefloor image contained in *Lovers Rock*, Goto's gaze may have been unwelcome in a space dedicated to bassline-powered freedoms. So, given that portraiture provided common ground, the photographer set up a makeshift studio adjacent to the dancehall area, in front of the club's noticeboard. Acquiring some roll ends of backdrop paper, he tacked them up and took images of youth club members on their way into the dance, inspired by the still, quiet Dutch paintings he'd seen at the National Gallery in central London.

The negatives sat in a box for thirty-three years. In 2013, they emerged into the light. Five years later, the images from *Lovers Rock* were exhibited elsewhere in the borough, in a disused unit within Catford shopping centre. Goto's portraits were accompanied by a new commission. With few suitable youth club locations left in the borough, photographer Des Willie depicted young people in a variety of locations: the community-focused Hill Station Café; at the annual Lewisham People's Day; and in various shopping centres.

I did a couple of voluntary shifts at the exhibition, which meant that I watched fully grown people walking in with their shopping bags and coming face to face with depictions of their teenage selves. I was chatting with two women who pointed out details: this person they knew from school or church; that cardigan they had as teenagers; the way kids back then would often have a lollipop on the go. I told them how amazing I thought these youth club pictures were, getting a bit drenched in imagined second-hand emotion. One of them put me straight. 'Look at them,' she said, in a way which managed to be simultaneously off-hand and urgent, nodding towards one of the photographs. 'They look worried. This was a very bad time.' The pictures changed in front of me, and what I perceived as stillness now looked like stress. I dropped into a different kind of understanding. 'I can see it in your eyes,' the woman said, walking off with her friend. 'You get it now.'

16

1976: BLUE LAMP DISCOS

I was looking for reasons to return to Northern Ireland. An opportunity arose through a misunderstanding. The people behind Rudimentary Records in Belfast invited me to DJ at an afternoon event they were running at Lavery's, the well-known pub in the city centre. I'd been liking and sharing so many social media posts by mutual friends that they thought I'd moved over. I accepted, happily, because it's always a joy to share favourite records with fellow music heads, and because I'd have an excuse to return to the Linen Hall Library. There were archive boxes I wanted to open.

Specifically, I was looking for information about the Royal Ulster Constabulary (RUC). After a good breakfast at Maggie Mays café near Botanic station, I arrived at the Linen Hall and walked up the wide stairs towards the fourth floor, where the Northern Ireland Political Collection is held. A permanent collection, *Troubled Images*, transforms the walls into what the curators call a 'vertical gallery'. Posters shout 'Stand Firm' and 'All Party Peace Talks Now' and point fingers in all directions, causing an effect that is indeed vertiginous – at least for me.

The RUC had been formed after partition, at the end of the Irish Civil War, replacing the Royal Irish Constabulary. Remaining a predominantly Protestant force, the RUC ceased to exist in 2001 as part of the peace process, and was renamed and reconstituted as the Police Service of Northern Ireland, with an active policy of recruiting more Catholic officers.

RUC Box 1 Ephemera contained layers of snapshot context: scribbled notebooks, newspaper cuttings and information on training courses, including one for officers in 1980 on Kodak photography. A bright yellow leaflet issued by the Chief Constable's Office outlines how to avoid being taken hostage, while another, 'Take It from Here: Have You a Future?', explains how to avoid getting killed on duty. Wallet-sized, a calendar reads, 'thank you to all our security services', alongside quotes from the Bible and the Queen. A logo hovers around the dates: a red hand inside a star with a crown on top.

Youth club references appear in the ephemera with regularity, including a pamphlet distributed by the force around Glen Road, Belfast, in 1974. Quoting an *Irish News* story, it stated that 120 children playing table tennis, billiards and football had miraculously escaped injury when their Tuesday-night youth club at St Teresa's primary school was hit by an unstable home-made pipe bomb. The pamphlet concluded with the admonishment 'your neighbourhood has tolerated the foolhardy but murderous antics of the provos for too long and many of you know the criminals responsible for this outrage', followed with a request to call the security forces' confidential telephone number.

Each year, the RUC released an annual report. Some copies were to be found in the maroon Ephemera box, and some were missing, while others were available behind a locked wooden door in the microfiche room. Grey machines, looking like oversized first-gen Apple Macs, were humming and whirring in analogue harmony. Rectangular strips of brown negatives contained compressed A4 pages, ready to be inserted into a pull-out drawer, magnified and shown on the screen. Scrolling through decades of information in this time-capsule environment resulted in a disorientating feeling, somewhere between car sickness and information overload.

I was searching for three words – Blue Lamp Disco – and I didn't have to look for long. Between 1974 and 1993, the RUC ran regular events under this name in youth clubs and schools across Northern Ireland. Police officer DJs, some in uniform and others wearing sportswear or special Blue Lamp t-shirts, would play pop records on turntables housed in wooden boxes and placed on trestle tables. On either edge, a revolving blue lamp offered a visual statement of the obvious. Their existence was very well known across the whole of Northern Ireland, later prompting Belfast poet Martin Mooney to use the words nostalgically as the title of his 2003 collection.

By 1978, the RUC had acquired twenty-six 'disco units', including a mobile set-up with a trailer. A year later, attendances would reach a high point, with 1,588 'well-supervised discos' for a claimed 225,405 attendees, where teenagers could 'meet and mix with others from their own area without intoxicating liquor being available'. It's necessary to approach any Troubles-era document with what you might call an 'open mind', but even if you halve the figures, the number of estimated attendees is still considerable.

The RUC's Community Relations Branch (CRB) was behind the disco lights. The unit came into existence a year after the Hunt Report, which was established to urgently examine policing in the context of bias against the Catholic population. The committee made several recommendations. These included demilitarising the police, disbanding the particularly contentious Ulster Special Constabulary, and that 'activities in the field of community and youth relations should be stepped up'.

Youth clubs were considered a vital location for CRB operations. A leaflet deep in the RUC Ephemera box is undated, but the photograph on the front, with women in headscarves and men with sideburns, has the look of the very early 1970s. It begins by explaining how hard the violence has been on the police, describing the emotional labour of conveying bad news to loved ones and witnessing 'frightening hatreds', before arguing for collaboration between the police and the community to restore normality and 'create an improvement in the quality of life for all of our people'. This is why, says the leaflet, the police are 'organising with the community Blue Lamp Youth Clubs, where local policemen are involving themselves in sporting and recreational activities with teenagers so as to build trust and civic pride'. A tagline, 'Say Peace, Say Police', is written across the bottom of each page. Nine officers comprised the inaugural staff, which doubled within a year, according to the *Belfast Telegraph*, with fifty-five full-time officers working for the CRB by 1976.

Running entire youth clubs can't have been sustainable, because the offering gradually shifted into disco promotions. The decision may have had practical roots, but it occurs to me that there may have been an emotional subtext too. Parachuting into existing clubs with a mobile disco may have ensured that individual officers and their superiors could police the emotional connections they made with young people – never entirely becoming youth workers, with the deep connections and advocacy true youth work involves. The *Belfast News Letter* in October 1975 had an explainer feature on the phenomenon, positioning Blue Lamp Discos as part of a drive against teenage drinking. The first of these over-fourteens events had opened in January in Antrim, said the writer, with other centres in Ulster now running Blue Lamp clubs.

'Blue Lamp youth clubs and discos are being set up all around the Province to keep the youngsters out of the pubs and at the same time let them have a bit of fun,' the reporter wrote, adding that the name stemmed from the lighting traditionally hung over the doors of police stations. 'Each member is issued with an identity card which enables him to get into the disco, which ends at 11.30 p.m., and no teenager is allowed in if he has been drinking heavily.' Bangor's Blue Lamp offering had opened the previous July and attracted nearly 1,000 members. Sgt Dick Russell stated that the Antrim club ran discos and karate classes, and had club rooms open most nights of the week for its 400 members, while the Ballymena disco night for under-eighteens that had run in test mode over the summer would officially open in October.

A year later, *Belfast Telegraph* journalist Ivan Little wrote a feature on the discos, headlined 'The Policemen Who Are on the Pop Beat', describing 'the RUC's ever-expanding but rarely publicised Community Relations Branch'. He reported from a disco at Tullycarnet, in east Belfast, where three RUC officers were doubling up as DJs, taking their turn on the decks while two policewomen stood at the side. 'With increased demands on manpower in the face of the deepening security crisis, it is clear that the police are pinning great hope on the branch . . . there are secondary benefits for the police themselves. Young people, they say, are beginning to see them as human beings and not ogres, and adults from community associations have begun to realise they have a part to play in crime prevention.'

In 1979, the RUC engaged with 480 different youth clubs, running discos and a mobile cinema, offering over 220 screenings. There will have been some who sensed dissonance in this description, less than a year after Amnesty International called for an inquiry into allegations of RUC brutality towards mostly Catholic suspects at Castlereagh police station, and a widespread belief – later evidenced – of collusion between the RUC, the British Army's Ulster Defence Regiment and Loyalist paramilitaries in murder.

Youth club discos gave senior brass something positive to discuss. The *Derry Journal* in April the same year quoted Chief Constable Sir Kenneth Newman batting off criticism of his force as 'less than fair'. His speech to the Belfast Rotary Club praised the force's 'extensive' campaign to bring people together and provide healthy outlets for their energy. 'Last year,' he said, 'nearly a quarter of a million teenagers attended our Blue Lamp Discos, to provide one example of our community work. I have made and will continue to make it my responsibility to see that the RUC is equipped to carry out all its duties impartially and imperceptibly.'

There is evidence that RUC officers and their mobile disco units did enter culturally Catholic areas, although the clippings tend to show this in terms of resistance. A December 1975 report in the *Belfast News Letter* noted local Sinn Féin complaints that discos in Armagh were being run to recruit 'teenage spies and informers'. The RUC rebuked the claim, stating that the dance parties were a 'serious attempt by the police to help the young people of the area by bringing them together for a few hours of harmless enjoyment each week'. This sets off a series of thoughts in my mind about the logistics. Would there have been behind-the-scenes conversations where guarantees would be sought from the relevant community figures? Would the SAS have been hiding in bushes or unmarked cars lined up in the street? I knew someone who knew someone in the Met Police, and asked if it was possible to make some discreet enquiries. A reply offered the perspective of one ex-RUC officer. Local police, they said, would usually have been aware that a Blue Lamp Disco was planned, and in more hostile areas might have supplied a plain-clothes officer. Sometimes, they said, the local force didn't even know about the event until it was taking place.

The Gaelic Athletic Association turfed the event out of its building in Portaferry, according to the *Belfast News Letter* that same year. 'Roman Catholics, Protestants and members of the RUC came together at a weekly disco,' it wrote, 'but when the GAA's governing body heard what was happening it immediately warned local officials to end the dances – even though the RUC brought its Blue Lamp Discos to the village at the invitation of the local Gaelic club to help boost its funds.'

In an example of how a simple youth club disco can cause outrage, a member of the Democratic Unionist Party complained, with Councillor Douglas Hutchinson claiming that Blue Lamp Discos at Armagh Technical College were 'destroying the morals of young people in the town'. Decrying rowdyism and drunkenness, he claimed that windows were being broken, doors banged and liquor bottles left lying around.

The club dancefloor was an important platform for conservatives to display moralistic uproar and was also of use to those more obviously involved in the world of sales and marketing. Teenage dancefloors were evoked in campaigns aimed at the young. Coca-Cola took a lead role in the youth club market, sponsoring NAYC disco-dancing competitions across all the nations of the UK in the late 1970s and early '80s, including in the North of Ireland. English company KP Snacks launched a new line of strongly flavoured circular crisps called Discos in 1970, with early packets offering a competition to win one of 150 portable transistor radios.

Discos – the events, not the crisps – were also a valuable resource for RUC recruitment campaigns. Various versions of the same newspaper ad appeared in the mid-1970s, featuring pencil-drawn community relations officer 'Paul Walters', and which described his working week in the style of a day-by-day diary. Monday has conversations with a festival committee and a local youth club about purchasing their own disco unit, 'thus releasing the RUC's own Blue Lamp Disco for a new club somewhere else'. Tuesday and Wednesday brought stones through windows and a nail-bomb attack respectively. Thursday was training for the RUC athletics team, and Friday was disco day, testing equipment and taking it to a youth club. 'We're very proud of the Blue Lamp Disco idea,' read the copy, as if spoken by an officer. 'It's worked extremely well. It gives us a chance to get to know the kids in an informal way, besides giving them something to do in the evening. In addition, we find it eases the teenage drinking problem.'

Police Beat magazine carried an article in 1979 titled 'Terrorism – A Point of View', discussing the motivation for armed struggle and looking at how democratic society copes with such activity. In the concluding section, the writer lists some of the anti-terrorism methods used in Northern Ireland, concluding with the work of the 'large' CRB. 'Every effort is made to bring the two communities together. The thinking is that if the police can win over the young terrorist before he becomes hardened to a life of crime that the recruiting base will be severed – a "hearts and minds" campaign.' Strategic anti-terrorist work included the youth, officially.

———

Author Neil Trelford attended Blue Lamp Discos as a teen-age Mod on an estate in the town of Antrim, as the decade shifted from the '70s into the '80s. He remembers police in their civilian clothes playing pretty much the same music as the other youth clubs, maybe with a slightly greater focus on the ABBA- and Nolan Sisters-type pop-dance music, but also throwing in some punk and Mod anthems, despite their inevitably political interpretation. There were exceptions, 7-inch lines that could not be crossed. '"Alternative Ulster" by Stiff Little Fingers – I don't recall the Blue Lamp playing that,' said Neil when we chatted.

His memoir, *The Youth Club*, describes how being into music could offer an identity different to the one fixed at birth. But what did he think youth clubs offered specifically? 'A sense of actual community spirit in the younger generation and a level of acceptance – that you could have a voice and an identity that didn't bring you into any sort of jeopardy. It was a space where you could grow and develop. Not just the music scene, but the sheer fact of having opportunities for sporting activities or arts and crafts.'

Economics played a part too. Neil describes himself and his friends as coming from working-class families. 'Youth clubs were a safe haven which was relatively low cost. Private clubs or stuff that went on at leisure centres, they cost considerably more. They [youth clubs] were affordable, and it gave your family reassurance that you weren't wandering the streets. It gave them a break from being concerned about you.' His comment propels me into the mindset of motherhood. I get a tiny glimpse into the ways that being a Troubles-era parent would have amplified the anxieties that come hand in hand with having children. I can't truly understand, of course, because I didn't live it. But I get a sense, along with a new appreciation of how valuable youth clubs would have been for the rest of the family too.

Music allowed young people to blur the spatial boundaries of Catholic or Protestant life. Neil attended Blue Lamp Discos at the Greystone Community Centre, which was 'somewhat neutral in terms of the religious side', and at Parkhall High School and the First Presbyterian Church in Antrim Town, which were less so. 'The core group of friends that I grew up with were from both sides of the community. We went and did everything together, and this was just another outlet, so you got that blend going into all the venues.' Given that Antrim was a relatively safe place for police and soldiers to live, there were also kids whose parents were in the British Army, meaning a handful of white English and a minority of Black British young people in the mix.

The experience of negatively racialised youth in England offered a mirror that could be peered into from across the water, and which gave both a soundtrack and a sense of remote solidarity. 'If you were to pick anything to try and represent what it was like for a Northern Ireland youth club, at least in my era, go to any song by The Specials,' said Neil. My eyes widened when he said this, because band members attended youth-run youth club the Holyhead, in Coventry. 'The Specials were interracial and they sang about everything. Whenever we listened to them, we thought, "They're singing about us," y'know? The Specials forged a real sense of hope for our community. It was a fusion – "This is what's possible." These guys had done it and they're representing it.' New awareness washes over me: of a connection between young men burning cars and throwing stones in Handsworth, Toxteth, Moss Side and Brixton and their peers across the water, in terms of both their lived experience and the hope that bands like The Specials signalled.

In 1981, when the group's 'Ghost Town' went to number one in the UK charts, the RUC reported that 1,116 Blue Lamp Discos had been held, working out to around twenty for every week of the year and attracting almost 153,000 young people. Reported numbers stayed above a thousand discos per year until the middle of the decade. Belfast visual artist Lesley Cherry attended a Blue Lamp Disco around this time, when a mobile unit provided the music for her primary school leavers' party. 'I thought it was amazing,' she told me, recalling her pink dirndl-style skirt, royal-blue sandals and Kelly Marie's pop hit 'Feels Like I'm in Love'.

Decades later, Cherry recreated a Blue Lamp Disco for the opening of her video exhibition of the same name. It took place at a gallery, The Station, which as the name suggests had a prehistory as a workplace for police officers. In the videos that comprised part of the artwork she mimed to songs, including 'Breaking the Law' by Judas Priest. 'The irony of the RUC using youth outreach during the Troubles was fascinating,' she said, 'but it wasn't until I was older that I realised this, the way we continued to use entertainment as a tool to normalise what we were going through.'

Cherry's *Blue Lamp Disco* was designed as a piece of art that commented on real-life experiences of enjoyment and simply getting on with things. 'The escapism and the music were so important,' she told me. 'The discos seem to have been written out of history, a forgotten part of the Troubles. Obviously they were aimed at one section of the community, for obvious reasons,' she said, 'but I like to think they were at least trying, even if the RUC and the political agenda was predominantly Unionist.' For younger children they were great, she said, adding that a Catholic friend of hers did attend the discos in her area of Monkstown, just outside Belfast, as her mother considered them safe.

In 1986, the RUC claimed there were 658 discos for 80,000 dancers, alongside the once national and now Belfast-based Disco Dancing Competition, which attracted thousands of entries and had TV personalities acting as judges and presenting trophies. By 1990, the Blue Lamps were running low and, in 1993, the CRB was replaced by Community Affairs. This new branch had a wider remit, including crime prevention, domestic violence and the RUC band. The police beat no longer included youth club discos.

It's possible that the RUC's offering was many things all at once, including a response to the huge popularity of music and dancing with the young, and a strategic response to violence, enacted by a state which took a particular view about where the violence came from and how it should be controlled. Dancing is a connective activity, and these sessions may have contributed to feelings of warmth and happiness within groups of young people who were under a great deal of pressure. Even within the RUC it would have been multifaceted: an opportunity for music-loving officers to do something fun with people who liked you, and, for others, public relations work or steely intelligence-gathering.

17

1979: LONDON GAY TEENAGE GROUP

Adults across time and space have proactively created places where teens can meet. On occasion, the youth have done it for themselves, and the UK's first official youth clubs for queer teenagers fall into this category. As always, a confluence of events and energies led to these specific outcomes, and we're going to pick our way through the stories, starting with an incredible woman who helped lay the foundations.

Rose Robertson was a south Londoner, a mother of two and a Second World War spy. Born in Deptford in 1916, she was recruited as a special operations executive in 1941, during the war. Among other things, her time in France conveying Resistance messages back to the Allies in Britain provided an opportunity for compassion and understanding that she might otherwise not have accessed. Her obituary in the *Guardian* in 2011 described a moment that changed her life: accidentally walking in on two male Resistance operatives in bed together. 'Rose knew nothing about homosexuality and was curious,' it read. 'She eventually plucked up the courage to ask them. Both men told stories of family prejudice and rejection. Their stories affected her deeply. She was shocked that parents could be so heartless towards their gay children.' Rose would turn shock into action.

Back home, she married, had children and moved to Catford, on the other side of Lewisham. In 1969, she formed Parents Enquiry, Britain's first helpline to advise and support parents and their lesbian, gay and bisexual children. For three decades, she answered phone calls and hundreds of letters each week, as well as running groups for young gay and lesbian people in her home. It occurs to me that wartime spy training endowed her with unusual empathy. Men and women who were part of this 13,000-strong secret organisation had been trained to successfully live a double life, and to maintain this even under Nazi interrogation. She must have understood, through her lived experience, the pressure of secrecy.

In practical terms, she created a small space in the public arena in which sexuality could be carefully, sensibly and sensitively discussed as something ordinary. With Rose making their case on TV, on the radio and in print, and with co-signs for Parents Enquiry from famous newspaper agony aunts like Marje Proops in the *Daily Mirror* and Claire Rayner in the *Sunday Mirror*, those who dared to create clubs might have felt a tiny bit safer. Responsible adults were advocating for them in public.

One of the young people who made use of Parents Enquiry was Maureen 'Mo' Hand, who grew up in a Catholic household in north London. Chatting on the phone, Mo took me back in time, describing the extreme bravery it required to broach the subject of homosexuality in the era in which Rose Robertson established Parents Enquiry. Diverting from straightness was considered so categorically appalling that extending kindness towards those who were even suspected of being gay, to use the terminology of the time, took significant courage. Being pro-queer risked being labelled queer yourself, and, in Mo's words, after she recapped a list of the slurs that were common at the time, 'no one wanted to be associated with that'. Rose, she said, would have got serious backlash. 'If she'd been around today, she'd have got a bloody MBE or a blue plaque. She saved so many lives.'

Nervously making the trip across the River Thames, Mo attended a group at Rose's house on a curved section of Honley Road in Catford. The Parents Enquiry founder, she said, was a 'traditional little old lady', and her home was warm, friendly and welcoming. 'There were two other young women there: a middle-class girl, well educated, and a woman who was dressed head to toe in leather. I could hardly look at her, I was so scared. It was all tea and biscuits and "How are you feeling?" She normalised that there was nothing wrong with us. We were loving beings and deserved to be treated with respect.' It was, said Mo, the first time she'd felt like she was part of a community. 'To have an older woman who was a mother figure was amazing – that someone of her generation could be so supportive. It enabled me to think that there was hope for my own mother and my own family.' When Mo's mother finally realised that her daughter's 'boyfriend', Sean, was just a cover, she was distraught. Fortunately, Parents Enquiry was there for the adults too, and Mrs Hand was able to telephone Rose and receive reassurance. 'I think it really did help her to understand that there was nothing wrong with me.'

Word about Parents Enquiry travelled. By June 1980, the *Cork Examiner* was quoting Rose in a piece about a constitutional challenge to continued criminalisation of homosexuality. In it, she described seeing two or three 'Irish homosexuals' every month, who told her they'd left their home country because of the legal situation. 'In her experience,' said the unnamed reporter, 'there was far greater reluctance on the part of young Irish homosexuals to tell their parents than there was in England. The thing that seemed to be uppermost in their minds was that it was totally illegal.'

*

I spoke to Mo on the landline from where she lives in rural Wales, because the internet's too shaky for anything else. Her professional life doubles up as a timeline of liberational milestones, predominantly in London, where in 1987 she was appointed as a paid youth worker for North London Line, the first full-time gay and lesbian youth group in the country. The service ran five days a week, with three full-time workers and part-time colleagues, encompassing a young trans group – the first in the UK, says Mo – as well as catering to a wide variety of needs. Groups were run for those who were both gay and disabled, and the Camden Black Lesbian Group was also set up. It encompassed a service for gay and bisexual male survivors of sexual abuse, and the Positive Young Gay Group for those with HIV, at a time when now-unimaginable fear and stigma was directed at those with the diagnosis. Afterwards, she spent twelve years working for the Powys youth service, and now runs a dog hotel surrounded by fields and mountains.

It's a long way from 1970s Camden, where she grew up with a Northern Irish mother, herself thrown into single parenthood when Mo's father died. At the age of seven, Mo was expelled from her Catholic primary school for 'deviant behaviour', or, in other words, trying to kiss a girl in the playground. Homophobic pressures shaped a remarkable teenage life: by the age of seventeen, Mo had been a member of Camden skinhead gang the South London Aggro Girls, or SLAGs, an apprentice for Arsenal Ladies football team, and the drum major of Camden Majorettes, running twice-weekly choreography and drum sessions for between fifty and seventy girls in the function room of her Catholic youth club.

Underage bar work took her into Oxford Street nightclub Spats, which has its own storied place in the history of UK youth culture, creating space for jazz dancers or hip hop break-ers. Visiting Rose Robertson in Catford set Mo on a path that led her to attend and then help run some of the UK's earliest gay youth groups. 'In a way,' she said, 'the youth service saved my life. I was a kid going nowhere from a working-class single-parent family, living in central London, with access to every drug going and best friends with prostitutes. A little thug, really, every youth worker's nightmare. I could have ended up in a very different place.'

Where she actually ended up, or perhaps started out, was the London Gay Teenage Group, known as LGTG. A pioneering youth-led club, it catered mostly for young gay men, but was also open to young lesbians and those who'd now be described as trans. On arrival in 1978, she was deeply disappointed to find it was so heavily male. On the other hand, she was amazed that young people were running the club themselves. 'It was self-run, before the youth service started doing participation. It was like going into a family. One of my missions was to get more young lesbians in. Because I was working at Spats, at this night-club, every time a young person walked through the door I'd say, "Have you heard about the London Gay Teenage Group? We meet on Sundays."' Slowly, more girls arrived.

It was 'a fun place', she explained. Discussion groups on anything and everything were an important part of club life, which makes sense given how vigilant many of the members would have been about what they said, or communicated, in the outside world. Welfare needs were high and the group attended to these in an organic way, offering counselling to members, including those whose mental health issues were serious enough to describe the club as literally life-saving. 'Quite a few young boys there were rent boys, so they had a safe environment to talk about what was going on,' said Mo. 'We had quite a few survivors of sexual abuse, boys and girls, and it was a sanctuary for that very vulnerable group. It grew and grew.'

In 1979, aged seventeen, Mo undertook a Youth Opportunity Programme with the Camden Girls' Project, which was run by experienced youth worker Jane Dixon, quickly setting up the Camden Young Lesbians Group. The group would meet at 6 p.m. on Monday nights, explained Mo, with older women in youth worker roles, on hand to welcome members into the space. There would be informal chats – how the week had been, what school had been like, problems with parents – and a reading group that included books by famous gay women. Tutors supported them in the emerging technology of videography and they had their own cameras and drum kits, and a music studio courtesy, she said, of now-unimaginable 100 per cent grant aid. Club members shot films, produced music and made posters containing positive images across intersections of race, class, gender and sexuality. A set of cards was produced to create a game where teams had to convince a panel to give them funding – a smart bit of gamified training. Trips took place, to mid-Wales or Brighton. Other times they'd just watch a video or get on with planning events, including London Gay Pride.

It strikes me as an industrious place, where young people were working hard while having fun, an image that sits at an angle from the youth clubs I experienced in a mainstream part of the suburban 1980s, which contained plenty of freeform dossing. This difference is telling: a reminder that youth clubs can act as a sideways glance at the world that allows us to see what's needed. The kids at LGTG would also have required unstructured hanging out, given the pressures they experienced in everyday life. Even as it provided relief, this kind of youth club required work.

Absences can communicate information too. Mo's experience at the frontier of youth clubs for LGBTQ+ teenagers offers useful and important perspective on how mainstream clubs worked for those on the margins of sexuality: the need for separate spaces speaks to societal failure. It also shows us how even these DIY spaces, hand-carved out of stony refusals to acknowledge the existence of gay teenagers, found it hard to cater for girls and those whose lives were complicated by racism. There were battles within the battle.

But, first, let's see how Mo's youth club came to exist in the first place. Even the concept of officially sanctioned clubs for gay teenagers was extremely controversial in mid-century Britain. The reasons were social, legal and cultural. The Sexual Offences Act of 1967 only partially decriminalised the bedroom, with sexual intimacy between men under the age of twenty-one remaining totally illegal in England and Wales. It was outlawed for all ages in Scotland until 1980, and in Northern Ireland until 1982.

Laws preventing sex between women did not exist because the House of Lords decided in summer 1921 against publicising the possibility. 'I am strongly of the opinion that the mere discussion of subjects of this sort tends, in the minds of unbalanced people, of whom there are many, to create the idea of an offence of which the enormous majority of them have never even heard,' stated the Earl of Desart during the debate. Blackmail, agreed the lords, was a risk in a country where 'in all innocence and very often as a necessary consequence of the shortage of small houses, they have to have the same bedroom and even sleep together in the same beds'.

Step changes in equality often occur when like-minded people organise. However, the main campaigning groups working towards equalising the age of consent in the 1970s feared creating space for teenagers would contribute to the existing conflation of homosexuality, hypersexuality and paedophilia. Complicating matters was the open existence of the Paedophile Information Exchange (PIE), which we encountered earlier at the NAYC's conference, and which had successfully infiltrated some gay rights groups, according to Dr Clifford Williams, author of the brilliantly detailed history *Courage to Be: Organised Gay Youth in England 1967–1990*. The existing campaign by gay activists to lower the age of consent in the service of equality was ambushed by adults who wanted to abolish it entirely.

Brave individuals and groups appear in Clifford's book, in which he pieces together disparate timelines through analogue-era data: committee minutes, newspaper reports and interviews with people who experienced it all. In the year after decriminalisation for over-twenty-ones, nineteen-year-old John Holland tried to set up a youth group in Wolverhampton. Unilateral action didn't work, but failure led this young man to form a local branch of the Campaign for Homosexual Equality (CHE). Admission criteria were under his control, and he set the entrance age at sixteen.

Clifford found that the UK-wide CHE had discussed setting up a club for teenagers in 1974, but agreed that this was not possible, even though there was sympathy for the idea. Such a group, they felt, would need to start under the protective umbrella of an existing council-approved youth club, recognised by both the community and official bodies. Existing youth clubs were not the route through which history happened. Maybe no one asked; maybe individual clubs bolted their doors out of fear or ignorance. The archives are unclear. But in the absence of a welcome, teenagers decided to do it themselves.

In Liverpool, in 1972, members of CHE had set up a youth group. The need for this was removed when the main organisation accepted under-twenty-one-year-olds, despite the risk of legal action should under-twenty-ones couple up. Comedian and broadcaster Paul O'Grady, who found fame as Lily Savage and was later awarded an MBE, attended aged seventeen, which may well have brought extra volume and colour to proceedings. In the early 1970s, CHE in the capital had set up befriending service London Friend, which had an under-twenty-fives youth group meeting on Friday evenings in Islington. London Friend split from the CHE in 1975, according to Clifford, and a few of the younger ones from the group joined forces with a handful of under-twenty-ones who'd been meeting in the safety of south London's Oval House Theatre café.

A youth-led movement began to take shape around the affordable and welcoming coffee bar of this London community arts institution. By 1975 or '76, this emerging group of gay teenagers were also meeting high up in a council tower block between Old Street and the Euston Road. Living there was Philip Cox, a creative activist who'd scribble Gay Switchboard numbers in telephone boxes and on walls everywhere he went.

Another early attendee was soon-to-be actor and founding presenter of Channel 4's youth culture show, *The Tube*, Gary James, who states he was the first openly gay presenter on British television. His memoir *Spangles, Glam, Gaywaves & Tubes* tells the story. He'd been alerted to the LGTG's existence by secretly scouring his first copy of *Gay News* for every single bit of information it contained, which meant reading everything from the contents page to the classified ads. The latter contained information about the newly formed LGTG. Going down to the phone box in his home town of Tunbridge Wells, Kent, he dialled the unknown, acquired the details and got himself up town for the next meeting. Inside the flat there were 'twelve or so young guys present, all checking each other out and marvelling at what for most of us was the first time we'd been amongst our own kind in a safe environment. It's impossible for me to convey just how much this meant to us. It wasn't a social gathering – it was a revelation.'

Founder Philip Cox believed that a teenage group should be run by teenagers but had turned twenty-one. So, in winter 1976, after setting up a management structure that allocated all responsibility to group members and finding space in premises used by sexual health organisation Grapevine on the Holloway Road in north London, he walked away. The newly arrived younger ones were in charge, whether they liked it or not.

News spread, mostly through Gay Switchboard and Lesbian Line, but also through friendly agony aunt columns in mass circulation newspapers and magazines. Problem pages doubled up as a kind of national information service, offering sensible intel on subjects that would be swerved by schools, which offered minimalist or non-existent sex education. This was my experience in the mid-1980s, being brought up Catholic and learning almost everything I knew about the subject from the problem pages of teen mags like *Just 17* or *Mizz*.

The LGTG began to receive phone calls and letters from otherwise isolated young people who didn't live within reach of the capital. In response, members set up a pen pal network, so that aspects of youth club life could be delivered to people's homes through the medium of a white envelope. There was a pen pal brochure, available through sending a stamped self-addressed envelope. In return, the sender would receive details of potential letter-writing friends, formatted much like platonic classified ads.

Pen pals were commonplace in the 1970s and '80s, and there were multiple schemes across all sectors of society to facilitate this pre-internet version of a DM. I had a variety of pen pals, some of whom lasted longer than others. The youth club I attended in the south-east London suburbs took us to a national Methodist Association of Youth Clubs (MAYC) event at the Royal Albert Hall. The culmination of the evening involved throwing home-made pom-poms with our name and address into the crowd, as an invitation to a potential correspondent, and collecting one in return. In the decades before data protection, this was considered totally safe and entirely wholesome. I picked up a pom-pom from someone called David, and probably wrote to him the next day. I don't recall our paper-based friendship lasting long, which was also the case for the letter-exchange with a couple of Army squaddies that my friend Maxene and I befriended on a day trip to the seaside. Longer lasting was correspondence with a German girl I met on a family holiday in Cyprus.

Interestingly, in the context of the LGTG, my German pen pal was the first person to discuss sexuality with me. She wrote to tell me that she was bisexual, but that it was okay, because 'she didn't fancy me'. I recall being shocked by her confident self-awareness and slightly offended, all at the same confusing time. *Courage to Be* author Dr Clifford Williams was one of the teenage LGTG pen pal crew, writing to a peer in Scotland.

Likes and dislikes were shared in their letters, with the Scottish correspondent upping the ante when he sent the analogue version of a dick pic: an outline of his penis drawn on the writing paper.

Clifford had grown up in a Quaker family in the southern suburbs of London, attending Cubs as a kid and later joining a Baptist youth group with the now eyebrow-raising name of Crusaders, which offered 'loads of sport and activity holidays', he told me when we spoke one autumn afternoon. By secondary school, he was avoiding the existing local youth clubs because 'they were heterosexual. I wasn't interested in what they did.' Instead, he joined the Young Liberals.

Politics wasn't really satisfactory for him either, so in 1978 he went to Sutton Library, which stocked *Gay News*. Hidden behind the counter, the act of accessing it was an awkward kind of coming out. The newspaper contained a listing for the LGTG. He wrote them a letter, to which they replied. 'I don't think I had much hesitation going,' he said, 'because it was well away from where I lived.'

The club, which he attended for two years, was then taking place for three hours every Sunday in two small rooms on the first floor of 296 Holloway Road, above the Theeba takeaway. On the other side of the front door was a welcome and a shrugged but explicit indication that the person who was showing him around wasn't trying to pick him up – this needing to be explained at a time when being homosexual was conflated with 'sexual predator'. In order to try to keep actual predators out, the group came up with a number of proto-safeguarding processes, which were broadly adhered to: that over-twenty-ones had to say farewell (unless they stayed as part of the management committee), and that new members had to be met by two of the existing crew, if this meeting took place away from the safety of the club itself. This, and the presence of what Clifford describes as 'some formidable punks', offered some protection.

By 1979, when Clifford attended, the LGTG had grown to a shifting group of around fifty members on a Sunday and twenty on Wednesday evenings. 'It was crowded, like a party where you're crammed into someone's house,' he told me. 'There wasn't a lot of room for anything, no pool or table tennis. Darts would have been terribly dangerous.' His memories of the club's first HQ centre around meeting people, having cups of tea and coffee, and milling around the office. Volunteer youth workers organised trips to gay discos, as well as away-days to Norwich, Luton and Boulogne in France.

Other youth clubs benefited from their collective strength. Clifford described occasions when the LGTG would go and visit their supposedly heterosexual peers elsewhere. A sex education discussion group at Albemarle House in Essex sounded especially lively, and led to at least one of the apparently straight Essex boys quietly joining the pen pal scheme.

Several members would go on to great acclaim, along with others who'd contribute to society through youth work, social work or, like Clifford, writing books. Pop star Jimmy Somerville of pop heroes Bronski Beat and The Communards was a regular, as was Andy Bell of synth-pop duo Erasure, who'd win Best British Group at the BRIT awards in 1989. Renowned choreographer Sir Matthew Bourne OBE also attended, and a number of members were involved in making an influential 1983 documentary, *Framed Youth*, where the young film-makers went out on the street to interview straight people. The group offered an access point to establishment culture – for example, when a group of LGTG friends went to see their peer and later TV presenter Gary James performing at the Royal Court Theatre.

Fire damage to the downstairs takeaway in summer 1979 necessitated a move. After some hesitation and discussion by the committee at Manor Gardens, a charity providing welfare services to the people of north London, they were allocated the organisation's dilapidated old laundry building, on the condition that the group spruced it up and repainted the walls. Here, the LGTG looked more like a standard youth club. There was finally room for a pool table and table tennis. Trips provided opportunities to attend the NAYC's annual events or go to Germany for a conference about understanding the minority experience, along with a group of young east Londoners from Bengali families.

Teens at Manor Gardens would clump together based on their subcultural affiliations. Punks along the wall, and the ones who, back then, would be described as 'camp' in another corner. People would bring along records to play on the club turntable or just hang out, discussing news and gossip. While everyone there identified – in the terms of the day – as gay, lesbian or bisexual, it was unusually diverse across other cultural or demographic identifiers. 'It was a huge mix,' said Clifford, on our second call. 'Different classes, ethnicities, views, lifestyles, religions. We had all that diversity and difference, but we had that common bond around our sexual orientation. We were a group pretty despised by society. Most people thought we were deviant, criminal, sinful, immoral. To a certain extent, being a punk, I celebrated that. I tended to be a bit rebellious.' Clifford delivered another piece of sobering contextual information. This was also the period in which serial killer Dennis Nilsen was active in London, murdering at least twelve boys and young men between 1978 and 1983. It's frighteningly easy to imagine him scanning a crowd and immediately discounting the confident gaggle of kids from the LGTG. They had friends; someone would notice if they went missing.

A few days after chatting, Clifford sent me an email. The subject line stated 'rare footage', and, further down, the email explained the content. In 1979, LGTG members had gained access to a video camera and made a film for local council committee members, who were deciding whether or not to support the official registration of their youth group. The link clicks through to a grainy black-and-white film. It opens with flickering white static, before a group emerges, with Tom Robinson's 'Glad to Be Gay' playing in the background. A serious-looking young man called Robert is holding a microphone, while others walk in and out of the room. He explains, in a gentle Scottish accent, that the group are attempting to gain formal registration from the Inner London Education Authority (ILEA). This was being held up, he said, by the ILEA's concerns about registering an openly gay group.

He describes LGTG's purpose as providing 'a relaxed atmosphere away from the commercial scene', before the camera – a little shakily – pans to a group discussing possible destinations for an upcoming trip. Robert interviews his friends, asking one how they found out about the group, while another suggests that the group was not so different to other youth clubs. 'I am human,' says the interviewee dryly, waving his hand as evidence. A nervous, young-looking contributor says that parents have a right to know if their children are gay, but that he wasn't going to tell his mum because 'if she found out one of her sons was like that, she'd kick his head in and throw him out into the street'.

Towards the end of these seventeen minutes, which convey a charming ordinariness about this extraordinary place, Robert speaks directly to the ILEA committee who formed the film's audience. 'I hope this film has shown you there is a great need for a group such as the London Gay Teenage Group. Without it, gay teenagers would not feel able to openly discuss their problems,' he explains. 'I for one do not want to see the London Gay Teenage Group close.'

On the other side of the static that ends the clip was a decision. The result was sent to the group on ILEA-headed paper by the admin officer of the Islington Area Youth Office in September 1979, a few months after the group had received a grant from the London Union of Youth Clubs. This pioneering stamp of local government acceptance allowed the group access to a youth officer and provided a doorway into further acceptance.

Justifying their existence had taken a lot of work. Negotiations had been going on for two years 'at all political and administrative levels', according to *Something to Tell You*, which included a potted history of the LGTG when it was published in 1983. Meeting over twenty different committees and preparing accompanying documentation, the experience was both 'a clear illustration of institutional prejudice' and 'a valuable opportunity to discuss the issues with a very wide range of people, helping them confront and overcome fears and prejudice'. Leaders from the Scouts made the effort to attend meetings, to argue against LGTG being officially recognised.

In 2018, Clifford became a voluntary youth worker himself, working with a group in Winchester after they asked to interview him about growing up gay, a process that got him thinking about his teenage youth club experiences, and which led to his book. They'd been working on a project about Hampshire's LGBTQ+ histories, and he took them to the archives, including those at Magdalen College, Oxford, Bishopsgate and the LSE. After that trip, he persuaded the lead youth worker to take the group to Gay's the Word bookshop, which was just up the road. 'They were so excited,' he said, 'because they'd seen it in *Pride*.'

Youth clubs, through the lens of the LGTG, can be seen as responses to the world, and as world-shaping. 'In terms of history, it's a big landmark event,' reflected Clifford, thinking back on the story that he lived, and to which he's given so much of his life through his research and writing. 'This was the first officially recognised group to have a paid youth worker, possibly in the world. Looking back on it, I'm amazed the group survived – all the pressures, the lack of money, the legal situation being somewhat fraught.' It was a multiplier event, with members creating new spaces and others elsewhere in the country starting their own clubs once they knew it was possible. In a simple way, too, hundreds of people derived strength and inspiration from passing through the doors.

In a small and sideways fashion, the LGTG may have affected my life too. Around 1986, aged fourteen, I met a boy at a house party hosted by someone from my local youth club. I don't know if he knew about gay youth groups, but I do know he went to see LGTG's Jimmy Somerville in his band Bronski Beat, because I went with him on what I thought was a date.

It became apparent that this was not the case when I went over to see him at his mum's house the following week, during which he spent the whole time cuddling his friend – a boy – in bed. The openly gay frontman may well have worked some confidence magic on his audience as well.

18

1982: AN UNEXPECTED CORNER OF PIRATE RADIO

A strong creative impulse, and the resultant notable output, was evident in the UK's first youth groups for LGBTQ+ teens. Members made compilation tapes and zines, and LGTG co-founder Phil Cox initiated *Gaywaves*, the UK's first gay pirate radio show. He and future *Tube* presenter Gary James came up with the idea and spent four years writing and recording sketches, making jingles and recording their favourite music onto tape before actually finding a way to air them. Eventually, the pair made a connection with influential pirate station Thameside Radio, which would broadcast from tower blocks across the city, including from Phil's flat.

'We used to hide their aerial equipment amongst his washing to disguise it from the Home Office, who would regularly raid broadcast sites,' shared Gary James, when I emailed him, adding that Thameside would sometimes hold high-peril parties where listeners could turn up at a live broadcast, with the person undertaking 'van watch' on the balcony offering a semblance of protection against unwanted guests who would shut them down. 'Phil's bargaining enabled us to occasionally sneak in some of our recordings, although I think the most we achieved was the occasional news item, which was largely in exchange for them using his flat,' he said, reflecting back into the far past.

In May 1982, the pair started a weekly show on another station, Our Radio, pre-recording it onto cassette tape as a way of limiting the risk of being caught on air during a raid. 'It should not be underestimated just how difficult things were back then to get broadcasts out,' said Gary, when we spoke. 'In this day and age of internet and open access, people don't think twice about making and putting out their own content, but back then it was actually a criminal offence and we risked arrest and prosecution to make our shows available.'

In John Hind and Stephen Mosco's brilliant book *Rebel Radio* – which contains the world's best appendix: an outline of how to build a pirate radio station – Cox describes the joy of making the shows, and of meetings in dark railway stations to hand over the tapes. The *Gaywaves* co-founders lost touch, and Cox died in 1992, but the shows didn't die with him. He'd given his archive to the British Library, and, in a detail that speaks volumes, had ensured that copyright for the relevant sketches and jingles was correctly attributed to his *Gaywaves* co-pilot Gary James.

Some of the energy generated by teenage groups was creative and social. In Manchester, it became organisational. Paul Fairweather had set up the Manchester Gay Teenage Group in 1978, aged twenty-one. He was already an experienced activist, using youth theatre to propel him from Birkenhead to Oxford, where he started working at the UK's second Gay Switchboard. Coming to Manchester to work for the CHE, he quickly and quietly set up a weekly teenage group in a 'grotty basement' on Waterloo Place owned by Manchester University. 'We'd drink coffee, chat, talk about things,' he said, describing a demographic composed in large part by young gay men aged sixteen to eighteen. 'It was mainly non-students, people nearly all living with their parents. There was nothing for young people. Mainstream youth provision were very reluctant to do anything for them.' On Fridays, the group would go to the gay disco held at Manchester Polytechnic's Aytoun Street building.

By 1980, the group had moved to Bloom Street, now in the heart of Manchester's Gay Village. With space provided by the Gay Centre, support from the Centre's part-time sessional worker and an upper age limit of twenty-one, they offered talks on sexual health and on finance, haircare and leaving home. There were opportunities for activism, with Manchester Gay Switchboard and Manchester Friend. The group became Lesbian and Gay Youth Manchester, which turned into Proud Trust, who now deliver youth work and offer one-to-one support, alongside a national training and inclusion programme for schools. 'Proud Trust have this amazing building, raised two million quid for it,' said Paul, ever unassuming despite now having the letters 'MBE' after his name. 'They support LGBT groups across Greater Manchester and beyond. It's sort of the succession of the group I set up in '78, really.'

New entities were emerging by the early 1980s, like the Tyneside Gay Teen Group in Newcastle, which received funding in 1983. As groups stabilised and took root, members and their networks became available to researchers. Previously invisible lives could be turned into data, which itself could be used to argue for equality. In London, in 1983, the GLC funded youth worker academics Lorraine Trenchard and Hugh Warren to create the London Gay Teenage Group Research Project to look at the lives of young lesbians and gay men in the capital. Young people and the author–researchers co-created a questionnaire and used a proto-street team to distribute 2,000 copies to pubs, clubs, discos, meetings and events, with volunteers also handing out copies to friends and family. A poster and info pack was sent to all the youth clubs on the London Union of Youth Clubs' mailing list – numbering 'about' 1,100. The fact that, in 1983, there were over *a thousand* youth clubs affiliated to this one umbrella organisation counts among the most remarkable details in this eye-opening story.

Trenchard and Warren's research aimed to identify the needs of young lesbians and gay men in London and to make recommendations. Their book *Something to Tell You* published data about young people's experiences alongside cute, wry cartoons drawn by the teenage participants. One, for example, showed two Edwardian-era ladies sitting next to each other, with the caption 'Shall we go home for a statistically abnormal evening?', while another shows an openly gay teacher, with a pig flying outside the window.

The youth service was proud of its ability to move with the times and address the changing needs of young people, wrote the authors. 'This flexibility and the voluntary nature of the relationships help the young people feel safe, and can take into account all the factors that may have limited personal growth and education within the school system.' The book concludes with three recommendations concerning information, education and resources, all based around a simple starting point: 'A prerequisite for improving the lives of young lesbians and gay men is the need for the recognition of their existence.'

Legal barriers reappeared in 1988, when Prime Minister Margaret Thatcher's government outlawed the 'promotion' of homosexuality 'as a pretended family relationship' by local authorities and schools through Section 28 of the Local Government Act. The law was imposed at the worst possible time for public health messaging around HIV and AIDS, which were both on an upwards trajectory, and ensured that schools couldn't safely share information or advice. It remained on the statute books for fifteen years.

Other laws shifted with glacial pace towards equality. It took until the turn of the millennium for parity to be achieved, when the Sexual Offences (Amendment) Act 2000 changed the law, making sixteen the age of consent for everyone. Legislative and social changes eased the pressure on this aspect of youth work, and the LGTG faded away, gradually replaced by happily unremarkable offerings in mainstream youth clubs, which increasingly made space for their LGBTQ+ members. The internet, obviously, also created opportunities for digital togetherness.

Worldwide, however, it's clear that gains in equality can be temporary. Hate offers quick dividends to politicians derelict enough to unleash it. These stories of youth clubs for teenagers marginalised by sexuality are a reminder that it is always possible to make space for those who need it, and that those moments come in waves, sweep people up and generate energy. They also signal something irrefutable. If necessary, the forward motion that creates such environments will unfurl again, like it always has.

PART THREE
CLASSIC YOUTH CLUBS, THE LATER YEARS

19

1983: THE LEAGUE OF JOI BANGLA YOUTH

Youth clubs that catered more specifically to South Asian youth would catch, and generate, an incoming cultural wave. The story begins with the Federation of Bangladeshi Youth Organisations (FBYO), an umbrella organisation that was formed in 1980, a practical outcome of the anti-racism movement of the previous decade.

Organisations wanting to join this national association were required to accept the FBYO's aims and objectives. These were as follows: 'to help young people nationally to reach full maturity as individuals and to assist them to play a full part in society and to make a contribution to the social and economic life of the Bangladeshi community'. Groups had to have at least fifty young members, as well as a constitution or written rules. Members were required to keep records, involve youth members in the running of the group and allow the FBYO to inspect clubs' activities.

By the middle of the decade, there were seventeen affiliates across England, including in Birmingham, Sunderland and Luton, with the majority in London's East End. Clubs were working hard for, and with, local teens. The Bangladeshi Youth Organisation in Bradford, for example, ran a youth club seven days a week, offering music, video film-making and drama, with three women workers who made regular home visits to 'try and help with any problems'. In London, a film workshop, Contrast, offered training to young women and men in video and film-making, alongside screenings and seminars, with the specific intention of correcting media bias. Groups across the country fielded sports teams, mostly football, and the FBYO ran tournaments that brought together young people from different parts of the country. Nationally, the organisation was also making concerted attempts to set up clubs for girls, recognising that the combination of racism and sexism required special attention.

Transparent frankness comes through in a 1985 report by the FBYO. Reading it gives me a new understanding of the difference between reports that frame reality in flattened language, because they're written for funders, and those that are community-facing. Baked-in tensions between grassroots work and officialdom pop off the page. The report looks to the year ahead, stating that the FBYO will campaign for change in the 'antiquated law determining what is "political" and what is "charitable". At present, the law says that it is charitable to alleviate the symptoms, but political to attempt to work at the causes.' Examples are given: that it is political to try to stop a racist attack and charitable to help an injured victim. Describing the law as 'pathetic', the writer makes clear the difficulty for organisations dealing with racism to get charitable status. The politicised roots of the FBYO, based as they were in the anti-racism movement of the 1970s, were, unsurprisingly, still evident.

One of the youth groups affiliated to the FBYO was the League of Joi Bangla Youth. 'Most of the groups in the Federation had been formed by young men who'd come to this country aged thirteen or fourteen and had taken part in the anti-racism movement,' explained community activist, researcher and League founder Ansar Ahmed Ullah when we talked. 'We were formed slightly later, not by young men who'd come from Bangladesh, but by either British-born or

British-bred Bengali young people.' The League of Joi Bangla Youth was, he said, the first youth organisation by and for British Bengalis, meeting in the common room at the Montefiore community centre in east London from around 1984.

The racism that forced the FBYO into existence remained in some youth clubs. 'In the 1970s, there was a sense of hostility. Many Bengali young people stayed away from youth clubs that had white young people,' said Ansar. 'I think this changed by the mid-1980s, when Bengalis started to have their own youth organisations, even their own youth clubs. That barrier was crossed, and youth clubs became open to all.'

As a twist on the classic youth club, the League would lead to the formation of at least three separate outfits: the popular Joi Bangla Sound (later renamed Joi), dancers Joi Bangla Crew and indie-rock outfit Joi Bangla Banned. 'Most of the people involved in the League were into fashion, music, going out, that kind of stuff,' said Ansar. 'We wanted to connect with young people who perhaps weren't fluent in Bengali or weren't aware of the cultural heritage because they were growing up in the UK.'

Bradford-born, before moving to Brick Lane in east London, brothers Haroon and Farook Shamsher joined the League and formed Joi Bangla Sound in 1983. Community work became orientated towards the dancefloor, and the group toured local youth clubs, bringing together Bengali music with hip hop breakbeats. The five dancers of Joi Bangla Crew – two young women and three men – created choreography and put on performances for mixed audiences of young Londoners.

Photographs of Joi Bangla's youth club excursions adorn the walls of the Tower Hamlets archive. Taken by Raju Vaidyan-athan, who was a little older than the young organisers behind the League of Joi Bangla, the images exude positivity. The photographer has thousands of pictures, he said, 'especially of the youth club'.

'What is your relationship to youth clubs?' I asked him, when we talked. 'I've got a broken, dysfunctional family background,' he said. 'Around fifteen I started going into a youth club, playing table tennis and just hanging around. The youth worker helped me find a place to live, because I was in a bit of a homeless situation. Then, later on, I became a part-time youth worker. I'm still living in the flat that was a halfway house for kids that the youth club started. When they closed it, I managed to get the tenancy.'

In a few packed sentences, Raju has shown youth clubs to be a kind of circular economy. As a young person in the mid-to-late 1970s, he received support and practical assistance that had a long-term positive impact on his life. He then passed that on, training in youth work and taking a role with the Bangladeshi Youth Movement's inaugural youth project in Tower Hamlets and, until 2012, other projects elsewhere in the borough: Robin Hood Gardens and St Matthias in Poplar, and Saint Andrew's Wharf and Cottage Street on the Isle of Dogs.

As a youth worker, and, later, after having studied film and photography at Guildhall in his thirties, Raju would take photographs and pin them up on a big board that was on show in the club, making the walls an informal gallery space, reflecting young people back at themselves. 'When the council shut the youth club, they threw everything away,' he told me. 'I found out within hours, contacted the refuse people, and they told me where they might have thrown everything away. I went and retrieved the boards with the photographs. I still have them, under my bed.' Raju's youth-club-generated home is doubling up as an archive, I think.

'What would you say was the role of youth clubs for young people in your area,' I asked, 'around the time Joi Bangla were combining hip hop, early house music and dance into their youth club forays?' 'When I was growing up, young Asian kids never went to youth club,' he said. 'We thought, "It's not for us."' There was a youth club next to the football pitch he used, but he never went in. 'We looked in from the outside,' he said. 'I used to hate it because I could hear them playing table tennis, and I always wanted to play table tennis. It was one of those things – young Asian kids thought youth clubs were only for white and Black kids. Then [someone] opened one room in a church hall and said, "Come in, come in." There was an Asian member of staff. For us, it was heaven-sent, playing table tennis, running around or whatever. Youth clubs at that time for young Asian kids was a big thing.' Apart from hanging out, meeting friends and the opportunity to meet other youngsters through inter-club football tournaments, he added, it was there a lot of the community workers and councillors got their start. 'It was a political grounding too.'

'Is there anything else we should talk about in relation to the subject of east London youth clubs?' I asked, as we finished chatting. He paused. 'It all became a bit . . . racialised,' he said. 'When I went to work in Poplar and the Isle of Dogs, we insisted the staff had to be multiracial so the users would be multiracial. But a lot of the east London youth clubs became religious, geared towards a religious grounding, so straight away you're excluding some people. Youth clubs should never be exclusive. They should be very inclusive.'

Leaders of all faiths have long generated social spaces so that young people could learn more about religion – just think of the heavy Christian focus of the Settlements and the Mission

Houses a hundred years earlier, or the many Methodist youth clubs. Youth clubs are powerful places, and, as Raju says, should be as inclusive as possible.

In 1987, more than half of the Bangladeshi people living in Britain were fifteen or under, compared with one fifth of the British population as a whole, according to a newspaper report from the time. Under the headline 'A Young Generation Begins to Fight Back', it positioned Bangladeshi youth organisations in terms of the National Front, which led marches down Brick Lane. Nahid Huda, a member of the League of Joi Bangla Youth, was quoted. 'Only now is this generation fighting back,' she said, referencing novelist and director of the Institute of Race Relations Ambalavaner Sivanandan. 'Migration happened and we are here because you were there.'

As house music arrived from Chicago, Joi Bangla added their own elements, releasing 'Taj Ma House' in 1988. John Peel played the white label on his influential BBC Radio 1 show, and their follow-up was named Single of the Week in primo rock publication the *NME*. Joi Bangla's 'Deep Asian Vibes' sessions at the Blue Note have gone down in cultural history, and there's now a blue plaque outside Haroon and Farouk's family home on Brick Lane. A UK-wide scene generated by and catering to South Asian teens drew heavily from youth clubs, using them as a resource, a playpen, and for what might be called 'audience development', going on to influence the mainstream at the time, and, decades later, entities like Daytimers and Dialled In.

'We were interested in all things Bengali and the history of Bangladesh,' added Ansar Ahmed Ullah. 'It was a time when Bollywood and bhangra were strong in the Asian youth scene and there was no Bengali artist. People credit us as being part of the Asian underground music scene. I think people saw it was a breath of fresh air. People felt proud we existed, and that we were pioneering.'

The history of independent music venues often sails close to the youth club, as do the histories of sound systems, dance-halls and nightclubs. One such location would be the Medway Indian Centre, or MIC, which operated in Kent at the same time as Joi Bangla were bringing new sounds and ways of being into East End youth clubs. Based in rooms with low ceilings, it was run by a man of South Asian heritage known to one and all as 'Sandy', primarily as a social space for Indian taxi drivers, above the Twin Dragons Chinese restaurant in Chatham.

Attracting mostly white English youngsters, with bands and audiences coming down after school, it was 'a packed room full of fifteen- to eighteen-year-olds, plus a few people as old as twenty-two', according to writer and musician Vic Templar, who wrote in compelling style about MIC in the zine *Noise Grunge Garage*. There was a quarter-stage in the corner, a pool table, a bar and, on the wall, American wagon wheels from the weekly Blue Montana Skies cowboy club that took place there, recalled musician, artist and poet Billy Childish as we talked in his light-drenched studio in Chatham Dockyard. He was working on two paintings at once and drinking big mugs of green tea, with oil paint, brushes and half-squeezed tubes on the table around him, and canvases stacked up against the walls.

Childish was a regular, playing with his band Thee Milkshakes, and later releasing a live track, 'Club M.I.C. (Instrumental)'. Other bands were put together by teenagers living in the dock town and making the most of the avail-able space, attracting a soubriquet – the Medway Scene – with

Childish in particular acknowledged as influencing later artists, including Kurt Cobain and The White Stripes.

Our conversation covered personal history, opinions on art, money, creativity, religion and empire, and was interspersed with many unrepeatable anecdotes about other artists and musicians. Then Childish began riffing on the subject of squats, and how awful they really were. 'Anything that's good looks after itself,' he said. 'When you look at anything utopian, I'm really suspicious.'

Sensing an opportunity to divert the conversation back to MIC, I jumped in. 'What was the utopian version of this quasi-youth club, and what was the dark side?' 'If you were going to look for one, it's this great little venue. It wouldn't be very utopian, but it'd be a big plus, this space where you did whatever you wanted, where you got the door money and there was no one ripping you off . . . We're back to the very simple thing of somewhere to go, something to do.'

'What might be the minus?' I asked. Childish paused. 'I don't think there is a minus, which is strange. You might have to ask one of the taxi drivers. He might tell you the minus was having us there on a Friday night and ruining the bingo.'

Walking back through the dockyard, I pass a ship's figurehead, now erected as a statue. It comes from HMS *Wellesley*, a warship launched in 1815 from India's Bombay Dockyard. As I head off towards the nearby caff, I'm struck by the layering of all these elements, and how Empire showed up in the youth club, both in Chatham and within these early South Asian youth clubs in the 1980s.

Chatham Dockyard was a central location for building and repairing the British ships that created and maintained colonialism, which was brutal for many of those who were colonised. The decline and then eventual closure of the docks in 1984 had a harsh effect on the local economy. A community social club was opened up by a man of South Asian heritage offering safe downtime for British Asian taxi drivers in this part of Kent. The invitation was extended to Kentish teens, who in different ways and for different reasons, needed space to be themselves. Offering paying custom, albeit massively underage, the kids turned the MIC into an entity that was part youth club, part genre-generating grassroots music venue, and wholly remarkable.

However, it's important not to lump superficially similar safe spaces together. Being shouted at on the street for dressing like an arty punk is in an entirely different category of threat to racist violence. But no communal entity is an island, and the story of the MIC helps illustrate the interconnected nature of youth clubs, community centres, social clubs and loosely commercial venues that welcome all sorts, as well as the way that the creation of safe spaces can have unexpected outcomes that spread way beyond the original intention.

At national level, politicians were pushing for changes that would safeguard the youth clubs being used by Joi Bangla and MIC indie kids alike. In December 1983, John Watson, Conservative MP for Skipton and Ripon, tabled a question in Parliament. Would the Secretary of State for Education and Science introduce legislation along the lines suggested by the Thompson Report on youth and community services?

The report he was referring to was already more than a year old. *Experience and Participation: Report of the Review Group on the Youth Service in England* outlined recommendations, the first of which being that the youth service had a duty to help all young people who have need of it. Local authorities and voluntary organisations should, said the authors, work together to address patchy provision. Most importantly, it advocated for a statutory basis for the youth service, stating that it should be funded 'at a high level'. Offering a new definition of youth work's purpose – to provide social education – it noted that both the inner cities and rural areas needed special attention, and also highlighted the needs of girls, 'ethnic communities' and young people with disabilities. Listing out the ways the youth service would achieve success, the Thompson Report mentioned the need for activities, advice, action in the community and access to vocational and life skills. The first item on the list, though, was 'association', followed by a phrase in brackets – 'a place to meet' – which could easily be replaced with another: youth club.

Junior Education Minister Peter Brooke answered his backbencher in the blandest of terms, saying as little as possible through phrases including 'under consideration' and 'announced as soon as possible'. Labour MP Dale Campbell-Savours pushed for more, asking if the minister knew that youth clubs throughout the United Kingdom 'operate in difficult financial circumstances, suffer great hardship and have to survive from week to week', adding that youth clubs 'ensure that many young people are taken off the street, where they could engage in anti-social activities'. A reply came in the language of bamboozle economics, stating that the government's plans 'should' allow 'the great majority' of local authorities 'in aggregate' to maintain past levels of provision, 'provided that costs, especially pay, are contained and resources are managed effectively'. In short, Thompson wasn't going to happen. It was another lost opportunity at government level, leading to losses that would play out on the ground.

20

1984: A CREATIVE CULTURAL POWERHOUSE

Generation X would be better described as Generation Y, as in Y for Youth Club. Ask anyone in that demographic, and they'll look to the left, as memory kicks into action. There would have been somewhere near-ish, even if they went only once and quickly spun on their heels because it was, to quote a friend, 'a more violent version of school'. In direct and specific ways, open-access youth clubs supported globally powerful art, culture and creativity, and they did so despite the lack of government funding and scant recognition of their role in the cultural ecosystem. For those whose parents were lacking spare cash for music lessons or art equipment, the youth club could be an especially powerful stairway to a creative life.

Like a kind of tuning fork, youth clubs responded to the cultural vibrations. Club members, whether in Southend or Southampton, could share and absorb emerging music, style and culture. For those energised by then-new US hip hop, artists including KRS-One articulated routes into an artistic life through the 'five pillars' of playing records, rapping, movement, artwork and 'the knowledge', or learning about the culture. This new impetus, along with the substructures provided by the men and women behind the UK's myriad reggae sound systems, provided a solid foundation for early-1980s teens to build on, bolstered by the practical instruction of punk – 'this is a chord, form a band' – which was still reverberating. All of this could be practised in the youth club, as if art and culture were aspects of active citizenship, not something to be passively consumed.

Also at play at this time were the adjacent benefits of unstructured hanging out and the motivating role of boredom in the pre-internet age, both of which made the youth club a place of great potential for creativity in all its forms. Handheld LCD games like Pac-Man had begun arriving in 1982, but were expensive and therefore rare. TV, video and computer games were almost entirely static, consumed at home or in amusement arcades. Warmer than the street, with subsidised snacks and understanding adults, youth clubs offered plentiful scuffed-up space for people of a similar age. It was a situation that would inevitably lead, for better or worse, to ideas. Action followed.

In the mid-1980s, those running youth clubs at a national level increasingly began to foreground art and creativity. Sport looked after itself, with table tennis, snooker and football well catered for in the country's youth clubs. Establishment networks with the ability to set and enact strategic aims began tuning in to the increased interest coming from young people themselves. Conferences, publications and events all contributed to a sector-wide push for the arts.

The NAYC had been promoting crafts and practical forms of creativity for as long as it had existed, with these activities taking up space on youth club schedules alongside sport or camping. For many years the creative arts were delivered in tandem with sport, the two areas being organised through a single committee, instead of having their own space for discussion and planning. The arts at national youth club level before the mid-1980s looked like one half of a coin, not a full currency.

In 1984, following in the footsteps of margins-powered groups including Joi Bangla or the LGTG, to whom art and music were central, the NAYC launched a new Arts Festival. Catering for 300 young people and their youth workers, the event was sponsored by Mecca Leisure and featured workshops on mime, dance and drama, and competitions in photography and journalism. Star power was in evidence: *Coronation Street* actor Kevin Kennedy, who played Curly Watts, was an adjudicator for the drama section. 'I was only too pleased to be asked to help,' he said at the time. 'I was involved in youth theatre myself and I consider it very worthwhile.'

Subsequent to the Festival, NAYC gained funding from the Gulbenkian Foundation, which had been set up by the British–Armenian oil man and philanthropist of the same name, and built a programme of training and network-building alongside the now-annual Arts Festival. Commercial sponsors got on board, with stalwarts Mecca Leisure joined by others, including household brands Brooke Bond Oxo Ltd and Coca-Cola, along with the Abbey National Building Society and aluminium company British Alcan Tubes. The effects played out in local clubs – for example, a three-day workshop in Rhydywaun County Youth Centre in mid-Glamorgan, Wales, offered taster sessions in 'art and craft', video film-making, judo, photography and disco dancing. 'Though perhaps a little early to consider it a trend,' wrote the Welsh Association of Youth Clubs, 'there has been an encouraging response from all areas for more creative activities.'

Regions began rolling out their own versions. In Gloucester-shire, an arts team was formed in 1985 to take art, drama, dance and mixed media to clubs across the county. Six workers made more than seven hundred visits to ninety clubs over a nine-month period. The response was declared 'very positive' and, in language that points towards an increasingly outcomes-focused world, 'young people's enthusiasm for the arts was demonstrated'.

Turner Prize-winning artist and NTS radio presenter Mark Leckey is well known for his 1999 dancefloor video opus *Fiorucci Made Me Hardcore*. He attributes his visual acuity to time spent at Hope Farm Disco, held in a 'very modern' Methodist church whose youth club allowed access to the stimulants of music, fashion and dancing in the early '80s. 'It's where I forged my interest in culture,' he told me, as we drank tea and chatted. 'I don't really remember adults being there. I just remember it being full of kids.'

Ellesmere Port, right on the edge of Liverpool, was the location of an earlier youthie, as clubs were known in the north-west. It sounds like a renegade spot, with young adults from the local Sutton Way gang ensuring access or denying it. It was purpose built, 'a very 1960s municipal building', with a pool table and perhaps – the memories are vague – some boxing. In an echo of factory girls drinking cocoa and Mods eating toast at Weekender youth clubs, Mark – unprompted – mentions snacks as 'a big part of being there'. Youthie was a place to hang out for those in their middle and late teens, right up to people in their early twenties. 'Compared to a lot of those kids I was more innocent,' he said, digging deep into blurred memories of fights, stolen car radios and magic mushrooms grown in the club's field. 'That's where I lost my innocence.' In memory, adults are very much in the background, almost invisible.

'I have a vague outline of someone being there, someone you didn't want to upset. I think there was a respect there for the person who ran it.'

'It's interesting,' I said, 'that you had access to this unchaperoned, or under-chaperoned, space in which young people were in the majority, which was somewhat lawless but also somewhat contained. I'm wondering, what carried over from this into your life as an artist?' He paused before replying. 'I grew up in this working-class culture and then I went to art school, where I was inculcated, indoctrinated into middle-class values of behaviour, humour and culture. As I've got older, I've realised that when I was young, I *had* culture. It was there in your parents, but it was also at places like youth club. You'd be introduced to music or fashion in a very sophisticated way, in advance of the music press. I grew up with something very expansive and hungry, which had its own ambitions and was for sharing. It was communal.'

Rich culture was available, miles away from establishment validation. Youth club topped up his creative storehouse in ways not shared by most of his peers at art school, at least some of whom had been cushioned from harsher social realities by growing up at a distance from poverty. In terms of visual culture, youthie operated as a kind of stage, or catwalk, as well as – for Mark – a sideways boost into academia.

'There was a different style every week,' he recalled. 'When I was fifteen or sixteen, it's the peak of casuals, scallies. There was a period when it moved incredibly fast. At one point you'd be wearing golf jumpers, then the next week looking like a geography supply teacher, or wearing a deerstalker hat. When I got to art school everyone was talking about semiotics, learning how to read art. I'd already had a foundation degree in reading visual language.' Youth club was, he explained, a 'pipeline', but there are caveats. 'I'm celebrating all this stuff,' he said, 'but there are reasons I left my home town. I wanted a little bit more. These are conflicted feelings that I've never quite got to resolve.'

In the now-familiar reverberation, Mark has returned to the fold. He runs the Music and Video Lab, where teenagers can come and make music-adjacent video art in Toxteth, Liverpool. 'We did one last year in Redruth in Cornwall, and in Margate. The Liverpool one is ongoing. It feels very much like a youth club when you're there. I feel like a youth leader. It's quite hard to adjust. I initiated it because those kinds of initiatives aren't going to come from governments or local authorities any more.' Like so many others, Mark picked up the signal, ran with it and, eventually, in his fifties, looped back.

The word 'evident' means obvious. But none of the obvious-to-me benefits of Hope Farm Disco or the youth club in Ellesmere Port would be easily explained by an official evaluation. Youth clubs' visible effect on art, like everything else in this corner of the world, operates with a time lag. Perhaps this is because youth clubs as entities share certain characteristics with teenagers as a demographic. A small group of young folk can take an hour to walk to shops that are only fifteen minutes away, because, as a poet friend once said, teenagers walk in spirals. Youth clubs might progress similarly.

———

Despite the active unwillingness of Margaret Thatcher's government, youth clubs in the mid-1980s were becoming a generative location, contributing to the emergence of the UK as a leading location for art and culture. In the 1950s, they'd been envisaged and funded largely as a way of controlling teenagers, specifically the Teddy Boys. This time round, youth clubs were going to respond to and welcome various 1980s versions: indie kids, pop fans, goths, casuals, and the b-boys and girls, rappers, breakers, graffiti artists and DJs involved with electro, hip hop and early house music.

Bristol music legend DJ Krust has had a creative life since his teens, first making it into the charts with Fresh 4, alongside friends Suv, Flynn, Judge and Lizz E with their 1989 hit 'Wishing on a Star'. A leading light in Bristol's mid-1990s jungle scene, notably with his tune 'Warhead', he ran the influential Full Cycle record label and was an original member of Roni Size's Mercury Prize-winning Reprazent outfit. He remains an in-demand DJ and producer, and recently curated an exhibition, *This Is Jungle/D&B: The Origins of Bristol's Music History*, at Bristol's Centrespace Gallery. He remembers youth clubs' formative role in his own artistry, and the rolling back of investment.

Aged ten or eleven, he was sent on an errand to Eagle House youth club in Knowle West by his seamstress mum. It was a sizeable space, attached to a working men's club, with table football, snooker and pool, a tuck shop and outdoor space for football, basketball and netball. 'I walked in,' recalled Krust. 'My brother was there, playing chess in this huge place, and I remember just feeling like it was important, and thinking, "I can't wait to get there." By the time I got there, the place was fucked. In four years it totally deteriorated.'

Before arriving at youth club, Krust and his friends had made use of the available space at school. Inspired by 1982 hip hop movie *Wildstyle*, the group persuaded teachers to give them a room, which they spray-painted. They then put down the lino necessary for b-boys and girls to dance on, and ran school discos once a month. Outgrowing school – 'there was always going to be limits' – they approached Eagle House.

'I think it was an easy sell,' Krust remembered, when we spoke one evening. 'Their job was to keep us off the streets, to keep our minds occupied. We'd bring other kids into that space. They gave us this jumbled-up room. We cleaned it up, organised it and started practising.' A youth worker supported them, recognising the specific creative and cultural interests of the schoolkids in his orbit. Dave was cool, said Krust, a 'tall, softly spoken giant. He was alright, and that was the thing that made Eagle House okay. He never really said no. He had that attitude of "Let's find a way."'

Youth workers, or those who instigate youth projects, are a particular kind of human. A teacher friend uses the phrase 'central casting' as shorthand to describe how similar archetypes – the eager brain-box; the clown – would appear in her classes year in, year out. I feel sure that central casting has been sending out youth-worker types for centuries, perhaps even millennia. Youth workers have a view on what young folk might need, and they attempt to provide at least some of it. The conditions in which they operate are time-specific, as are their assumptions about what they are doing and why, but I'm pretty sure that the undercurrents are the same: to attend to needs, and a firm belief that the kids are alright.

And so, with a strong, supportive adult on the sidelines and one of their mates on the door, the entity that was becoming Fresh 4 emerged into reality. It did so organically, through a simple set-up in which the four friends could take part in learning by doing. Accessible youth club space allowed them to create something approximating a club night: Krust and friends played records on belt-drive turntables and rapped over and around the beats on a cheap microphone. Girls were allowed, in gender-constrained fashion, to try a bit of singing. The artistically minded in their crew created spray-painted backdrops, while those with high levels of physical skill battled each other with brand-new dance moves absorbed from films and what writer, critic and artist Lucy Sante astutely described as the 'great invisible telegraph of youth'.

Fresh 4's youth club parties got so big they had to move from their small room into the main hall. This they outgrew too, and once they'd found their way into a squat on St Luke's Road, they exited the youth club entirely, swapping ping-pong and the tuck shop for high-energy squat parties and space to learn music production with influential producers Smith and Mighty by hanging out in the back of their Ashley Road studio, a rarefied post-youth club situation.

It was a moment when their youth club disco began edging beyond the margins of emerging culture and touched what had already been sanctified as 'real' or 'proper'. Such proximity made Fresh 4 more real too – the beginnings of a transformation from ordinary teenagers to individuals who'd cause a nudge and an eye-widening when seen out and about; something *extra*ordinary, amplified. Within the emerging street-level arts and culture, it would become possible to invent your own job based on skills you'd learned and practised in the youth club.

Youth clubs, to varying degrees, sucked in a communally aware self-starter culture. Having this space, said Krust, provided a 'home from home', a phrase that is especially relevant to teenagers whose single mum is maybe working two or three jobs to keep the household afloat, meaning that she's probably not at home when they get back from school. 'We were the original latchkey kids,' he said with a grin. 'Key under the plant pot or the mat, come home, make dinner for ourselves.'

It felt good, he said, to be in a space where you could be noticed and appreciated. 'We come home from school, no one's at home, and we're not getting that attention. We're going to the clubs to make something of ourselves, to big ourselves up. You could be recognised for the little things you were doing.' Decades later, the influence endures. 'Every time I start something, say a kitchen-table business, it's still that DIY mentality. That's what I learned from Knowle West and the youth club.'

'Is the youth club a DIY space?' I asked, to clarify. He nodded. 'Yes. If you want to do something, *you* have to do it. My mum isn't buying new clothes, she's making them. If I asked my mum, "Can you buy us a turntable?" she'd say, "You want a turntable? Go and make it." And if you can't make it, go and make something you can sell, so that you can buy a turntable.' The Irish family he grew up next to had a similar mentality, he said. 'Work hard, make things from what you've got around you. No one's giving us stuff. We're looking around – how can I use this environment, this space? It gets you into action, straight away.'

DIY, then, in this cultural context suggests grassroots community creativity, not the act of putting up shelves. Under this lens, the bringing together of the three letters is plural, not singular: do it yourselves – an appropriately communal and creative response to the prevailing individualism of the political time.

That individualism was summed up by senior Conservative minister Norman Tebbit's response to the suggestion that unemployment had caused the 1981 riots and uprisings. 'I grew up in the '30s with an unemployed father,' he said, in the age-old way that powerful people parade personal histories of hardship. 'He didn't riot. He got on his bike and looked for work, and he kept looking until he found it.'

Teenagers in the mid-1980s would have had to clock up significant miles cycling to get a job, especially if they lived in areas suffering higher than average levels of unemployment. In 1984, the NAYC reported that there were 1,180,500 unemployed young people under twenty-five. 'Throughout NAYC's history the Association has been pioneering in the world of work and employment,' it wrote, offering some backstory, describing clubs for factory girls in the early 1900s that campaigned for better working conditions and noting that, throughout the 1930s, the 'personal aspect of unemployment and strategies for overcoming the problem through Girls' Clubs' were addressed. As we've heard, by the 1970s the NAYC had initiated Community Industry, repeatedly describing it as being for those who'd probably be unemployed 'even in better economic times'.

By 1984, many unemployed young people were turning up at youth clubs in the daytime, with both clubs and youth workers unprepared for their needs. At government level, there was concern that unstructured free time unleashed by unemployment would lead to trouble, and money was found to open youth club doors to those on the dole. The NAYC launched the all-caps DAYSPACE, with the year's annual report explaining the rationale: 'The programme seeks to bring together in networks those who are working with the young unemployed, so that they can share resources, exchange ideas and information and undertake joint ventures.' The NAYC appointed a full-time worker to develop the scheme, as well as running a quarterly newsletter and schemes to retrain youth workers for work with the young unemployed. The latter would be managed by the Greater Manchester Youth Association and the Merseyside Youth Association, with funds from local authorities and the European Social Fund. Efforts to deal with unemployment through the youth club seemed focused on damage limitation.

In Northern Ireland, in 1984, a different youth service plan was launched under a sensible name: Practical Action. Something needed to be done, after all. Unemployment was the highest in the UK, standing at 17 per cent. An ad in the *Belfast News Letter* the following year, promoting Practical Action's presence at the 1985 Youth Festival at Balmoral, explained the idea: 'We are an appeal to the private and public sectors but NOT for money, but for resources such as equipment, manpower and expertise, to support projects for young people who would otherwise be unemployed.'

The Thatcher government was concerned about more than just dole queues. A 1984 letter to Sir Keith Joseph, then education secretary, regarding the Review Group on the Youth Service underlines the prime minister's view. A national youth service advisory body was unwelcome because it would 'likely become a troublesome pressure group'. A subsequent line gives a sense of how starkly politicians can prioritise self-interest over the national good, in this case as it relates to unemployment: 'As you know, we recently abolished the Careers Service Advisory Council on these very grounds.'

Once again, social conditions were generating youth clubs for problem youth whose problems were largely caused by society. At the same time, youth clubs themselves were in the firing line.

21

1985: CRISPS AND ORANGE SQUASH FOR NEW TOWN YOUTH

The United Nations deemed 1985 International Youth Year, although you wouldn't have known it in Britain. In Canada, the government allocated £8m in support of the initiative. The UK government, however, offered only £250,000. The sums should come as no surprise: the UK was six years into a Tory government led by Margaret Thatcher, which, for people born in the 1970s and '80s, conjures up a range of words, with the simplest of these being 'divisive'. After she died in 2013, hundreds of people of all ages and backgrounds lined the streets with hand-drawn placards, booing or turning their back on the funeral cortège. For those born in the 1990s and 2000s, a shorthand is useful: Thatcher was a steadfast supporter of populist leaders and regimes. In the mid-1980s, this meant personally and politically backing South Africa's apartheid regime and the Pinochet dictatorship in Chile. She was also big on spending cuts, at least when it came to public services.

While selling off public assets and cutting tax, her government also restricted local councils from raising the money they needed to deliver the services required in their area. Previously, councils would apply a local form of taxation to cover the shortfall between central government grants and what was needed locally. Working out how much money they needed to generate, councils would allocate each property in the area a 'rateable value', applying an equation that set the rates for the year, which householders would then pay.

Labour-run councils, in particular, were accused by the Conservative government of overspending. Regular tabloid stories about 'the loony left' helped the narrative, as councils in economically deprived areas were scolded by right-leaning columnists for wasting money on funding for feminists, homosexuals and people of colour. The idea of introducing powers to limit individual council budgets, though, was controversial, because it centralised power and damaged local democracy, and so prominent Conservatives MPs campaigned against the Rates Bill. Despite opposition, it passed through Parliament in 1984, after the government pushed it through the House of Lords by summoning many of their members who rarely attended. The bill's success pitted some councils, especially those which had scooped up more left-wing councillors in local elections, directly against the government. In Westminster, Conservative MPs wanted to slash spending. Locally, there was a desire to fund groups and projects deemed socially valuable, which, of course, included youth work.

In 1985, fifteen councils refused to comply with the new rules by deciding not to fulfil their legal responsibility to set a balanced budget, in a moment known as the 'rate-capping rebellion'. The rebellion failed, though, and the metaphorical taps that could be turned on locally were definitively turned off. The effects were felt across council services.

A visit, in International Youth Year, gives a sense of the scope and scale of clubs. In 1985, Her Majesty's Inspectorate visited Coventry. The city council at this time had a Youth Resource Centre, which operated as a kind of community treasure chest. It included camping, games and hiking equipment, materials for handicrafts, guitars, drum machines, drum kits, PA systems, wind instruments and what was described as 'Asian music'. Pentax and Canon cameras for photography and video were there for the borrowing, along with two types of computers – the ZX Spectrum and the Commodore 64 – and minibuses, plural.

'Becoming an adult can be a difficult process at the best of times,' wrote the HMI report's author, in a section about the value of youth work. 'It is doubly difficult to discover a sense of authenticity and purpose in a period of social and economic instability,' they continued, noting the decline of the city's manufacturing base and its motor industry. 'As young people compete for scarce jobs and resources, many come up against unemployment, racism and homelessness – those three negative ingredients of contemporary urban social experience.'

Critiquing specifically the offering for 'young Asian and Afro-Caribbean' British citizens, it was noted that staffing levels and the quality of facilities were less than adequate in those areas of the city where these young people lived. Specialist provision for Asian girls was heavily centred around sewing and flower arranging, as well as 'the preparation of tea and *burfi* and listening in another room to some of their own records'. While these activities could be criticised for confirming rather than challenging the domestic role of women, the report noted that 'young women might not be allowed to leave home to associate socially for much else. The youth worker has to strike a balance between meeting the needs of the young women and honouring the cultural imperatives of the community.' Two things strike me at once: that respecting cultural imperatives is essential, and also how easily, in all parts of society, girls' needs are considered conditional.

Unemployment continued to wreak havoc, and, to differing degrees, jobs were in short supply everywhere across the UK in the mid-1980s. Most people left school at sixteen or seventeen, and only 15 per cent of school-leavers in 1985 went to university. Between 1979 and 1985, unemployment for under-twenty-fives went up 167 per cent, according to Huddersfield MP Barry Sheerman, who raised the matter in Parliament, declaring that there were over a million under-twenty-fives out of work. However, unemployment came with a fortnightly social security payment, as well as easily accessible housing benefit, which was not capped in the same way as today, and emergency grants. The vast downside involved low self-esteem, high anxiety and an upwardly spiralling chance of long-term poverty. Those not signing on undertook poorly paid, insecure placements on the government's Youth Training Scheme, which was known by its initials, YTS. It paid less than the dole and often just led back to the dole queue. In March 1985, schoolkids rebelled against a government plan to make YTS compulsory for the young unemployed, with 3,000 schoolchildren in Cardiff and 30,000 kids in Liverpool skipping class and taking to the streets. Over 2,000 young people, from across the sectarian divide, also marched in Northern Ireland.

There were still large numbers of youth clubs, for those who went after school and their unemployed peers. The NAYC's affiliation statistics for 1985/6 showed 6,693 member youth clubs, with 626,629 members and over 40,000 youth workers, albeit the vast majority volunteers. This wouldn't have been the full total: other organisations offered an umbrella association – for example, the National Association of Boys and Girls Clubs, or the Federation of London Youth Clubs.

Peterborough, in the east of England. Approximately 70,000 families had moved to the area in the years after new town designation in 1967, a backstory also shared by Milton Keynes and Northampton. Subsequently, there were families from all over the country who were in special need of social spaces in which to meet each other, given that everyone was a 'new kid'. Lincoln Road offered a number of options. It was an old street in the north of Peterborough which housed City Centre, a council-run building, and the Asian Cultural Centre, run by co-ordinator Ansar Ali with two generous priorities: 'To provide a base for activities for the Asian community and to offer a rich source of culture to those who are not Asian.' Individuals, friendship groups and demographic crews moved between clubs and centres with varying degrees of osmosis. Elsewhere in Peterborough, Mrs Hussein organised the Goulistan Girls Group, initially from the back room of a house and later in mobile classrooms in a school playground. Framed as an educative, not social, setting, girls learned to read and write Urdu, explore religious scriptures and learn practical skills like needlework and housekeeping, as well as letting off steam by playing cricket or tag.

The Young People's Theatre Company (YPTC) was another of these spaces, using the drama of teenage life to attract members to their sessions. Based at Bretton Woods Community School, in an area of Peterborough that ranked highly in the English deprivation indices, it was started by the school's head of drama, Yvonne McGuinness, in 1980 and was funded by the Peterborough Arts Council. A set of images by documentary photographer Russell Boyce shows a banner with a forward-thinking provocation – 'Boys will be boys, girls will be girls: innate or learned?' – and an off-stage moment, with a boy in an Adidas tracksuit deep in concentration, in charge of sound effects. Teenagers in Tacchini and Nike Cortez engage in improvisation, and a girl who reminds me of myself screws up her face after smoking her first cigarette.

A teenage version of Andrea Brace can be seen within the frame of these images. Now, she's in the digital square of a video call, filling me in on the details. The group would gather to create productions like *Grease*, but, more importantly, to discuss, create and improvise drama about, say, masculinity or teenage feelings. There was plenty of rich dramatic material outside. 'We were challenging young people, and a lot of people wrote us off. The group was able to get people who'd have been out on the streets, where we were causing mayhem,' she said. 'Somehow, out of the chaos, a group of young people were able to explore themselves and their identity in a way that made you feel valued.'

'What kind of chaos were you collectively creating?' I asked, sensing teenage comedy. 'Well,' she said, and laughed, putting her head in her hands. 'It's embarrassing. We'd be hanging out at this big bus stop. We were the Bus Stop Lot.' Her next comment sums up the way that childhood and adulthood overlap for those in their early teens, with details that evoke how kids entertained themselves before the internet. 'We'd just hang around smoking, phoning the Speaking Clock or listening to the music you got when you pressed 1 and 6 on a public telephone. There'd be people sniffing deodorant, glue. A lot of the breakdancing would be down there, or we'd be running round playing [childhood staple] forty–forty.'

Within the theatre group, things were different because their teenage entropy was grounded and directed. 'It was purposeful, useful, challenging. All this energy you have – you can use it. You can tell your stories.' Andrea's own story needed some telling. She'd moved to the town from Manchester when she was seven. Her dad left home, and the country, soon after. Family life became difficult and she was suspended from school and kicked out of home.

'I was told I was too emotional, loud, and I was made to feel this was a negative. When I got to the theatre group, I realised I was right: I'm allowed to have a say. I'm allowed to stand up for myself and to call out misogyny, although I wouldn't have known that word.' It's heavy stuff, travelling back to teenage trauma, and Andrea paused and said something amazing. 'It gave me an outlet so I didn't have to carry that feeling around with me, that distress I felt in my life.' I think of the youth club as having so many functions – for example, a sanctuary or a place of social education. Talking to Andrea has given me a new understanding of what space can do: provide a framework to hold and share a burden, lightening the load.

Youth theatre was a kind of spark-plug. One of the YPTC group, Cheryl Fergison, went on to work as an actor, winding up in *EastEnders* as mid-2000s character Heather Trott. Others went off to teach, including Andrea, who trained as a drama teacher and then became head of drama in a comprehensive school, getting the kids to do Shakespeare or make up their own plays. On the morning of our call she was teaching Forum Theatre to her Year 9s. It's a radical and politically charged technique, pioneered in the early 1970s by Augusto Boal in Brazil during a military dictatorship, in which audiences and actors can jump into a scene and create new or different routes through the story. 'They're the same age I was when I was introduced to it,' said Andrea, describing how the lesson's topic – homelessness – had led to a discussion. 'I told them the journey, about changing direction and being in control of that. I wanted them all to have a voice. I had education through youth clubs and youth theatre, where people would say, "Have your say!" Now kids are being told, "Shut up, behave, sit down."' She paused and sighed. 'When did we go back to the 1970s?'

Her comment got me thinking. Schools and youth clubs are different entities, each offering their own opportunities, relationships and dynamics. There are many ways to be a good teacher, and those who do this important job are animated by the good and the bad bits of it, even if they disagree about what the good or bad bits are, or were. Education is always in flux, for a complex set of reasons. Sometimes schools are underpinned by a wide range of beliefs about how to educate teenagers, with differences both between and within schools. Some lean heavily on the external – uniform or haircuts – with others operating on the assumption that students can wear different-coloured socks and still be good at maths. At other times, variance is knocked out, with a greater degree of homogeneity between schools and a focus on strict behaviour policies. I believe that leaning too heavily on compliance, especially if it comes at the cost of critical thinking, is counterproductive at the best of times. And when the politics of hate and division gains traction, internationally, it can be downright dangerous.

A five-month solo photography exhibition, *New Town Youth 1985*, took place at the Peterborough Museum and Art Gallery almost four decades after the events depicted. The pictures had been shot by Russell Boyce when he was twenty-three and were shown informally at the time, pinned on boards in the City Centre community space. Boxed up, the negatives moved with Boyce from house to house until he attended a Covid lockdown talk by Lisa der Weduwe from the Museum of Youth Culture and Geoff Broadway from the Living Memory Project. 'Geoff and Lisa talked about the notion of archiving work for the future and how this is disappearing because of digital,' explained Russell, when we spoke. 'I thought, "Oh, I've got an archive in my attic." I went and got the box of negs, got in touch with the museum, and it blew their socks off.'

The black-and-white pictures, shot with a Minolta 100B camera, capture a moment in time beautifully. They offer yet another example of how the youth club allowed older young people to practise their art form, in this case photography. As with John Goto's *Lovers Rock* photographs of Lewisham youth, Raju Vaidyanathan's shots of Joi Bangla and Jake Bernard's pictures of the Holyhead in Coventry, Russell was drawn to this rich and easily accessible part of community life.

Andrea's theatre group is there, of course, alongside images that document the YTS scheme. It's the shots from the weekly Friday Club session that form the heart of Russell's collection, though. Evocative and universal, photographs show young teenagers on bikes, front wheel up in the air, waiting for the building to open, and friends sitting on low walls, resting their heads on each other's shoulders in the teenage way. In others, two boys giggle over a birth control pamphlet, while others with feather cuts read informational material about sniffing glue. In the doorway of the tuck shop at ten past nine, an older man is holding ketchup and brown sauce, perhaps to put on someone's chips. The handwritten price list shows that drinks include a super-affordable orange squash for eight pence, while crisps and chocolate bars are all under 20p, with Lion Bars being the cheapest. There is a police-run rifle club, where members could learn how to load a gun and shoot at a target. Russell's subjects mostly ignore his camera, some more studiedly than others.

When not at Friday Club, Russell was working, teaching evening photography classes at the Arts Centre and working in a clothes shop. He had crossed paths with lead youth worker Brian Healey, who, in time-honoured style, had drawn this young photographer into the youth club orbit, with the idea that Russell would offer informal photography sessions. 'Brian was a fantastic guy, a great believer in giving young people space to be who they are, without restriction. He liked that it was really multicultural. He'd say if one person got something from it, it was a success.'

Armed with a tiny £150 grant from Peterborough Arts Council, Russell went down to Friday Club, hung about and gradually got to know the members. Acceptance had a price. 'I was just around and I always had my camera with me,' he said when we conversed. '"Let's borrow your camera, Russell," and I'd be a bit nervous because it's my only camera.' He winced at the memory. 'They'd bugger off with the damn thing and photograph each other's backsides with it,' he recalled.

'What do you think the Friday Club did for the young people who attended,' I asked, 'including you?' 'I think it gave them space to be themselves, whatever that was. There was a lot of self-policing going on. If something was going on, they controlled it themselves, and I think the youth leaders allowed that to happen. They had authority amongst themselves to resolve their differences.' He paused. 'For me, it gave me an enjoyment of life. At the time, things for me personally weren't very good. The vibrancy of taking pictures of people, just being around them and having a laugh, it made me feel good when I felt bad.' It was, he said, 'a springboard' into the rest of his life, which involved thirty years as a photographer at the world's most famous news agency, Reuters.

Russell was aware of the ethical and political choices he was making about his subject. 'Often people want to see poverty porn,' he said. 'What I wanted was the fact that young people were grabbing opportunities: theatre or breakdancing or helping one another. The vibrancy for life was amazing, and I think that comes across. The passion for them to achieve, and I think it's as true now as it was then for young people.'

The mural on the outside wall of the club depicts one version of that remarkable vibrancy: tracksuited b-boys mid-dance next to Escher-influenced squares and planets, a compromise image that brings together those caught up in new hip hop and electro and those who were still listening to Pink Floyd. Inside, a cluster of breakdancers are turning the floor into a performance space, with friends sat about on soft chairs, watching or waiting their turn. A section of Russell's images titled 'Local Bands' shows rockabilly types with flat tops and Billy Idol-style quiffs. Mods, goths, rockabillies and fusions of these are screaming into the mic, leaning back into their guitar-playing or posing for proto-album covers in front of posters that ask 'What's Caging You In?' (the stated answers include poverty, unemployment and racism), while another contains the slogan 'Crush Poverty Not People'.

When the images were retrospectively exhibited, though, it was the wall-to-wall smoking in evidence in his youth club photography that attracted the most comment.

*

222

There was a lot of smoking. Government surveys at the time showed that, in 1986, 10 per cent of eleven- to fifteen-year-olds in England smoked, with 22 per cent of their fifteen- to eighteen-year-old siblings doing the same. This strikes me as highly unlikely, having been within the lower age bracket at the time of the survey. If someone with a clipboard had asked me that question, I'd have shaken my head, lied and reached for another Polo mint. I vividly remember the first time I smoked. I was fourteen, standing outside the back door of the house I grew up in, with two friends. One of them held out her cigarette and asked if I wanted a drag. It wasn't a question; it was a test. I passed, albeit with a lot of coughing, and quickly taught myself how to tolerate and then enjoy cadged fags and the odd purchase of ten Silk Cut. I recall non-smokers as a minority among my peers and remember only one friend who refused the 'Do you want a drag?' test, which, shamefully, I enacted on her. If you didn't smoke, you had to either hide the fact or have a really good reason not to. Asthma, by the way, was not considered a valid excuse.

What we didn't know, of course, was that the tobacco industry was watching us, tracking teenage smoking and developing 'starter brands', according to paperwork unearthed by academic Stanton Glantz. I was simply responding to adult influence, in an alarmingly direct way. Philip Morris set out their stall fifteen years earlier: 'A cigarette for the beginner is a symbolic act. I am no longer my mother's child. I'm tough. I am an adventurer. I'm not square . . . As the force from the psychological symbolism subsides, the pharmacological effect takes over to sustain the habit.'

It is not surprising that the images from Friday Club have tobacco swirls coming off the edges, or that we pushed the habit onto each other. Adults working in the tobacco industry were using their education, intellect and creativity to ensure we complied and, in this way, were involved in a particular form of youth work. Photographer Russell Boyce was a rare non-smoker, but even he brought cigarettes with him, placed in his shirt pocket to indicate that he was alright – maybe even an 'adventurer' – and occasionally to hand out to the kids in a then-reasonable barter of acceptance.

Children live in flux: in both the future that adults haven't yet encountered and the past adults are leaving behind. The youth clubs offer space for this gap to be bridged.

The perennial difficulty of articulating the value of youth clubs can sometimes be overcome by talking money. The business case is the worst of all cases when trying to articulate the value of any community space. But economic arguments can be made, if necessary. Arts-based activities practised in clubs nationwide may have widened the base for both artists and potential audiences. Prioritised in the following decade by New Labour with their 1998 Creative Industries Mapping Document, the arts-based aspects of the UK's GDP would regularly outperform the economy as a whole. At the time of writing, according to the House of Lords, the sector known as 'the creative industries' generated £126bn in gross value added to the economy, employing 2.4 million people.

22

1986: BOXING GETS KNOCKED OUT

Youth workers and youth club members were engaged in a fight for survival. An Inner London Education Authority (ILEA) List of Registered Youth Groups in 1986 shows that many were holding on. Tower Hamlets alone had forty-five full-time youth workers employed by the council, with nine youth centres, six adventure playgrounds, seven non-local-authority youth organisations and another eighty-eight part-time and voluntary youth organisations. Many of these were youth clubs in the obvious sense, while others would be better described as projects, with workshops or activities, or which aimed to address unemployment or community education, or were carved out for girls and those we'd now describe as LGBTQ+.

Youth clubs have always offered a variety of activities to cater to a multiplicity of possible members, as would have been the case in Tower Hamlet's myriad clubs for youth. Boxing, still available in mid-1980s clubs, brought certain demographics into the orbit of adults who might direct their strength and energy into formalised fitness and fighting. Soon, this would be blocked.

In early summer 1986, an ILEA report had landed in London Youth Committee pigeonholes. Greenwich Area Youth Committee had asked the ILEA to urgently investigate boxing provision because of the health risks. Included was a summary of the British Medical Association's working party on the subject, who viewed availability of the sport for children 'with deep concern'. Boxing had been banned in schools two decades earlier, but the ruling did not apply to the youth service. The ILEA reported that the sport took place in statutory, council-run clubs and in voluntary youth clubs, sometimes as part of a specialist boxing club and other times alongside ping-pong and pool. In the former, 'serious' boxers were as young as ten years old.

Under the heading 'Boxing and Youth Service Objectives', various arguments were outlined: the sport was said to foster self-discipline, fitness and courage, attracting boys and young men who 'may not respond initially to other activities in the youth service, and channel energies which may otherwise be used more destructively'. On the other hand, the infliction of physical damage was noted, along with the risk of personal injury, including of the permanent kind. Additionally, 'It stresses a particular kind of "manliness" and excludes girls and young women, at a time when the youth service is seriously concerned to decrease sexism.'

Legal advice followed: essentially, the ILEA must take reasonable care to ensure that young people were not harmed unnecessarily. In the section titled 'Possible Future Directions', I sense the local authority protecting itself, a committee-based sidestep, holding gloves up to the face. 'If it is felt that boxing should be encouraged only in a limited way, it could be withdrawn from statutory clubs and focused in only one or two (voluntary) [their brackets] clubs in each area. Some areas already take this approach, in order to decrease accidental "exposure" to the activity.'

Dr David Dee is a social historian at De Montfort University, Leicester, who has written books and papers about the relationship between sport, leisure and immigration. My knowledge of boxing is limited to ringwalk tunes, and so I email him some questions to help me get a sense of the background context. He was off on paternity leave but was kind enough to reply with some thoughts.

Boxing had become a key component of youth institutions in the late Victorian era, particularly when university Settlements arrived. Cricket, football, rugby, gymnastics and boxing were a key part of the offering, he told me, 'often driven by public school, middle-class ideas of *mens sana in corpore sano*, or a healthy mind in a healthy body.' The idea, he explained, was 'to improve young people physically and to improve their self-control and apparently innate aggression'. His own research showed that boxing would sit alongside film club and more sedentary activities, and that this remained the case until the 1950s or '60s. 'In Scotland, it was very common for Catholic Boys' and Girls' clubs to be set up in inner city areas. Famous boxers, like the World Champion Benny Lynch, started in such institutions, which remained common until the 1960s, when young boxers started off in amateur boxing clubs.'

David then told me about Irish trainer and former professional boxer Brendan Ingle, who moved over to Sheffield in the 1960s, setting up St Thomas's Club in the city's Wincobank area after being asked to do so by a local priest. The idea was to keep youngsters off the streets, and while it began with discos and other youth activities, it soon changed into a bespoke boxing gym, attracting large numbers. 'His gym is famous for helping "wayward" youths like Herol Graham and Prince Naseem Hamed get into boxing,' he said, 'and propel themselves to the top level domestically and internationally.' This connection between roots and fruits explains the tradition of boxers – and, for that matter, other sportspeople – supporting or creating youth programmes once success has provided them with financial stability – for example, Anthony Joshua offering free boxing classes for young people through his Clean Herts Community in Watford.

Equitably gendered exercise suffered as youth clubs remained boy heavy, despite the female-centric roots of the whole youth club enterprise in recreational offerings for factory girls. Attempts were made to address this. The NAYC's Girls' Work Unit had been set up in 1978, and was replicated in the regions. Within a few years, this aspect of the national organisation's work had created structural change. The London Union of Youth Clubs (LUYC), reporting on their formal Girls' Work policy in the early 1980s, outlined the impact. Catering directly to nearly 40,000 girls in over 650 London clubs, they wove girls' work into every aspect of their organisation, including staff training and management. A 'woman field officer' was appointed to 'establish a balance of resources' in clubs that were often skewed towards boys, in a youth service that was frequently male-dominated. The effort paid off, and the majority of senior staff and committee chairs in their organisation were women.

The LUYC ran girls-only adventure weekends and two amazingly ahead-of-their-time offerings: girls' football, decades before the Lionesses crashed into the national consciousness, and a DJ training course for young women, which must have been one of the first anywhere in the world. Tiny revolutions were taking place, on the edges, with young people whose gender, ethnicity, sexuality or employment status attracted harsh realities. Gains were again temporary, however, as the national Girls' Work Unit was KO'd in 1987, in yet another cost-cutting round.

23

1987: FRIDAY NIGHTS AT THE METHODIST YOUTH CLUB

In my early teens, I attended a Methodist youth club on the edges of the London Borough of Bromley. As well as offering weekly space to me and my siblings, it functions as a portal through which we can see inside a very ordinary example of a youth club at the time. Drinking squash, sneaking cigarettes in the car park or standing around a trampoline on Friday nights, we were inhabiting a space made accessible by a combination of individual effort and national leadership, made local by parents, teenagers and neighbourhood volunteers.

I'd discovered the existence of Orpington Methodist Youth Club in a neighbourly way. Two sisters walked past my house, and I asked them where they were going. Encouraged by my mum, I joined them, paying the 50p entrance fee to the parents who ran the club and who welcomed us in from behind a trestle table in the church's concourse. Between 1985 and 1988, Friday night meant youth club. When my sister turned twelve, she joined me, and we'd walk ten minutes down the road for an evening of giddy social time or playing ping-pong, all fuelled by cartons of raspberry juice, accessed through tiny, stabby straws, and cheap crisps. Once a year, the club hosted an all-nighter, with a range of activities including a band and a spray-painting corner for graffiti, which being unventilated caused us to lose our voices and gain an extra 20 per cent in hyperactivity.

Each summer our youth club joined over 10,000 over-excited kids for the Methodist Association of Youth Clubs'

(MAYC) annual jamboree at the Royal Albert Hall, at which, as previously described, thousands of kids flung green and yellow pom-poms into the air in order to gain new pen pals. Ancient home-made videos shot by a tech-savvy teenager on 8mm film a decade earlier and uploaded to YouTube give a flavour of the event. Some footage captures the worship and the live performances, but the majority of the screentime goes to secular fun: gangly teens jigging about under colourful trade-union-style banners, young men play-fighting and rolling about in the car park before the coach left for London, and what the voiceover describes as 'a ritual of fountain baptism', aka throwing each other, the youth leader and their banner into the fountains in Trafalgar Square.

In 1987, an actual television crew made a three-part programme for Thames TV, titled *Who Believes in Orpington?* The programme notes described a new series, referring to our town as 'one of the largest commuter suburbs in Greater London' and using it as a way of finding out what residents thought about religion, church and churchgoing. In the 1960s, Orpington had become a by-word for bellweather lower-middle-class voters, an idea expressed by New Labour in the 1990s in the phrase 'Mondeo Man'. The cultural shorthand had moved on, but the town remained at least vaguely typical of a broader picture, and the media men from the telly were using us as a way of suggesting trends. Episode three was called 'An Air of Indifference' and focused on the youth. The TV researchers found their subjects at two youth clubs. At one end of the high street, behind the Walnuts shopping centre, was The Saxon, which had opened in 1982 with a garage that provided motor maintenance classes; at the other, on a residential main road, the Methodist church and our youth club. I remembered the programme only very vaguely, a blurred half-memory.

Like so much else, *Who Believes in Orpington?* is not on the internet. It is, however, available in the extensive televisual archive at the BFI's Mediatheque on the banks of the River Thames. Watching it involved some hardcore time travel as the footage reopened forgotten memories. The opening shot showed a fold-up pool table at The Saxon youth club, where a girl, whose hair was tied with a huge white scrunchie, was lining up a shot. The wall behind was covered with artwork, including a big piece of yellow card with paper-mounted photographs depicting trips and activities.

One of the main interviewees from The Saxon was tuned in to politics and alternative music. Wearing jeans, DMs and a customised bomber jacket with CND badges and three bar towels sewn onto the back, her hair was cut short and gelled upwards into tiny spikes. The camera crew followed her into WHSmith's. She selected a cassette tape in the record department and went for *The Circus* by Erasure – which, in a neat bit of youth club circularity, featured Andy Bell, who attended the London Gay Teenage Group. The voiceover gave a sense of the context: 'A common complaint amongst young people in Orpington is that the town offers them very little to do. There isn't even a cinema. Providing youth club facilities is one way in which the churches have thought they can help. Too often, though, these clubs have closed because of vandalism. One that survives and attracts large numbers is the Methodist Youth Club.'

While interviews with Saxon club members were filmed in the familiar setting of comfy municipal chairs pushed up against a wall, the Thames TV people asked us to sit around a table for a more formal discussion. And there I am, in a black-and-white top, with gold hoops and a thin gold necklace, and a pink lipstick that was either Rimmel's Twilight Teaser or the slightly less cyanosis-adjacent Pink Shimmer. The interviewer, whom I remember as suave in a disconnected way, encouraged us to discuss whether or not there was anything to do in town. There were murmurs in the negative, and I chipped in, my fourteen-year-old voice high and fast, with an unhelpfully optimistic question–observation: 'There's a sports centre?' I was chided by my table-neighbour, who pointed out that there's nothing open after 10 p.m., and the conversation moved on.

Did we believe in God? Apparently, I did. My younger self began disagreeing with one of the young Methodists around the table, attempting to counter his view of Catholicism as 'high church'. And then, oh dear, I heard myself say the following: 'I go to Catholic school,' I said, and giggled apologetically. 'In the first four years we did the religions we'd never have anything to do with, like Buddhism and Islam. We never got to learn about the religions we might possibly have to do with, like Church of England or Methodism.'

At this remove, I understand what I was trying to do: make a bid for connection with my youth club peers, who shared a faith background that was different to mine. I did so in the time-honoured way, by trampling over others. Reflecting on this discovery, once I'd got over the mortification of having held this view, and of it being committed to film, I came to a few conclusions. Teenagers pick up ideas, some of which might be reactionary or divisive. Conversation, in a safe environment, allows for discussion and subsequent shifts in perspective – especially if a sensible adult has a quiet word.

Pinboards behind the interviewees' heads speak to the differing demographics at Orpington youth clubs: there's a DSS poster behind a boy at The Saxon who is talking about religion being pointless – 'It's not going to get you a job,' he said – while sitting next to a girl in triple denim, who giggle-glares off camera at her friend, who appears to be kicking her. At the Methodist church there's a poster for one of their international fundraising schemes, with the words 'Go Ghana' printed in red, green and yellow over a map of Africa.

A week after watching *Who Believes in Orpington?*, I walked down from the railway station to the church. Opened in 1953, nearly a half-century after Methodism arrived in the town, early advocates having held services in a corrugated-iron building known as 'the tin Tabernacle', it's now got a glass-fronted extension and community café. There's a nursery school in one of the halls and, in an act that speaks to both high street decline and the importance of community space, Barclays Bank has taken over a back room in lieu of the now-closed branch. Carolyn Licence ran the Methodist Youth Club with her husband Robin and four others: Pauline and Ron Friend and siblings Andy and Anne Orchard. It was a group effort, which involved substantial engagement from these individuals, who also had jobs and families to look after. I imagine that it must have been fun as well, nicely communal and no doubt offering plenty of comedy at the end of the working week. It would, after all, have been social for the adults too.

Now, Carolyn is in the church café, directing Barclays customers to the back and fielding questions about a leak in the toilets. She might have left youth club behind, but as a lifelong picker-upper of communal tasks, she's now on the church's property committee and has inevitably picked up the bulk of the work. Adults like Carolyn and her friends make the world go round.

I remember her as soulful and sensible, a lively adult with kids my age who made it her business to create a youth club that was warm and welcoming. She's as sparky as ever, taking me on a tour of the building and reminding me what happened where. I feel like we're walking past decades-old versions of ourselves, lounging on padded chairs or standing about with the adults in the kitchen. The hall is, of course, smaller than I remembered, but is essentially unchanged and could be swapped out for almost any of its type and time. There's wood panelling to waist height, windows along one side, and a stage. This triggers a memory of doing sound effects for a play and pressing the doorbell a page too early. The actors styled it out, and I realised that jobs that required real-time accuracy were not for me.

Carolyn had grown up in youth clubs herself. She met her husband when they both attended Methodist youth club in the 1960s, in West Wickham, between Bromley and Croydon in outer south-east London. The club offered gymnastics, music, table tennis and football, and an annual sailing trip to the Norfolk Broads. 'What did you get from your youth club?' I asked her. 'Fun, loyalty, exploration,' she said, adding that mixing with boys, without the expectation of a relationship, was particularly important, given that she attended an all-girls school. 'The club offered the sort of things you can't buy. People were so keen to widen our horizons.'

A short history written for the Orpington Methodist Church magazine in 1952 explained that there had been 'juvenile activities' before the Second World War which continued throughout the conflict and were maintained 'in the face of so many difficulties'. Carolyn picked up the baton from a couple who had been running the successor club since the 1970s. 'Before, it was very much "This is a Methodist youth club and shut the doors." We didn't want that,' she said, with the quiet determination that I imagine she's been bringing to life since day dot. 'There was quite a rough element of Orpington youth that would try and get through the door. We decided it was probably easier to invite them in.'

The club flourished in small-town ways, attracting a mixed demographic of around a hundred kids, including myself, my sister Nathalie and my brother Jim. One of the people who also attended Orpington Methodist Youth Club was Fran Sweetman. She was friends with my sister, and so we grew up in and out of each other's lives, part of a broader friendship group that allowed for more fluidity than the rigid and entirely artificial separation dictated by which year group you were in at school. We're still friends, so it was unsurprising when I bumped into her in the local park. We got talking about youth club, and she dropped quickly into our shared recollections, adding colour and detail to the elements I recalled: that the alternative was hanging out in the multi-storey car park and that she also used the club to rehearse the band she'd put together, or remembering our friend who would always put The Blues Brothers or Joe Jackson on the club stereo. 'People were falling over themselves to share their music,' she said, 'in the hope that other people would feel the same way about it as you did.'

Kids are amazing at finding connections, she observed, making a link between how our generation used physical space and how her children use social media to enable camaraderie. It's friendships, though, that she remembered most powerfully, recalling peers who were bullied at school but flourished at youth club. 'You could choose people, not just having to be friends with the people you'd ended up with because you're in the same form at school.' We giggled about the ways some of us used youth club as a way to practise courtship, through the medium of 'snogging people'.

'There's the hope of romance,' she said. 'Your hormones are firing up and it's the start of you wanting to broaden your horizons. You're leaving your parents behind and starting to explore relationships.' She paused, and a leaf dropped from a tree onto our other friend's head, causing her to scream like a teenager, until she realised it wasn't a creepy-crawly. Recovering from our middle-aged moment of drama, Fran continued, suddenly serious and moved by adult understanding of our childhood selves. 'It wasn't just romantic relationships. It was being around stable adults, families that weren't volatile. For some of us, that was a relief.' In our case, and no doubt for many others, youth club offered family, belonging and kinship. It allowed us to come home.

24

ANOTHER SHORT REWIND, TO CLUBLAND

Methodist churches have a surprisingly central role to play in this story, the telling of which requires a short rewind back to the start of the timeline. As with other churches and organisations, Methodists focused on the poorer areas of London, opening their West London Mission in 1887 and a Settlement, like those created by universities, four years later in Bermondsey.

From the 1940s onwards, church leaders built a network of youth provision to rival that of the local authorities, understanding, among other things, that young people would be the churchgoers of the future. Much of this can be traced back to one youth club that became internationally famous. It had a zingy name: Clubland.

In the beginning, there was just a Friday-night Bible class for six boys. Probationary minister Jimmy Butterworth began the group in his landlady's basement in south London in 1922. He had grown up in Lancashire and was thirteen when his dad died by suicide, which, of course, created a terrible full stop in his life. Almost immediately, school was replaced by long hours and low pay at a local dye factory. Joining the Lancashire Fusiliers, he saw two years' active service in the First World War, including, briefly, at the Somme. Volunteering for the remainder of the war in rest huts, where soldiers on leave or recovering from injury could meet for recreation, he met professionals including youth workers and chaplains. After the war, Butterworth became a Methodist minister, propelled by spirituality and an intense commitment to social work.

Early life experience ensured Butterworth never grew above five foot, and it seems that he turned this to his advantage, using his stature to charm and disarm those around him. In ways that remind me of the youth groups that followed, Butterworth and his growing group gained the use of disused cellars in a church basement on Walworth Road in south London. They cleared out debris, acquired furniture and turned the space into a clubhouse. A youth parliament was convened to make decisions and take action. Bringing in skilled professionals, the growing membership had access to carpentry, chess and film clubs, and visits to talks and exhibitions.

By 1927, Butterworth had been formally ordained and had a well-established club, as well as a growing network of supporters who'd read his three books or his articles and newspaper interviews. Benefactors emerged, magnetised by his achievements and proximity to working-class youth who were separated from wealthier parts of society by invisible class barriers. Similar distancing is palpable today in phrases like 'hard-to-reach youth', who are only hard to reach when those doing the reaching are removed from them by social, economic and cultural circumstances.

A skilful networker, Butterworth applied serious graft to his fundraising. Funds rolled in, and Butterworth commissioned a new church, designed by famous architect Edward Maufe and open to the congregation from 1929. Youth club rooms underneath the chapel were central to the plans, and were laid with parquet flooring and fitted out for snooker and table tennis. Over the following decade, the Reverend Butterworth would acquire adjacent derelict properties, build the theatre and gymnasium and develop a committed membership of juniors, seniors and officers.

Queen Mary, the Queen Mother, officially opened the building in springtime 1939, a flamboyant moment captured on black-and-white cine film. The theatre, gymnasium, library, 'parliament room', art room and a classical central quadrangle signalled loud and clear that the youth of south London deserved the best. It offered the kind of quality you'd expect from exclusive members' clubs – Walworth's Soho House, as it were – with volunteers running art, sports, music, debating and drama activities. American senator-to-be Robert Kennedy made his first speech in the building, aged thirteen, during an event for the children of international diplomats based in London, his father being the American ambassador at the time. Six months after the official opening, war returned. Bombs dropped by the Luftwaffe destroyed the chapel, and the surviving club rooms were requisitioned by London County Council to house the Blitz homeless. Clubland continued many activities in other parts of the building, however, and church services took place every Sunday.

Clubland's magnetic and widely celebrated successes in the early days may have encouraged top-brass thinking. In the era before widespread local authority youth provision, Methodists already had a significant foothold, with 3,400 clubs for over 110,000 young people in 1933. In 1943, the Methodist leadership set up a Youth Department aimed at the twelve-to-twenty age group. Decision-makers merged the Sunday School department and the faith-focused Wesley Guild, which had nearly 2,000 local branches and over 133,000 members, with a monthly magazine and, foreshadowing those mid-1980s photographs of Peterborough teenagers, a 'pen and camera club'. By combining the religious and educative intentions of Sunday School with a group conceived as a 'Young People's Society' that held regular meetings for 'devotional, literary and social purposes', they created something that nodded towards the youth clubs of the decades ahead. The merger also attended to the church's strategic drive for Sunday School teachers, faith leaders and congregational growth. By 1945, the Methodist Youth Department claimed to be one of the largest church-based youth organisations in Europe.

Mark K. Smith, whom we met earlier running local authority youth clubs in Amersham, has written extensively on faith-based youth work, and I requested confirmation: was I right in thinking that the Methodists were particularly big in the youth club world, as opposed to, say, Catholics or Anglicans? 'Catholics would have a completely different terminology and the Church of England had youth clubs,' he replied, 'but the Methodists were the biggest by far.'

Clubland's physical space was rebuilt after the war, with Butterworth spending nearly twenty years finding the necessary funds. Deciding that money would be more easily raised from wealthy people in the USA than in post-war England, he took a boat across the Atlantic and immediately began making friends. In relay fashion, one person introduced him to the next, and the benefactor trail inevitably led him to Hollywood. No one knows exactly how he met super-celebrity Bob Hope, but it's tempting to imagine Butterworth's hard-earned smarts in action in LA, maybe slipping off during a studio tour, perhaps hoovering up scraps of info to ensure their paths crossed, or maybe even, mock-innocently, knocking on his dressing room door to introduce himself. Either way, Butterworth was able to tell Bob Hope his story, and Bob was all ears, perhaps recognising elements of his own early life in another part of south-east London. He agreed to come and see the club, and, nine months later, the promise turned into a reality. Hope was mobbed on the streets of south London and sold out the London Palladium, with proceeds going straight to Clubland.

In 1955, Reverend Butterworth gained official National Treasure status when he was featured on the hugely popular TV show *This Is Your Life*, in which a celebrity was surprised by a man with a big red book and forced to sit in shock while everybody they'd ever known appeared one by one from backstage. He became, said his son John, author of Clubland history *The Temple of Youth*, a respected guest in the board-rooms of both Chelsea and Arsenal football clubs. 'Both teams visited Clubland and took an interest in Clubland teams,' he told me, describing visits from well-known players. 'He had a talent for talking his way into the company of people who could help Clubland in one way or another,' he explained. 'Actually, he hated having to do it but saw it as a necessary means to an end.'

The names of supporters in the Christmas newsletter of 1960/1 show that Clubland's shine continued to grow in the years after Butterworth was anointed on television. Movie megastar Douglas Fairbanks Jr 'represented both the British and American Board of Clubland governors', while the chair-man of Chelsea FC represented British donors at the reopening of the new club. Richard Attenborough was club president. Other photographs show Butterworth standing in-between an admiring Alfred Hitchcock and a radiant Cary Grant, and perched in front of mop-top era Beatles and UK rock 'n' roller Billy Fury, who surround him like the arc of a rainbow.

Correspondence between the youth officer of the Methodist Association of Youth Clubs (MAYC) and London County Council (LCC) in December 1960 shows Reverend Butterworth enquiring about the new building grant money made possible by the Albemarle Committee, whose recommendations for massive youth service investment had been accepted in spring that year. The letters in question are stored in a grey box at Manchester University's John Rylands Library and are between Reverend R. C. Bedford of the Methodist Youth Department and Reg Keeble, youth officer at County Hall. The former wrote to explain that Butterworth was 'a real pioneer', that he had been doing youth work in Walworth for forty years, and that he had 'built up a remarkable community despite bombing and other misfortune'.

The task of rebuilding had been financed via voluntary sources, noted the letter. Mr Butterworth had travelled across the United States at least twice, raising money, and had the support of everyone from Bob Hope to the American ambassador, and, as far as the writer knew, he had never received a penny in grant aid from either the Ministry of Education or a local authority. 'The position now is that the workmen have been "called off" because there is no money left . . . and at last [Reverend Butterworth] is thinking of grant aid.' There were two problems, which were carefully skirted around. Firstly, that the work had already started, which made it ineligible for Albemarle money; and, secondly, that the remaining work was on the 'club Chapel', not the main youth club space. The writer explained the exceptional nature of the situation. 'This is not a Methodist Church in any ordinary way,' he wrote with something approaching a plea, one which illuminates the class framing underpinning youth clubs, especially in England. 'It is the club members' Chapel, just as a public school has its own chapel.'

Butterworth wasn't alone in attempting to tap into this new stream of government cash. The existence of special LCC leaflets about building grants for Methodist youth work suggests that church clubs applied regularly for state funds. The Temple Street Methodist Church in Keighley wrote to the Methodist Chapel Department in 1961, describing a large schoolroom upstairs in their church that they wanted to transform into a youth centre. Costs involved removing dividing walls between vestries and altering central-heating pipes, making a serving hatch from the kitchen and a proscenium for the stage, as well as decoration. Asking for funding towards 75 per cent of costs, under the heading 'Albemarle Youth Club', they put in a bid for £1,224. Commercial entities responded to central investment as it flowed down to council level. Dexion Ltd produced beautiful leaflets explaining how architect-designed modular buildings could be turned into youth clubs, and posted them to church leaders, in the hope that marketing materials might translate into paid work.

Albemarle money percolated down throughout the rest of the decade and into the 1970s. Guidance from Staffordshire County Council's Education Committee explained that at least 25 per cent of the cost must be met by the applicant or their sponsors. It was expected that premises would be used five evenings a week for groups of at least twelve members within the fourteen-to-twenty age group. 'The accommodation and facilities provided must be primarily for the benefit of young people and membership must be open to young people served by the area in which the premises are situated.' Young people across the UK benefited from this important caveat, which ensured that

Methodist churches could expand and update their built environment, but only if they opened it up to all, regardless of faith.

With a specific mention of the Methodists, the local education authority waived the usual requirement that grant-generated clubs, or in other words, those paid for by the taxpayer, be held in a charitable trust. Bespoke conditions were created that trustees 'should confer with the Local Education Authority regarding the disposal of the premises'. In a paragraph that gives a sense of the economic gloom at the time, the council outlined the process if land, buildings or equipment were sold or ceased to be adequately used. Giving a grace period of twenty-one years, it stated that the local education authority may require repayment, but 'where the value of the land, buildings or equipment shall have depreciated since the date of the making of the grant, the LEA shall not require the repayment of more than the appropriate portion of the grant'.

Methodists impacted youth worker training too. Westhill, their teacher training college in Selly Oak, Birmingham, had an outsized role, sending youth and community workers out into clubs of all denominations and none. Principal lecturer and head of the Youth and Community Work Department between 1960 and 1977 was Fred Milson. He became nationally prominent, part of a push to professionalise youth work. He imbued trainee youth workers with a youth-centred approach, authored reports and wrote books, including *Youth and Community Work*, that placed youth work within a Christian framework, albeit one that cautioned against evangelising or, to use his phrase, 'spiritual scalp-hunting'. It remained on the reading list for decades.

At least ninety Methodist churches and projects received Ministry of Education Youth Service building grants between

1963 and 1971. Committees all over the country successfully applied for money to build, extend or renovate youth club spaces, or to purchase equipment, on the understanding that they opened up the space to those outside their congregations. Sums ranged from a few hundred pounds to tens of thousands. Five clubs – Westow Hill in Upper Norwood, St John's in Halifax, Central in Loughborough, Union Street in Maidstone and Downend in Bristol – each received government grants of between £865,000 and £1m in today's money. The figures listed, on typed sheets in the archive, suggest that Methodist churches benefited from land, buildings and renovations equivalent to over £5.5m, adjusting for inflation, during this period.

Clubland's name does not appear on the list of churches gaining building grants, but Reverend Butterworth managed to get the money together somehow. In return for significant donations, he offered a name, carved in stone, on the wall at Clubland. The wall is still there, and reads like a Who's Who of celebrity: Cecil B. DeMille, world champion boxer Gene Tunney, Richard Attenborough, Laurence Olivier, Vivien Leigh and Gracie Fields being just a few. Other celebrity supporters on this south London Rushmore include Bing Crosby, Cary Grant, Sybil Thorndike, John Mills and Charlton Heston. Queen Elizabeth, the Queen Mother, officially opened the new building with its rebuilt theatre, gym and open-air playground on the roof in spring 1964. Clubland was flourishing.

Actor Michael Caine was the most famous of the club's alumni, returning in January 1969 to film a documentary special for LWT, titled *Candid Caine*. The camera tracked him turning a corner as a red bus went past, with a plinky-plonky rendition of the theme tune to his hit film *Alfie* playing all the while. In the voiceover, he described his part of south

London as rather like the Lower East Side of New York or Ménilmontant in Paris, as he walked up the steps and through the door of Clubland.

Reverend Butterworth was filmed in a back pew of the church, describing, with verve, how Caine would hang around outside Clubland's theatre, trying to catch sight of the action. 'The number of times I cleared him out are innumerable. And then one day he said, "Do you think I could have a part?" And sure enough, as soon as he got up there, I thought, "He's got something."'

Halfway through *Candid Caine*, the actor walked onto the youth club's wooden stage, slowly, all alone, big and grown but hands in pockets like a scrawny fourteen-year-old. Interviewers everywhere, he said, want to know the same thing: where did you start? He paused for precisely the right number of dramatic seconds and pointed to the floor. 'Here, right here, is where I started.' He continued, face shifting from deadpan to something approaching warmth. 'Also,' he said, 'this same hall is where we used to hold the dances on a Saturday night.' An actual smile appeared, despite himself. 'It was the first place I ever held a girl, very close, to dance with.' In the foreword to the Clubland history, *The Temple of Youth*, Caine called the Reverend Jimmy Butterworth 'the most important person I ever met'.

Butterworth's club had an impact locally and nationally, in multiple ways. The rise and decline of Clubland also offers a way of understanding changes that were happening more broadly in youth work, outside of the faith context. The reverend ran a disciplined ship, with strict rules and a clear connection between club work and church work. In a retrospective mini-doc, Butterworth's son described a new mood that began emerging in the 1970s, as youth clubs that existed because of state investment, run by youth workers who came through the new training programmes in the 1960s, responded to social shifts. 'New thinking in youth work,' he explained carefully, was to 'open premises up and let adolescents just sit around, smoke, drink Coca-Cola, play table tennis if they wanted to, dance a bit, come in and out as they pleased'. It wasn't a shift that suited Clubland.

Numbers dropped, families left the area, and Jimmy Butterworth retired in 1976, with his health in decline. The following year, he died. Walworth had lost a legendary figure. Albemarle money eventually ran out, something that can be seen in a letter from Methodist HQ to a youth officer in Stafford in 1979. While their application had been approved, 'there is not likely to be any money available until 1982'. Whether the cash ever arrived is unknown.

Once space has been built, it can continue to be used, changing in response to what the local community needs. After Butterworth died, a new minister, the Reverend Vic Watson, reshaped the offering. Appalled by racism and shocked into action by the 1981 riots up the road in Brixton, he started Methodist Leadership Race Awareness Workshops, or the appropriately growling MELRAW, initially offering race awareness training for police recruits. The church became packed and popular again, with the congregation travelling from miles around.

I recounted the history of Clubland for a reason: to show how connected youth clubs are across time and space, and how the existence of one can support the emergence of another. The more I found out about Clubland, the more it reminded me of another nationally famous entity that attended to the needs of young south Londoners, decades later, and which was also headed up by a charismatic and influential figure who was able to raise huge sums of money from wealthy patrons. While Camila Batmanghelidjh's Kids Company eventually became a kind of alternative version of social services, with a vast offering for families in its orbit and nationally renowned for pioneering work with young people at the sharpest end of society, it started out as a drop-in centre, just down the road from Clubland, in 1996.

Around this time, staff at Clubland began working on a plan to modify their in-house theatre. The idea was to bring it back to life for use by community groups, and in summer 1999 Kids Company took to the stage. Royalty was again in the audience, this time in the shape of Charles, then Prince of Wales. Batmanghelidjh was becoming the Butterworth of her time, with champions including BBC chairman Alan Yentob, Chris Martin from Coldplay, the artist Damien Hirst and UK prime minister David Cameron.

Discovering this direct connection between two extremely important nodes on the youth work timeline made my pattern-loving brain light up. I went looking for more detail about the Kids Company performance at Clubland, but the internet provided no additional detail, offering another useful reminder that not everything is online. I'd visited Kids Company while working on youth-run publication *Live Magazine* and knew a few people who'd worked there. I texted one of them, a woman I'd become friends with who now works as a writer and broadcaster, with a long-shot question. Even though this was before her time, did she know anyone who might know anything about the performance?

A reply pinged back, almost immediately. 'I was in it!' She had, it transpired, grown up in south London, in a terraced house down the road from Clubland and Kids Company. She attended both as a teenager, and in adulthood went on to work alongside Batmanghelidjh. Filling in the gaps required her to mine both her own memories and those available through the online memorial page she was running for Batmanghelidjh, who had died peacefully on New Year's Day 2024, a few months before our text message exchange. The process of uncovering the connection between Clubland and Kids Company, separated on the timeline by decades, and discovering my friend's connection to both made me think about networks in nature: the mycorrhizal ones that connect trees in the woods or those in other plant communities. Perhaps none of this connectedness within the youth club is surprising. It might be, literally, natural.

My friend went digging, and a few weeks later we met again. She handed me a brown envelope. Inside was a photocopied theatre programme that she'd borrowed from another Kids Company alumnus at one of the regular memorial gatherings taking place in the wake of Camila's death. Details slid out of the envelope like blossom. According to the programme, Kids Company was based in five railway arches on Grosvenor Terrace, open seven days a week. Up to 200 children attended, with 5,390 vulnerable young people supported each week through work in primary schools.

Kids Need Friends, as the show was called, was initially envisioned as a gift for the Prince of Wales, who had visited Kids Company in 1998. It was a 'musical documentary', based on difficult material: a traumatic real-life story of sexual exploitation. Originally a project for young people themselves, with the help of Brett Kahr – now a renowned psychotherapist, academic and author – and then-nineteen-year-old Oxford student Jonathan Sacerdoti, it morphed into the performance that took place at Clubland, on stage, replicating the way Michael Caine had surveyed his childhood self.

'When Camila asked me to write an original musical score about child abuse, I struggled to find a way to transform the inherently awful and un-musical subject of trauma into something that could be sung,' wrote Kahr in the programme notes. 'We originally intended that the musical would be performed entirely by children, but as many of the young people attending Kids Company cannot read sufficiently well or concentrate for long periods of time, this proved unrealistic.' Drafting in 'helpful grown-ups' meant West End professionals, including Sharon D. Clarke, who'd had three Top Ten house hits in the early 1990s, including FPI Project's hip-house track 'Rich in Paradise'. Awarded an MBE in 2017, she'd become well known for prominent roles in hospital drama *Holby City* and *Doctor Who*.

Funding for the show had come from National Lottery operator Camelot, while another forty-two companies were listed at the front of the programme. Investment banks and City firms including Goldman Sachs and the International Petroleum Exchange form a bulwark of those listed, along with Nike, Top Shop and the Disney Store. The Calouste Gulbenkian Foundation, which supported the NAYC in its mid-1980s expansion into the arts, appears alongside the Prince's Trust. The money had to come from somewhere.

On the final page, there's a plea for help, penned by Camila Batmanghelidjh herself. Kids Company did not receive government or local authority funding and therefore needed support from generous individuals, companies and trusts, she explained. During the months of June and July, their funding shortage was especially acute, at precisely the time when summer holidays made life riskier. The page ends with a sumptuous phrase that I can imagine being spoken aloud, like a charm: 'May you all feel generous!'

Physical spaces came into being, nation-wide, because the government turned on the money taps. Methodists built a kind of extension to local authority clubs, adding significant numbers of clubs to the total, particularly in England. Over time, the conditions changed and the Methodist church gradually swapped youth clubs for a focus on children and families. Mainstream, open-access youth clubs for everyone were on their way out.

25

1988: ECSTASY HITS THE FRIDAY-NIGHT DISCO

Music and dancing remained hugely popular in youth clubs across all the nations of the UK in the late '80s and into the '90s. A national report, *Providing for Young People*, from later in the decade, described Friday-night discos as a key part of the offering. 'When asked what forms of provision attracted high rates of take-up youth workers everywhere commonly replied "discos"; if you wanted to boost your number you organised a disco,' wrote the authors. 'This connection between high take-up and discos was so universally reported that it appeared almost a truism.'

The disco would eventually begin shuffling away from the centre of the youth club universe. Opportunities for young people to DJ and dance would be replaced, gradually, by environments that allowed for music production, in response to changing technologies and young people's interests. In the early days of this process, which would switch out one aspect of youth club life for another, acid house hit the UK. Dancing, particularly to house and early rave, would become conflated with drugs, and in the youth work context this led to the NAYC running conferences on the topic. On the ground, dance drugs presented youth workers with both challenges and opportunities. Illustrating this necessitates another short detour, which will lead us to a remarkable youth worker who'll help us understand more about the lively intersection between the youth club disco and the rave.

*

Located in Bethnal Green, in east London, Oxford House had been opened in 1884 by scholars and alumni of the famous university. Settlers began their work in an old school building, before moving to a purpose-built home. Designed for graduates and 'old boys' who wanted to volunteer in the area, the handsomely proportioned structure contained bedrooms, a dining room, a library and a court for graduates to play the sport known as Fives, which is a form of posh squash played with the hands.

When Errol Wynter arrived as a youth worker, during the centenary celebrations, he knew the long-running Oxford House youth club needed a revamp. Music and dancing were his chosen levers, fitting perfectly with the times. Under his watch, the late 1980s saw Oxford House host a popular weekly disco, where he'd be floating about, making sure no one was sneaking booze into the place. 'All the boys used to stand up against the wall,' he told me, miming boys standing up straight and leaning back, with their arms folded. 'Girls would dance. As a youth worker, you observe. One night, at this Christmas party, all of a sudden everyone's dancing. Boys are dancing. We were like, "Something ain't right here," and at the end of the night we found out they'd discovered Ecstasy.'

I can't overestimate the comedy and shock I felt when Errol finished that sentence. I was hearing, from a totally new angle, about a cultural moment I experienced as an underage acid-house raver in another part of London, even as someone mostly getting high on the music. As a youth worker, though, Errol's first thought was about harm reduction.

'We didn't know what to do, as a team. This is a new drug and these are our kids, our young people. How are we going to deal with this? We had to sit down and think. Imagine us in the room, we were looking at each other, all of us, all thinking exactly the same thing: "What's going on?!"'

The team decided that they needed to counter the new narrative that dance music required dance drugs. 'We were trying to put across the opposite message,' he said. 'You don't have to take a pill to enjoy the music. You just have to get *into* the music.' He emphasised 'into' in a way that made me think of the embodied knowledge of how music can move you without synthetic chemicals.

After some discussion, the team decided to run a workshop at the borough's rural residential centre, knowing that discussions about drugs would land more easily away from the norms and expectations of east London life. 'I'm not gonna sit here and lie and tell you it made them stop,' he said. 'It didn't. But some of them stopped, the ones that felt pressured. We made them know it was okay to say no. They were reassured. The ones who were doing the pressuring, we made them realise – don't force them. I'd have said it was successful.'

Success formed a basis of trust that would soon be built on. At the same time, Errol explained, Oxford House kids started going to raves. He paused, before explaining his very practical and youth-centred response to a situation that elsewhere was causing performative moral panic. 'We had a problem,' he said bluntly. 'How are you getting there?'

Raves like Raindance took place in the middle of a field in Essex or Kent. 'Not that far, but too far for them,' he explained. 'So I decided we're going to get a minibus and we're going to take them to the rave, and then we're going to pick them back up again. I was really concerned. There were young women, sixteen or seventeen, going into an environment where there were some really ruthless people who are gonna sell you Es, cocaine, cannabis. So I went and spoke to the parents.'

Families were mostly okay about it, knowing that the kids were going to go anyway. 'One parent, she was iffy. So I said, "What would you prefer, that he goes on his own? You don't know what's happening, and how's he going to get home?" She had a bee in her bonnet, but we got rid of the bee. I saw it as part of my role and I did it on my own time, setting my alarm for five o'clock in the morning to go and pick them up. I did that for about a year.'

'What do you think the young people got from accessing the raves?' I asked. 'Experience of life!' he said, with the confidence of corroboration. 'I'm in contact with quite a few of them on social media. You can see what they're doing with their lives, and I'm so proud of them. It makes me feel good.'

Errol's Raindance minibus rave excursions led to changes within Oxford House too. 'I realised that when young people reach a certain age, sixteen or seventeen, they start to divert from the youth club and they start to participate in adult entertainment, with all the risks that come with that,' he told me the next time we met. 'I wanted to keep them in the youth club for as long as possible. I also wanted to give them the ambience of going out to a club, not just a youth club.'

Oxford House director Tom Scott liked Errol's thinking and agreed they'd seek funds for his idea, which would turn the existing youth club dancefloor into a space that could, Bugsy Malone speakeasy style, be flipped between standard during the week and spectacular on the weekend. Years of fundraising and youth engagement, and months of construction, followed.

In November 1990, the Oxford House Youth Club reopened under the name Oxfords, with a nightclub-style space pointing to the future. Arsenal and England footballer Michael Thomas and two cast members from school-based TV show *Grange Hill* attended the official opening ceremony the following year. Twelve young people accepted roles as committee members and took responsibility for policies, programming and the day-to-day running of the club. Their peers requested workshops, including dance, music and photography, alongside skating (ice and roller), martial arts and kickboxing, and football for boys, girls and mixed teams. Budget constraints meant that only some of their wishes could be fulfilled by the club's after-school offering.

On weekend nights, though, it operated as a self-sustaining youth club disco, separated from influential East End nightclubs like Labyrinth only by the quantity of thirteen-year-olds. 'Kids were telling other kids, and we were getting 150 of them, some of them too young, not ready for youth club,' remembered Errol, 'but they've heard about it and they're climbing up the lamp post outside to see what's going on.'

A flyer from 1991 conveys the vibe energetically. The hand-drawn design features geometric shapes and knocked-back greyscale splashes. Photographs show someone in a denim jacket mid-mix on a Technics turntable; a line-up of girls on the dancefloor who look like they've been dancing for at least eight hours; and a boy with the curtains haircut of the time lining up a shot on the pool table. Under the caption 'Discussion group in full swing', there are kids with big jackets and folded arms, focused on Errol, who is looking happy under a baseball cap. Opening times were 7–10 p.m. midweek and 8–11 p.m. on Friday nights, with satellite TV, kickboxing, screen printing and opportunities to learn how to 'mix, dub and scratch music'.

The text then outlines the youth workers' intentions, which doubled up as a critique of existing practice elsewhere. 'We do not see ourselves as traditional youth workers,' it reads. 'We do not see our job as collecting subs, running the bar, banning individuals or telling people what to do. We see ourselves as social educators, motivators and advisors. We offer support, supervision and a shoulder to cry on when, and if, it's needed.'

A few months before Errol opened Oxfords, during the period I myself was a teenager, I went to a party near where I lived in the far suburbs of south-east London. Events spiralled out of control, and a boy I didn't know was stabbed. The situation was way beyond my daughter-of-a-nurse level of first aid, but I tried my best to keep him conscious until the ambulance eventually arrived. I learned a few weeks later, from the local newspaper, that he'd survived. I'd gained unwanted knowledge about the aftermath of random violence, and that being present when such things happened involved being called for police interview. An experienced youth worker would have been a welcome part of my life at this point. With the benefit of hindsight, I also wonder how youth work might have supported both individuals at the centre of this nightmarish moment, attacker and attacked.

Errol and I were sitting in the café at Oxford House. The building has been part of his life for decades and is just metres from his current home-from-home, the popular and locally essential Weavers Adventure Playground, which he runs. Life and work combine in a way that has made him central to his community, in the same way that faith leaders can become central, something evidenced by the number of people who stop by when they see me recording our conversation to tell me how important he is. Errol knows everyone, if 'everyone' means the men, women and children with life-roots in the vicinity. 'Oxford House, 1984, that was my first job, straight out of college. I had all these ideas. I wanted to revolutionise. I was very lucky. I had good bosses.'

Jamaican-born but living in the UK since the age of twelve, Errol is a friendly and open person, with knowledge and insights gained from senior strategic roles within the local authority and many years working at grassroots level. His own journey to Oxford House had been a complicated one. After suffering the British education system – see Bernard Coard and his damning 1971 book, which described widespread injustice – he joined the then-thriving rag trade as a pattern cutter. At night he'd attend evening classes at the London School of Fashion and, after hours, he'd follow the Duke Heels sound system, later King Edward Sound. 'We used to go all over the country, lift up the boxes, kicking it downtown.'

After some issues at work, where a promotion to the design department failed to transpire, he handed in his notice. Soon after, there was 'some trouble', which required a short time away. 'I started writing, putting my feelings and thoughts down in poetry,' he said. A community worker, Barbara Powis, was running Spitalfields Books and, in 1980, published his collection, *On the Other Side of the Fence*. 'Then I started to get invitations,' he said. 'The Howard League for Penal Reform invited me to give talks. I wanted to be a poet but I needed something to support me. Someone pointed out that I'd helped people with their parole applications and that I'd make an excellent youth worker.'

Errol volunteered at the Montefiore youth club in White-chapel, while his mentor wrote to every college in London, trying to get him an interview for a youth work course. The YMCA replied in the affirmative and, after completing the foundation year, Errol embarked on the two-year youth and community work course. 'It changed my life completely,' he said. 'I don't think I'd be sitting here, talking to you, if I hadn't gone to prison and written those poems. Before that, no one saw any talent in me at all. I made it my life's mission to work with young people.'

Chatting with Errol, I was struck by the source of his commitment, and how personal experience of the need for youth space is a repeated theme among the youth workers I've met in person or in the archive. I was thinking of one example in particular: a man who ran a youth club a decade earlier. While researching his club, I'd come across an earlier news story containing information I wasn't looking for: that as a teenager he'd stolen a motorbike with a friend. Full names and addresses were printed in the newspaper, along with details of their suspended sentences. I felt shame and humiliation transmitting off the page, and I understood in a new way this individual's later actions, which were to build a remarkable youth club that provided family, stability and safety for hundreds of local kids. Youth workers who've fallen off the edge of society bring a very special quality to their work: a lived example of alternative futures, of hope, and of recovery. I repeat here an observation I once heard, which relates to these themes of tenacity and staying power. 'Have you ever seen actual grass roots?' someone asked me. 'They are very long and almost impossible to dig out.'

Technological changes that would seriously democratise music-making were a few years away, as was the youth club as a place that regularly offered music production opportunities, but Errol had known which way the wind was blowing. In 1987, he persuaded the Oxford House directors to bend their existing artist-in-residence programme for painters or sculptors in the direction of youngsters' actual interests. The first musician-in-residence joined in 1987, offering sessions in guitar, bass, sax, percussion and keyboards, with a focus on African music and culture. In 1989, guitarist and producer Curtis Lugay took over, heading up a space where youth club members could play and record music. The appointment opened up a portal between young people testing out their aptitude for music and the existing musical infrastructure in the area. At the time, east London was both economically deprived and culturally rich, replete with powerful pockets of jazz, funk, reggae and soul. The area was perfectly positioned to receive the incoming signal of rave, and the existence of the Friday proto-club night and the studio offered another boost.

Lugay had appeared on reggae and lovers rock records, including Aswad's 1986 album *To the Top* and those of Brit-funk outfits Inch By Inch and Yeow Band. In 1988, he co-wrote Longsy D and Cut Master MC's 'To the Rhythm'. The tune marked a transition point between the fast chat MC styles of sound system pop stars like Smiley Culture and incoming rave. Fusing reggae samples with house and hip hop, the genres then adjacent and overlapping, it's an early example of UK rappers using their own accents. Later, in 1991, he'd release a tune with certified originators Shut Up and Dance. Released under the name Adé, it was titled 'Change the World'. If I had been a young person at Oxford House, I'd have been confident that the musician-in-residence was for real. Curtis Lugay was proper.

Stability offered by paid work that allowed for more, not less, time in the studio supported the creative output of the musicians who staffed these early hubs of music production. My guess is that it wouldn't have drained their creative batteries in the same way that other bread-and-butter jobs might have done. In this way, too, Oxford House formed part of the infrastructure that allowed bass-driven UK music to emerge.

'In addition to the development of my own music which has continued apace over the last twelve months,' Lugay wrote in the 1990 annual report, 'the residency was designed to fulfil the following objectives.' First in the list was his intention to enable young people with disabilities to become involved with the production of music. Then came his focus on what was then called 'computer music', aiming to increase digital literacy among young people generally and to help upcoming musicians develop their skills. A 'very large' number of young unemployed people were on the waiting list for courses. Four work stations, modified equipment to support young people with disabilities and cases to transport equipment were funded by a grant from Greater London Arts just before it was disbanded, along with money to cover the additional hours of those providing part-time support.

Youth club's supportive qualities extended beyond the teenage membership. Pirate radio stations were appearing across the FM dial, and Errol Wynter and his friends started their own station, Reflections FM, in the late 1980s. The station began broadcasting R&B and reggae, alongside community news and interviews, and there might also have been a period of, say, six months when the station operated from Oxford House's basement. Blind eyes were perhaps turned in service of the youth workers. It wasn't a sustainable scenario, of course, and soon Reflections had to find a new home in a local tower block. 'We found someone that let us have a room, and we paid the caretakers to put the masts up.' Errol and I took a walk around the building so he could show me where things were, in this same space, in decades past. He did so with a big smile, the kind that indicates sustenance.

At the same time that acid house, bhangra and rave were hitting the UK, a different kind of storm was hitting the youth service, emanating from the government at Westminster. Youth clubs and the youth service don't appear that frequently in Hansard, the record of parliamentary discussions, but there are more mentions than usual in the run-up to the Thatcherite Education Reform Act of 1988. The bill centralised and politicised education policy, creating a National Curriculum, introducing the origins of the later academies programme and moving accountability mechanisms away from local authorities. Legislating, among other things, for the abolition of the Inner London Education Authority (ILEA), it had knock-on effects on the youth service and, through budget cuts, on youth clubs themselves.

In the debate, MP Simon Hughes argued against the bill, mostly because of the effect it would have on provision for disabled teenagers. 'Let me finish on a personal note,' he concluded. 'Before I came to this place I was a youth worker in inner London for seven years, so I know of the vital need for that non-statutory service.' It is relevant, given the ongoing appearance of Settlement Houses in this story, that Hughes's youth work background included the Cambridge University Mission in Bermondsey.

The bill was debated a month later in the House of Lords. Baroness Faithfull, who'd been director of social services in Oxford, contributed in support of the legislation, while raising a point about the effects on life outside of schools. 'There is also the youth service, which is of inestimable value. At one time in my life I was a club leader and I know what this means to many young people particularly in the prevention of crime.'

The bill passed, and the following year a debate reached the House of Lords, with Durham educationalist and Labour Party peer Lord Dormand of Easington asking what steps the government was taking to ensure there would be a youth service after the abolition of the ILEA. Baroness Faithfull chipped in again, with a perspective on the youth club that persists today: that it's a weapon in the fight against crime instead of being a reasonable ask in any society – the creation of space for young people to socialise together. 'If we do not have a good youth service in London, we shall have more crime in the city.'

In 1990, a series of ministerial conferences took place to discuss the UK's youth service. An aim emerged, and it chimed with the spirit of the newly signed International Convention on Human Rights: youth work was to 'provide education that leads to an understanding of economic, personal, social and spiritual issues'.

The conferences were broadly ignored by those in charge of the purse strings, although one element – an increased focus on management targets and performance indicators – did make it through. Accountants Coopers & Lybrand Deloitte had been hired as consultants to write reports on multiple aspects of government. Between 1989 and 1992, contracts with the Department of Health alone cost taxpayers £3,683,703 (over £7.8m in today's money). The Department for Education and Science also commissioned a number of youth service reports from Coopers & Lybrand Deloitte, which, if the Department of Health reports are a good measure, would have cost, at the time, around £100,000 each. One, titled 'Managing the Youth Service in the 1990s', decreed in 1991 that performance indicators were necessary to ensure value for money, which was somewhat ironic given what the youth service could have done with £100k. The era of measurement had arrived.

Once again, the youth service was suffering from its lack of a legal or statutory basis. It's a situation summed up by one of our youth worker MPs, Simon Hughes, in a 1991 House of Commons debate on the future of the youth service. 'The youth service is not a statutory responsibility like education between the ages of five and sixteen. Therefore, local authorities have no obligation to fund a youth service. They have a responsibility to provide one, but not to provide the money for one.' His final sentence echoes through time like a somewhat stiff punchline: 'In a time of financial stringency, the non-statutory sector is inevitably badly hit.'

Annual reports have been written every year since Oxford House opened in 1884 and they provide official, funder-facing versions of the lived histories contained within the generations of people who passed through as young people, parents, staff or volunteers. Kept in the basement, where a short-lived pirate radio station might have operated at one point, they and other paper-based ephemera line the walls in sage-green boxes. The sound of trains going past filters through the walls, sounding squashy, cartoony, soft.

The annual report for 1990/1, which was for the first time also translated into Bengali and Somali, began with pressing financial context. Abolition of the ILEA and the introduction of the Conservative government's poll tax meant £1.4m worth of cuts to local authority grants, causing a shortfall of around £100,000 each year to Oxford House – or the average cost of one Coopers & Lybrand Deloitte report. Grants covering the musician-in-residence, Curtis Lugay, had evaporated, and the studio would need to become self-financing or be run by volunteers. Commercial 'computer music' workshops were being planned, and local musicians would be encouraged to hire the space to prepare demo tapes. The running and maintenance costs awarded to the brand-new youth facility were half those of the previous years, and the number of hours of paid part-time youth work were also reduced by 20 per cent.

In winter 1993, other worries shot to the surface. The racist, far-right British National Party (BNP) won a council by-election on the Isle of Dogs. Council elections don't generally generate a large turn-out, but 1,480 local people got out of bed to put a cross by the name of candidate Derek Beackon, who campaigned under the slogan 'Rights for Whites', employed grossly racist language and avoided public meetings because they attracted large crowds of protestors from the Anti-Nazi League and Anti-Fascist Action. He got eight votes more than the Labour candidate and was duly elected.

In what could arguably be seen as a consequence of the rise of far-right ideology, a few months later a nineteen-year-old student was battered in a near-fatal attack by a racist gang of twenty men, suffering horrific, life-changing injuries. Only one of the gang, eighteen-year-old Nicky Fuller, from nearby Bow, was tried in court, after his fifteen-year-old ex-girlfriend listened, appalled, to his bragging, wrote down everything he told her on two pieces of A4 paper and handed her notes to the police. He pleaded guilty to a reduced charge of violent disorder and was given a year's imprisonment. The attack took place in Weavers Field, the park directly in front of Oxford House.

Street-level repair work was required to make up for the damage generated by adults prepared to unleash hatred in service of political profit. At a majority Bengali youth project in Spitalfields and at Oxford House, youth workers collaborated on a programme of cross-community work under the project name 'Breaking Down the Barriers'. Interclub competitions in pool and table tennis took place, alongside music and art workshops and a joint visit to see Steven Spielberg's *Schindler's List*. A weekend-long residential retreat in Dorset allowed 'both sets of young people to mix freely' and was 'a resounding success'. These ordinary activities were, given what had happened, remarkable.

I'm telling you about this attack and the aftermath because, yes, youth clubs have had a major effect on UK music, sport and culture. But in extreme circumstances, like the one described, it's possible to see what this invisible public service really offers: social repair. As well as the cumulative benefits to young members, their families and youth workers, it enables a practical emergency response on the front line, just like ambulance workers or firefighters.

PART FOUR
AFTER DESTRUCTION COMES NEW GROWTH

26

1992: BYKER GROVE'S DOORS ARE OPEN

Youth clubs began taking centre stage as the location for prime-time television at precisely the same time as they were becoming the building-based versions of an endangered species. *Byker Grove* is the most famous of the televisual youth clubs, not least because it launched the careers of TV stars Ant and Dec, as the characters PJ and Duncan. Set in Newcastle upon Tyne, it was created by writer Adele Rose and executive producer Andrea Wonfor, airing on BBC One as part of children's programming strand CBBC. Eighteen series of the show were broadcast between 1989 and 2006, and by 1994 seven million viewers were regularly tuning in, with the show picking up consecutive BAFTA nominations for best children's programme.

The show quickly gained a devoted following who'd watch early teenage life play out after *Newsround*, catching up with the likes of Spuggie, Speedy and tireless youth worker Geoff, who sported spectacular sideburns. Early episodes set the tone for what would follow, with a focus on friendship dynamics, family discord and nascent relationships, reflecting the outside world through storylines referencing early-'90s hot topics such as joyriding, teenage smoking and eco-activism. Stories were variously humorous and hard-hitting, and, from series two onwards, a rival youth club, Denton Burn, was introduced to offer an additional mirror on *Byker* life.

Matthew Robinson has lived in Cambodia for over twenty years, making TV drama and movies for Khmer audiences. He produced the first seven series of *Byker Grove* and also directed multiple episodes, although, initially, he had reservations. 'Andrea [Wonfor] asked if I wanted to produce and direct a show about children in Newcastle,' he told me. 'I went to see her that same evening, and she told me that it was set in an out-of-school environment for eight- to twelve-year-olds. I pulled a bit of a face and said that you can't write interesting stories for that age group because they're not independent from their parents and they can't be left on their own. Stories with young people only become interesting when they have deep emotions, get up to pranks, do really bad things or really good things.' He paused and then continued, reflecting on the drama that forms the centre of so much teenage life. 'You don't fall in love at eight or nine. Probably a quarter of our story-lines were about relationships between boys or girls, or the gay issue – we got quite a lot of flak for that.'

After some discussion, Andrea Wonfor and Adele Rose agreed, and the age group for the programme was moved upwards, redrafting the original concept. *Byker Grove* would dramatise early teenage life, in a setting outside of school, so as not to clash with the BBC's long-running *Grange Hill*. A fictional youth club was the obvious answer, and once Zenith Productions succeeded in winning a commission for an initial run of six episodes from Anna Home, head of the BBC's children's department, they built a set in the corporation's studios in Newcastle. A dramatic but run-down building known as The Mitre, which had a prehistory as a bishop's palace, a pub and a nightclub, as well as the headquarters of the North-Eastern Coal Board, served for exterior shots. Gaining the go-ahead for two more series after the first was deemed a success, the BBC was persuaded to purchase the freehold of The Mitre.

A sizeable portion of the programme's budget was spent on refurbishing the interior, with PJ, Duncan and friends enacting teenage drama along the corridors, up and down the sweeping staircase and, in one *Byker*-famous scene, falling through a trap-door into the building's supposedly derelict basement.

One influential 1994 storyline saw fifteen-year-old Noddy kiss his friend Gary on the cheek in the cinema. Gary stormed out, leaving Noddy to pick up the pieces. Despite being an unreciprocated peck on the cheek that lasted less than three seconds, it was considered to be the first same-sex kiss on British children's television and caused a furore. The story was reported widely at both national and local levels. The *Belfast Telegraph* headline was representative – 'Parents Seethe at Gay TV Kiss' – while the *Shields Daily Gazette* reported that it 'led to complaints from scores of parents' and quoted right-wing TV campaigner Mary Whitehouse. Also quoted was Matthew Robinson, who acknowledged the complaints but refuted the idea that they were justified. 'It is a fact of life that some teenage boys feel this way about others and I hope that through this programme they will not think they are alone.'

It is worth pausing here for a moment in order to jump into the sidestream of an otherwise irrelevant familial detail, because it shows another point at which the family tree of UK youth clubs, real and imagined, converges. *Byker* producer Matthew Robinson had a brother, Tom, whose hit record '(Sing If You're) Glad to Be Gay' soundtracked the London Gay Teenage Group's efforts to gain official recognition. Other newspapers also made the connection, using it as a new angle to continue peddling fury about the *Byker* storyline. Matthew, who happens to be straight, was quoted, refuting the relevance of his brother's sexuality to the writing team's work. 'I also remember an editorial,' he told me, 'saying I should be shot at dawn, or at the very least sacked.'

Byker Grove dealt with young people's lives in the 1990s, and the young actors were encouraged to share ideas for storylines. It also reflected specific issues facing the youth service at this time. Sometimes a local councillor would drop into the story, such as when things weren't going right, when budget issues were raising their heads or when something significant happened, like a fire in the building. 'There was always this threat that it was going to be closed down,' recalled Matthew when we spoke. He recalled a major storyline around local authority cuts, with characters raising money and youth worker Geoff arranging for a couple of councillors to come down to see with their own eyes the importance of the place.

Even though it was a television programme, not an actual youth club, *Byker Grove* shared certain qualities with the real thing. The fictional club's rules allowed for members aged between twelve and sixteen. Similar strictures were enforced for actors, who had to be of the same age range, with characters written out soon after the person playing them turned sixteen. In series five, Dec's character, Duncan Sperring, left the show. 'It was one of our most touching scenes,' recalled Matthew. 'It was set at night, in Byker Grove. We had Dec's character saying, "But I love this place, it's my life." Geoff explained that the time had come, and he had to go. Actually, all these years on, I'm getting cold shivers down my spine thinking of that scene. It was very moving. The audience were absolutely in tears, judging by the feedback we got.'

Feedback arrived in the form of letters, and when kids would cycle up the curved path to The Mitre asking if they could join the youth club, or when they'd get their parents to drive them there to try and meet actors who were the same age as them, like Jill Halfpenny or Donna Air. The first 'Avid Fan Convention' took place at The Mitre in December 1993, with a long queue of teenagers lined up ready for the tour. Inside, they'd meet members of the crew, culminating in a low-fi kind of press conference where cast members sat behind a trestle table, ready to answer questions and sign autographs.

In the pre-internet world, fans had limited options if they wanted to get closer to the action. One possibility was the show's Ceefax page, Ceefax being the world's first 'teletext information service' and a combination of somewhat static proto-internet and the current red button service. The other was *Grove Gossip*. Copies of this monthly publication, which was put together by Matthew and ran to twenty-four editions, were available to anyone who sent a stamped self-addressed envelope to The Mitre. Up to ten thousand copies per edition were dispatched to fans, explained Matthew, who sent me a batch of examples to pore over.

Grove Gossip would have been eagerly awaited by teenage readers. It's a lively read, containing practical news about scheduled repeats, 'True or False' quizzes about cast, crew and the chaperones required by under-sixteen actors, as well as behind-the-scenes photos, gossip and tantalising storyline hints. The letters page shows fans writing in from Britain and Northern Ireland, and occasionally further afield. A fourteen-year-old from Bransholme, Hull, wrote in to say that she was profoundly deaf and loved the programme 'because it shows reality and has interesting acting', while another from Pontefract described getting her seventy-year-old nan to watch. 'She thinks it's really true to life and she especially likes the lush Ant McPartlin.' Other writers, including one Naomi from Birmingham, offered more practical comment: 'When PJ got hit and Duncan sobbed, Duncan should have phoned an ambulance right away and not taken ten minutes sobbing in front of the camera.'

During our conversations, I sensed a multidimensional scenario. Matthew was an experienced professional, having edited the Cambridge University newspaper *Varsity*, overseen many episodes of popular shows including *Emmerdale Farm*, *Coronation Street* and *Dr Who*, written *Crossroads* and directed many episodes of *EastEnders*, including the very first two. At *Byker Grove*, however, he was also a kind of youth leader, with responsibilities towards the young people. Being in a representation of a youth club made the situation, and the relationships, a bit youth-clubby. 'I think that's true,' said Matthew, when I put this to him. 'It had a profound effect on the young actors. I think most of them thought they were in a youth club anyway! They would grab the scripts to see what storylines they had, whizz through them. I tried to spread it out so everyone got a great storyline every two or three seasons.' This was, I reflected, very fair-minded, and also necessary in this uniquely youth-club-adjacent environment.

I wondered aloud whether or not the youth club is a particularly porous place, in which the world can easily make itself known, in ways that are different to the environment within a school. 'Well,' said Matthew, 'if you take school, or a well-run school, there is some opportunity for reaction between pupils, but not a lot. In the youth club, 95 per cent of the time it's outside the remit of adults. Within *Byker Grove* it was a chance to reflect what was going on in the outside world, and we did that wherever we could. But it was really more about growing up and young people finding their feet in this very confusing world. That's what we tried to do. Whether or not youth clubs generally do that, honestly, I don't know. I'm not that well versed, never having attended one.'

'Oh,' I said, 'so you didn't attend youth club yourself?'

'Maybe it's terrible to admit it, but I grew up in Huntingdon and Saffron Walden. I don't remember any, and I didn't have any connection with any.' He then paused, almost buffering, while a new thought appeared. 'Mind you,' he said, 'I started, when I was about thirteen, a sort of drama group for a few of my friends from grammar school. We managed to get the vicar to let us use the church hall a couple of times a week. We did various scenes from *Macbeth*, and my dad wrote a few plays to suit the members. It was the nearest I got to mixing out of school with my peers.'

'That's wonderful,' I said, slightly overextending into unsolicited familiarity. 'Your drama group was a youth club of sorts. You needed space to do something, you found adults who were prepared to offer space and support, which meant you were able to explore your interests.' 'Right, okay,' he replied. 'Well, I hadn't seen it that way. I just saw it as a chance to boss people around and develop my interest in drama. Even at that age I wanted to be behind the scenes, running things.'

The group ran for about two years and members received a newsletter that the teenage Matthew compiled and edited with great seriousness and notable flair, which appeared under the title *Godmanchester Junior Drama Club Times*. The two pages of the April 1958 edition were typed on his father's Imperial typewriter and copied, as a favour, by the headmaster's secretary at Huntingdon Grammar School. The newsletter included minutes from a group meeting, a list of auditionees for the play *Escape*, which included the scores each had been awarded, rehearsal and performance reports, birthdays, a letters section and a quiz. It looks a lot like a low-resource and very junior edition of *Grove Gossip*.

Matthew's newsletter, and the existence of his drama group, also reminded me of something I often think: that while not everyone who creates a teenage publication or enacts a school-age drama group will go on to have professional success in that field, almost every successful creative professional will probably have been part of something like this, however small and seemingly irrelevant, when they were very young.

Byker Grove became part of British television history because it offered an accurate and sensitive representation of growing up. 'I always said, for the first three years of the show, that the essence of the show was a bridge between childhood and adulthood and learning to grow up,' said Matthew, as we finished up. 'And Newcastle has seven bridges. I asked the designer to bring that visual theme in as much as we could. If you look at the first three series, you can see the main humpback bridge represented within the club and in many of the shots. Whenever we were shooting on location we'd try and have a bridge in the background. It's about growing up; it's the bridge of maturity, of learning to become an adult.'

'That,' I told him, before we closed our laptops after our online chat and headed off into the day, 'is an almost perfect summation of what youth clubs are all about.'

27

1993: SOUTH LONDON'S YOUTH CLUB SITCOM

Fictional youth clubs in the north-east cleared the way for a new sitcom. In July 1993, *What You Looking At?* was aired on ITV, in the Saturday teatime slot. It featured lead character Trevor Fry, aka Two Bad, and his younger brother Darren, along with other characters, including prominent girls – a lively three-strong crew known as the Wicked Sisters – and a deaf young person. Much of the comedy drew on the relationships between the young people, but also their interactions with the archetypal youth workers featured on the show. Staff characters at St Thomas's Boys' Club included twenty-five-year-old white university graduate Jane, who'd grown up in Berkshire and was nominally leading the club, injury-prone sports worker Lynford – played by ex-*EastEnders* actor Gary McDonald – and Mrs Williams, a no-nonsense British Caribbean woman who really ran things.

The show was popping with bright, saturated colours, an early use of computer-style graphics and an aesthetic popularised in cartoons, manga and hip hop videos by acts like Jungle Brothers, De La Soul and Monie Love. Like a confidently south London version of Spike Lee's *Do the Right Thing*, each episode began with a film-quality title sequence that panned down the Thames, past Battersea Power Station, before cutting to a Peckham estate, encompassing skateboarding, rollerblading, a dance circle and kids running down a fire escape, all before encountering the flashing blue lights of a police car and scarpering. Written by Trix Worrell, who'd created hit Channel 4 show *Desmond's*, it went out before the super-prime-time shows *Beadle's About* and *Stars in Their Eyes*. It was, according to the *Daily Mirror*'s resolute thumbs-up, 'a hit with both critics and kids'.

I went back to the British Film Institute's Mediatheque in London to watch the whole season of *What You Looking At?* Like so much else from that time, it's not on the internet. It took me about two hours to watch the first twenty-three-minute episode, because I had to keep pausing it to take in all the details: the Public Enemy and Kris Kross posters on the wall, or the stickers on the filing cabinet (Strictly Rhythm records and club night Jazz Bop), as well as the era-specific clothing, all baseball caps, dungarees and tucked-in long-sleeved t-shirts. By the end of the day I was swimming in the past, partly because I'm absorbent like that, but because the BFI's Mediatheque system includes the continuity announcements and adverts that were broadcast around the programme too, making the whole experience extremely immersive, a kind of reliving. It's probably worth noting which brands were attracted to the youth club framing. The ad break after episode one included Coors, the Ford Fiesta, a TSB youth bank account, Henara shampoo and Coca-Cola, a list which runs up and down the viewer demographics, speaking to youth-club-educated parents as much as their teenage kids.

Jokes acted as the vehicle for thematic strands. Youth leader Jane's idea to have a girls-only discussion group allows one of the Wicked Sisters to monologue about how they don't have any space in the club, that they're always getting shoved around, and that boys' sports always take priority. Eavesdropping, the boys line up to play imaginary small violins. And, in a detail that's repeated elsewhere in real-life youth club histories, this part of the show also had the Wicked Sisters removing the wheels from Jane's car. Another storyline, where nerdy new arrival Jai Singh explores his love of Elvis Presley, despite parental disapproval, allowed characters to offer ITV viewers an alternative take on the received wisdom. The King of Rock and Roll, said Two Bad, was a 'dead, fat junkie who stole Black music'.

The man who put words into the characters' mouths would become an honorary member of the British Comedy Academy and recipient of the Lifetime Achievement Medal from the Royal Television Society. Trix Worrell now lives on the south coast of England, where he moved after returning from a stretch in Hollywood, where his company Wicked Films produced films and worked with Fox, Universal, Disney, Whoopi Goldberg and Ridley Scott. Back in the early '90s, though, word had begun circulating in telly circles that the TV overlords were looking to replace Saturday teatime staple *Metal Mickey* with a new show. Trix didn't need telling twice, and leapt into action.

'I was searching for a young comedy programme I could devise, and a youth club entered my mind because they're very comedic,' he told me, explaining that, at the time, and in his role as a parent, he was in and out of Dog Kennel Hill youth club and adventure playground in the London borough of Southwark. 'They're very funny spaces.' He paused and chuckled, mentally inhabiting, I think, both the youth clubs he knew himself and the space he invented for young prime-time viewers. 'I thought it was a great place for solace, to go to and *be*, and you could hide. It was a nice place, it was comfort. Especially being young and Black in London. You didn't have to be on the street looking out for whoever the hell wanted to chase me and give me a good kicking, because that's what was going on at the time. It was a safe haven. You could be what you wanted in the youth club.'

What he injected into *What You Looking At?*, he said, was youth theatre, seeing the parallels between young people who come together to 'do drama' and the actual drama that inevitably takes place when young people are in the majority. 'In youth drama you can explore, via improvisation, all these issues that are swirling around you as a young person, as a teenager, and you learn how to explore it.' Youth clubs, he said, were an extension of the form. 'You get all sorts of young people coming together, issues are raised, you prod someone and they erupt – then people notice and talk about it. Whatever's going on, it's out there.'

One topic he put out there related to young people's experiences with constables and cars with blue lights, particularly those who experience a police force, not a police service. In the show, Two Bad is, through no fault of his own, constantly ending up in situations where it looks like he's committed a crime – for example, when he chases a mugger who has stolen a granny's handbag, and then ends up face to face with the police in a dead-end alley, with said handbag in his hands after the mugger ditches it and scales a wall to get away. 'That was deliberate. I wanted to burst that bubble,' Trix said, before dropping into a story of his own, about the hated precursor to Stop and Search, known as SUS, which allowed the police to act on the basis of suspicion alone, until the law was repealed in 1981. 'The first beating I got from the police was because of SUS,' he said. 'I was standing at a bus stop, there was this woman in front of me. She had no idea I was even there; she was just waiting for the bus, getting a bit pissed off with all these schoolkids. Next thing, a Black Maria turns up, they put us in the van, gave us a good kicking.'

At this point, Trix's voice went understandably quiet. 'So,' he said, with a slightly bleak chuckle that acted as a bridge back to the topic of his TV programme, 'I did another episode where it looks like Two Bad is doing graffiti. When I showed that to the audience, they went mad. Youth clubs were always seen as a hotbed of graffiti artists.'

I told Trix about the Bristol youth club at Barton Hill that helped nurture a generation of spray-can artists, and he immediately expanded on the point. 'Also,' he said, 'youth clubs were venues for sound systems. My brother made speakers for sound systems, even down to [south London icon] Jah Shaka. Youth clubs were places which transformed into a blues club on a Saturday, which was a way of the youth club making money too. A makeshift bar. The acoustics were terrible, but we didn't care. If the bass was rattling doors, frames, windows, it was doing its job.' I can see a big smile appear on his face. 'They were just sunny places,' he said. 'Great places to be.'

One strand of the show comes across as pretty surprising by today's standards: the ongoing theme of young people trying – in 1990s parlance – to 'get off with' the youth workers. Two Bad is constantly rehearsing pick-up lines on youth worker Jane, and the three main girls, the Wicked Sisters, are unabashed in their displays of affection towards Lynford, including one scene on the club's basketball court, where he tells them to stop being so forward, and, in response, they throw themselves at him, a bundle of cartoon limbs crashing against the court's wire-mesh edges. In another episode, Jane pretends to go along with Two Bad's attempted seduction, but it's clear to the viewer that this is akin to the olden days method of stopping your kid smoking by making them either eat a cigarette or smoke a whole packet.

What struck me, once I'd got over the shock, was that all of the adults in *What You Looking At?* are depicted as being beyond reproach. Yet they deal with the teenagers' innuendo and hormonal crushes in a way that would be, at the very least, unacceptable now, providing grounds for dismissal or even referral to the police. But, in essence, the youth workers are rolling their eyes, even if they're doing so in a way that we find mind-boggling now.

Trix's TV youth club was also a great place for some very early product placement, specifically in the corner of the club that doubled up as a tuck shop. Almost twenty years before Ofcom relaxed the rules on product placement on British television, *What You Looking At?* had characters snacking on KP nuts, slurping on Sunkist drinks and eating Bounty Bars, all laid out in front of a Zanussi fridge. 'I was telling Granada and LWT [London Weekend Television] that they could do product placement,' Trix explained, 'that we could get chocolate, things you'd associate with youth.'

'Was product placement normal at that time?' I asked. 'No, it wasn't at all,' he replied. The rationale for absorbing American attitudes to in-show advertising was two-fold, he explained. Firstly, he needed the money, because the high-quality visuals he desired were more expensive than your average thin-walled sitcom studio. Each episode of *What You Looking At?* included an opening sequence shot on location, which also bumped the costs up. But on top of that, he wanted to reflect the increasingly commercialised attitudes of young people in youth clubs and those at home watching. 'The language of those young people within the youth club itself was all about branding: "I eat these crisps or that chocolate, I don't eat crap."'

Thinking about money was necessary from a production point of view, and for audiences, but it also related to the situation on the real-world side of the screen. Trix described himself as 'very tuned into' the financial issues facing youth clubs. It was awful, he said, when they started closing, mentioning Thatcher and her sell-off of school playing fields. 'It's real estate, that's what it was about. I found it really galling that people making these decisions send their kids to private school, where they have grounds to play in, and where they have their own theatres, like Eton. That's why we have so many actors from Eton. I'm not knocking them, but how come we don't have that? I was very aware that youth clubs and adventure playgrounds were closing. I wanted to celebrate what they do and what they're about.'

The show also celebrated London as a city for all types of people. The Wicked Sisters give a sense of the show's approach to representation through the characters that comprised the friendship group: super-cool top girl Vanessa would likely have ticked the 'Black British' box on a diversity form, while Dawn would have ticked 'white'. The third member of the group, Elaine, would have ticked 'goth', an option that should surely be included on all monitoring forms.

I told Trix about a friend of mine who was a teenage goth and who, by the time *What You Looking At?* was airing, had been to art school and was running creative sessions in south London youth clubs. She has her own stories to tell about the youth worker's car getting nicked and becoming very good at both pool and table tennis as part of the relationship-building that youth work requires. 'What was your relationship with the goths?' I asked Trix, enquiring after the roots of the Elaine character. 'I really admired them,' he said, straight off. 'There was no way of hiding. They were so different, and they wore it out on the street; deliberately went out there and were themselves. As a Black person in a minority, there was no way I could hide. I was a target. They were a target for all kinds of things. I thought they were cool, how they dealt with it. Also, the music. I'm a musician, so I find something good in every genre'.

Trix drew on his own histories, as a young person and as a parent. However, the degree to which his own experiences fed into his life and work is pretty exceptional and is worth recounting. Trix's personal story also allows us to see yet another connection point between individual youth clubs and the wider cultural fabric of the country.

Remembering his own youth club on Telegraph Hill, elsewhere in south-east London, he describes the opportunities for culture and creativity, listing access to paint (and paint fights), putting together scratch bands with financially stable kids who had instruments, meeting girls, and learning how to roll a Rizla properly. 'You were encouraged. Before that, it was, "Shut up and sit down and don't say anything." Here, you had a platform to explore and be noisy and just be.'

It was a visitor, though, that opened the door that led to a life in theatre, film and TV. In the late 1970s and early '80s Martin Stellman was running a youth theatre group at the Albany in Deptford, alongside Brenda Moor, and had written the hit Mod film *Quadrophenia*. He knew the local youth clubs were hotbeds of new talent, and so when he was looking for a band for a show he'd written called *Down in Black and White*, he walked up from Deptford to Telegraph Hill and asked around. Trix: 'He said, "Can anyone read music?" And stupidly I put my hand up. I couldn't – I mean, I could work it out, but it would take me a while. He left a series of songs, buggered off, and said he'd be back in a week. We played it really cool but actually we rehearsed furiously and spiced up the songs. I added a brass section, and he thought it was great. That's how I got into the Albany.'

Interesting, I think, that a local kid needed an introduction to a local theatre group. But the issues known today as 'postcode wars' are not new, and I can well imagine that a youngster from the edge of Peckham might need permission, or an invitation, to safely head a mile or so down the road. It also reminds me how important it is to make sure that doors are truly open, not just theoretically so. It's also worth saying that Trix used his access to create more of the same, founding the Albany's Basement Youth Theatre Company, co-founding young women's drama group Second Wave, and also the Lewisham Academy of Music, which was replaced by the Midi Music Company under the leadership of Wozzy Brewster, a former member of the aforementioned Basement theatre group. When spaces are run by those who need them, or who know about the need first-hand, the benefits can be multiplied massively.

I've watched another film that Martin Stellman wrote, the sound-system-situated *Babylon*, numerous times. I already knew, therefore, that the credits thanked five Lewisham youth clubs, and that Stellman had worked on the script with these clubs, through round-table sessions, and knowing all this brought a possible connection into view. 'Yeah, exactly that,' confirmed Trix. 'I befriended Martin, so I was one of those passports into the youth clubs: "Come, Martin, come chat to these man."' As well as a credited role in the film, as one of Jah Shaka's men, Trix was present for an important moment in music history. The film's title track, 'Warrior Charge', was written and recorded by Aswad and produced by Dennis Bovell. 'I remember going up to the Mangrove, where they were mixing it. When they dropped that tune, that's when I realised the film was really going to rock it. *Babylon*, man, that was great fun.'

'It's really special,' I said, 'to be able to understand how your youth club facilitated your entry into cinematic drama simply by existing.' 'Martin opened up a whole world for me,' said Trix. 'I wrote my first play just on his say-so. I said, "I've got this idea for a play, Martin." I'd never written a play before. He said, "Just write it." He had no idea how powerful that sentence was for me. Because of it, I became a writer, even though I was dyslexic, dis-everything.'

In April 1994, the *Daily Mirror* reported that Trix's youth club sitcom *What You Looking At?* hadn't been commissioned for another series. 'Unfortunately, ITV reportedly claims it has no time slot for another series. Strange, isn't it?' wrote the paper's TV reporter. 'Especially as it managed to squeeze sad *New Baywatch* with its pathetic old storylines into the schedule.'

Youth-club-built relationships would be enduring. Later, Trix and Stellman would collaborate on a feature film, *For Queen and Country*, in which Denzel Washington played a British soldier returning home to south London after a tour of Northern Ireland during the conflict, or Troubles.

28

1995: FILMING BLAZED *IN COVENTRY*

Despite the decimation of the youth service, large numbers were still attending the clubs that were managing to hold on in the mid-to-late 1990s. A Department for Education survey in 1995 found that two thirds of young people had been involved with the youth service at some time, with 20 per cent of thirteen- to nineteen-year-olds involved when the survey took place. Another study by the National Foundation for Education Research, titled *Providing for Young People*, took place between April 1994 and June 1995, with authors Karen Maychell, Shalini Pathak and Vivienne Cato estimating that, at any given point, the youth service was working with some five million young people. Youth clubs comprised part of the picture, alongside other examples outlined in their report: a group for young Muslim women; a rural mobile bus project; and 'youth houses' that were more like friendly offices where local kids, who, judging by the syntax of their quoted comments, were from Liverpool, could come and hang out and use the computers, printers and typewriters.

The physical estate of youth club buildings had clung on throughout Thatcher's time in power but was now entering another period of active decline. Herculean efforts could be continued only for so long. Budgets were being slashed, with wholesale cuts in staffing, one local authority going from forty to fifteen full-time youth service staff. As well as losing trusted adults, millions of UK youth were cut adrift from previously widespread peripatetic dance or arts teams and the residential centres that had allowed kids from towns and cities to escape local pressures, often to somewhere semi-rural. Clubs that were previously open from Monday to Friday were reducing opening times. Local authorities were left with buildings they couldn't afford to maintain or run, or which weren't in the correct location to address local needs. Resourceful youth workers – 'we've become very entrepreneurial', said one quoted in the report – began looking towards mainland Europe, specifically after the UK joined the Single Market in 1993, with some making use of the European Social Fund.

Funds were still available, though, for short-term schemes aimed at solving particular social problems. Nearly £4m was allocated to the Youth Action Scheme between 1993 and 1996, which aimed to see if youth workers could reduce crime. The money didn't go into providing space or maintaining buildings, however, and had to be 'match-funded' by local authorities, therefore absorbing valuable resources. The availability of money to try to arrest criminality – perhaps a job better undertaken by the police? – must have been frustrating to youth workers running clubs on a shoestring. Academics claimed that the youth service needed to engage with the government's crime agenda, if only to 'grasp the nettle of evaluation', as David Smith and Ian Paylor wrote in *Youth and Policy* journal. Author and youth worker Sue Robertson, however, had managed one of these projects and came away with a specific view, expressed in her book *Youth Clubs*, which I've referenced repeatedly here. The youth service 'ought not to stray too far from its core business, i.e. clubs'.

The requirements around data collection ramped up in the early 1990s, even though such activity risked being both performative and punitive. This new reality showed up in a storyline in Trix Worrell's ITV sitcom (see previous chapter), in an episode centred around cuts, which included youth worker Jane bemoaning the extra work required in proving exactly who was attending her fictional club.

One youth officer in *Providing for Young People* described working out the cost – per young person – of their centres and finding that it varied between £4 and £300. 'There was concern that unit costs, if known, would be used as ammunition against certain types of provision,' wrote the authors, as respondents patiently explained a perspective contained in a different equation, attributed variously to Einstein and sociologist William Bruce Cameron: that not everything that can be counted counts. Data collection was time-consuming and moved youth workers away from face-to-face work. Dynamic-changing, it forced youth workers to act as surveyors, requiring them to enact potentially intrusive information-gathering on youth club members, collecting data about their characteristics and life circumstances. These new demands, and an increasing audit culture, were expensive, and the feeling was emerging that data must be acted on, if only to justify the expense.

An extended view appears through the cracks of the report, in an entry that describes a creative response to the conditions. 'In order to evaluate the long-term benefits of youth provision, and incidentally motivate current users, one authority was arranging reunions of ex-users at their still-running youth club,' reads *Providing for Young People*. One respondent, who'd left the club twenty-five years earlier, 'was talking about how he was beaten by his father, how he was expelled from school, but the one stable thing in his life was to go to the youth club . . . how useful it was and how he's going to make sure his son goes. What we do know is that it had a significant effect on these people's lives.'

Open-access youth clubs, where youngsters could hang out with their friends, in which youth workers could facilitate social education or empowerment for multiple generations of families and neighbours, and where the local community could feel assured that young people were being kept off the streets, were becoming a thing of the past. Government cuts, passed on to local authorities, were a major reason, of course, but policy changes aimed at centralising power and limiting state spending on public services were baked into law, specifically the Local Government Act and the Education Reform Act (both 1988). Both failed to adequately reflect the existence of the youth service, and both left the youth services to pick up the costs of change, including, in the former, the presence of the homophobic Section 28.

The Education Reform Act was having, as suspected by the handful of MPs who argued against it, a deleterious effect on youth clubs, particularly those that had benefited from free or subsidised space in symbiotic comprehensives. By the mid-'90s, some schools, particularly those in more affluent areas, were becoming resistant to youth workers coming in, regarding the youth service as catering for 'problem kids'. Newly empowered by the Education Reform Act, which granted school governors powers previously held by local authorities, school leaders were able to act on their prejudice and youth clubs were increasingly squeezed out of schools. Within councils, limited youth work resources were instead turned towards specific groups. Generally, these were described as 'disadvantaged', and included young people from ethnic minorities, girls, those with disabilities or considered to be 'at risk' of criminality, and those experiencing social or economic disadvantage.

In some areas, risks were especially high. The story of how Channel 4 broadcast a 1995 drama generated by a youth club begins with award-winning film-maker Adi Dowling. He was born in Dublin and moved to Coventry as a child. Leaving school aged sixteen in 1990, he undertook a BTEC media studies course. Dyslexic, he found the learning difficult to access. Next came a video training course at The Depot, a youth arts centre that drew heavily on the practices built at the sound-system-adjacent Holyhead youth club in the 1970s and '80s, followed by a Youth Training Scheme (YTS). The Depot had a 32-track studio and there was infrastructure. 'It wasn't about grades, it was hands-on,' he told me. 'I wanted to make films about raves, and they were like, "Here are the keys to the edit suite." For me, going into The Depot feeling like a failure, to be given that breathing space was unheard of. It didn't matter where you were from, or if you didn't have any money. I think the camera was £2 to hire it for the weekend, and there'd be times they'd let me have it for free.'

Adi's a no-messing kind of person, scathing about structural processes and individuals that push out pioneers, especially those who are working class, and of the concentrated power grabs that happen in small cities where opportunities are scarce. 'That attitude comes from being from an Irish background and not being nurtured,' he told me. 'It's down to you. And to be given equipment – that changes everything.'

In 1992, he'd use what he'd learned to make his first film, *A Hard Day's Night*, documenting DJ duo Parks & Wilson's influential residency at The Eclipse. He began promoting raves, mixing up the styles by booking big names like Grooverider alongside bhangra DJs. This period of Coventry life has since become the subject of retrospective documentaries, including his own multimedia exhibition, *House Is a Feeling*, as part of Coventry's 2021 City of Culture programming. 'I just thought, "No one's documenting this cultural revolution that's gone on in Coventry." I took that same attitude into the youth clubs in Wood End, Hillfields. I was letting them mess about, and eight months later they're working with Channel 4, with a canteen and make-up. They're primed, they knew how to be.'

Meeting me in the Belgrade Theatre, a partner organisation in his early videography work with The Depot, he described the city he lived in as a teenager as 'lawless'. Crack and heroin had arrived, pushing city life, for some at least, into the abyss. Adi would volunteer at youth clubs all over the city, including Yardley Street, in premises previously used as a working men's club. It was located just around the corner from a part of the city known as The Frontline, where he describes drug-dealing openly taking place. This proximity, of course, also created an alarmingly easy way for local young people to become involved in this aspect of economic productivity. He'd grown up in the areas he volunteered in, which meant it took only a few weeks of hanging about before trusted relationships could begin to be built, and so Adi became a de facto youth worker.

While early attempts were expensive – 'I brought down these walkie-talkies, and the kids robbed them because the drug dealers told them to' – trust was gradually built and creative relationships emerged. At Yardley Street, he showed kids how to use The Depot's video cameras. Noticing turntables built into a simple DJ booth left over from the building's previous incarnation as a working men's club, he brought down some of his jungle and hardcore records, letting the boys and girls play tunes, 'a big gang of us, all together, having a laugh together'. In around 1993, the group made a video for a competition run by The Depot, the youth club members becoming both 'technical and creative', as Adi described it. 'When we won, the place went mad. It was a big buzz.' Connections were being made between Yardley Street and TV production company Maverick by Enda Murray, a community youth worker and film-maker who'd made his own documentary with Ray Henry in 1994, about sound system culture and its connection to raves.

'Maverick had made something in Belfast. They saw what I'd made [with the video] and came down, said they were looking for something new in a rough area,' said Adi. 'Hillfields, the area the youth club was in, was more than rough. Rough would be a compliment.' Creative cogs began turning and the resulting drama, *Blazed*, was broadcast on Channel 4 in September 1995. The cast was comprised of mid-teens from the Yardley Street youth club, who'd also advised on the storyline and script during pre-production workshops, and was based around a day of escapades by two suspended schoolkids. *Blazed*'s credits included Adi, as technical assistant, and youth club workers Phil Moody and Abdul Shaikh, under the shapeshifting title 'Location Managers'. 'They were more than youth workers, they were important people,' said Adi, in one of a few subsequent phone calls. 'They could communicate with the young people. This is why getting rid of youth clubs is madness.'

Let's pause for a moment and imagine the behind-the-scenes work that would make it possible for a film crew with high-end kit and catering trucks to come into a youth club, in an area run by drug dealers. 'There was communication,' said Adi, explaining that youth workers brokered relationships between the outsider film company and insider personnel. 'Key people went out, saying, "We're going to be filming later. If you don't want to be seen, dadada." Camera crew weren't being taxed. *Blazed*, said Adi, made it possible for funding to follow and brought long-term benefits, of the kind that would be hard to see on an evaluation form. 'Maverick put their neck on the line,' said Adi. 'It brought a lot of confidence into the area, for the young people and their self-esteem. It allowed them to hold their heads up high about where they came from. None of those people in the film went on into the proper drug thing.'

It was very good for the community, he explained, but it was especially good for the kids because they saw the process from start to finish. 'A camera and messing round on decks at youth club went on to something broadcast on the telly, millions of people watching it. That was a big thing for the young people.' Adi paused. 'Imagine failing at school, and then being in a film. It was the same pattern that was happening with me.'

Many years later, when Adi's work was exhibited on a large scale as part of Coventry City of Culture, a lad approached him, introducing himself as one of the key Yardley Street youth and thanking Adi for what he'd done. The act of telling their story, said Adi, brought something out in the young people. It allowed them to understand where they came from, to celebrate what was good about it, and to learn about themselves in the process. It was, he said, in typically understated style, 'positive'. With very few resources, a handful of motivated individuals had made space on the ground, and in people's perceptions.

For a four-week period at *Live Magazine*, where I worked in the mid-2000s, there was a Saturday film-making club. Founder Sam Conniff, himself still in his twenties, roped in his actor friend Anton Saunders as a mentor and got to work. The participants were a small group of magazine regulars who weren't really interested in writing and wanted, or were thought to need, something different. They wrote the script, filmed it, and some appeared on screen. The result was *Tissue Paper Crew*, a nine-minute satire on gang affiliation, where the film's characters wore toilet paper around their necks and in their back pockets instead of the coloured bandanas favoured by local entities at the time.

In 2007, when the film-makers got to work, organised crime as it affected young people had become a pressing issue. A timeline of 'known gangs' in the area's SW9 postcode, compiled by author Simon Harding for his book *The Street Casino: Survival in Violent Street Gangs*, listed two groups in the period 1991–5. Six were included for 1996–2000, with two more added for 2001–5. In 2007, though, the list was long enough to require an A–Z, which ended with Young Thugz 4 Life and comprised a total of forty-five gangs.

A few weeks after finishing *Tissue Paper Crew*, one of the film-making group arrived at the office wearing a variety of purple bandanas, signalling membership of one specific grouping that appeared in Harding's A–Z. I have a strong memory of this moment because of the striking disconnect between the parody they'd been part of and this adoption of blaringly loud street-level insignia. Being realistic, you didn't need to be part of a gang to wear these items – you could just buy a bandana in the market – but wearing one was asking for trouble. A conversation followed that can be boiled down to this question–observation, which you can imagine being asked by someone with raised eyebrows: 'You just made a film that mocked the wearing of gang colours?'

The bandanas went away, at least in the office. The social context causing violence did not, and the following year Lambeth Council launched a five-year strategy to reduce 'gang culture', 'violent youth crime' and the custody rate for young people, in partnership with the police and health authorities. The council's leader described the dilemma facing young people on an estate where rival gangs operated. 'Join one gang,' he said, 'and the other is out to get you. Join the second and you become a target for the first. Join neither, and you're prey to both.' When I read this, I'm instantly taken back to the roots of the word 'club' in the English Civil War, and the people who courageously clubbed together when armies from both sides were rampaging through their homes and lives. Youth clubs that remained open in Coventry or Brixton, or in any area plagued by violence, were their direct descendants.

29

1997: BRISTOL'S BASEMENT

It is now commonplace for youth clubs to offer music production, through workshops or within bespoke recording studios. As we've explored, this was not always the case. Nestling within existing youth provision, the Basement in Ashley Down, Bristol, was a forerunner, creating space for musically minded teenagers in the 1990s. Local youth were able to record themselves on the mic or playing instruments, and learned how to sample old jazz, funk and soul 12-inches, using them as the basis of brand-new hip hop, house, jungle and drum 'n' bass records.

Resonant, due to similar conditions, with the Holyhead in Coventry decades earlier, it also connected members to welcoming pockets of the outside world, building energy, systems and structures that allowed a new wave of social and cultural impact to roll through the building, across the city, and out into the world. The Basement Studio's 1995 annual report has a graffiti-style logo and begins with a description. It is 'a youth music resource for marginalised young people which combines professional youth work practice with training opportunities in music, music technology, sound recording and radio production'.

This music-specialist project, up one of Bristol's many inclines, drew from culturally rich and economically deprived parts of the city, including St Paul's and Easton. A brief back-story would explain that it had started taking shape after a sustained period in which the parent club – Sefton Park Youth Centre – had become a hotspot for graffiti, breaking and music. Popular discos run by DJ Andrew 'The General' Williams and his crew, UD4, meant that the club was already connected through personnel, tunes and cultural energy to underground music venues like The Dug Out and Moon Club, which helped kickstart the careers of acts including Massive Attack. It was a node in the network, at junior level.

In the late 1980s, Sefton Park youth worker Graham Baker recognised that Andrew, his brother Ryan (later known as Mercury Prize-winning drum 'n' bass producer Roni Size) and their friends might need some redirection. He dropped a potentially teacher-ish phrase, 'Oi, what are you doing . . .', quickly followed by the youth worker equivalent, '. . . and what do you *want* to do?' The question played into the cliché at the time that teachers tell you what to do, and youth work-ers ask for your opinion.

The answer took a moment to emerge, because knowing what you want is mostly the preserve of adults, depending as it does on an awareness of what's available. 'I was asked that ques-tion,' Andrew told me, 'and I said, "I don't particularly know," not thinking we had loads of money or choice. Roni said, "How about some music stuff?" We done a bit of research, and that's how it started.' Young members went on the hunt for bits of carpet and materials to make their new space habitable, while the adults ran raffles to buy decks, a drum machine and a sampler. Volunteers helped clean, plaster and paint the base-ment and, when it opened, youthful energy flowed down the stairs and into the two sizeable rooms.

The Basement grew from these low-resource beginnings. It was to become famous, even outside of youth work. In

August 1997, at the Mercury Music Prize award ceremony, chairperson Simon Frith walked on stage to announce the results of the panel's five-hour deliberation. 'The judges would like to say, and this is speaking on behalf of all judges, that we do think that Radiohead's *OK Computer* is a classic album,' he said, to an audible intake of breath from the audience. 'But in the end we were agreed that the winner of the 1997 Mercury Music Prize is Roni Size with Reprazent for *New Forms*.'

In a post-win interview, Size announced that he was going to give the £20,000 winnings to the Basement, a decision that came as a surprise to his bandmates. 'No one saw that coming,' said his brother Andrew, who was then still on staff at the project. 'I was like, "You should have given it to me!"' He laughed. 'When that was announced, it put a highlight on us. So many people were coming through because of it. The Mercury Prize was a big thing.'

As well as a 'massive' effect on UK music, it also had impact locally. 'A lot of people have gone on to do better things because that resource was there,' said Andrew. 'You could learn how to use the equipment, but it was also a place to come, speak to the staff, who'd tell you about certain things: life, or who you need to speak to, or all those networking things.' The Basement team began running outreach packages city-wide – for example, with Avon Probation, the Trinity Community Centre and organisations dealing with youth homelessness. Gradually, other clubs raised funds for their own studios, and music production facilities began seeding the city like grass. It was a process happening nationwide, with spaces for music production appearing from the early '90s onwards in locations including Nottingham, at the Community Recording Studio (est. 1991), and, as we've already seen, at Oxford House in east London.

We're going to stay in this Ashley Down basement for just a little while longer. There were, of course, many other youth clubs in Bristol. To spend time here at the Basement isn't to suggest it was the only place, but digging into this one story in the youth club tapestry allows us to manage the material, to explore what was happening, and to try to understand how music production within youth clubs generally had such a strong effect on UK music culture, locally and nationally.

Women were at the controls of this early example of studio-based youth work from the outset. Sound engineer Gill Sargent had worked in recording studios and at events, including the long-running and free-to-enter Ashton Court Festival, Rock Against Racism and Glastonbury, and was joined by workshop organiser Mijanou Blech, under the guidance of Jane Staffieri, another musician and live-recording specialist who'd begun her own path in youth music in the aftermath of the St Paul's uprising a decade earlier.

Now, Gill lectures at music-tech school dBs. She described to me the set-up when the Basement Studio officially opened in 1991 as an independent voluntary organisation. She'd hooked together a 16-track reel-to-reel recording machine with an Atari computer and an Akai S950 sampler through a box, her DIY hack to answer a music-making need: for analogue and new digital equipment to 'talk' to each other, which existing technology couldn't affordably do. 'The kids loved it,' she said, describing the pace of work required in a room where you're translating the sounds in teenagers' heads, or from their 12-inch records, into new music. 'They'd be like,

"Do it now!"' she explained. 'Everything was very intense, so I learned to be really fast at what they wanted. Otherwise they'd get loud or over the top, and it wasn't the space for bombing around because of all the kit.' One hindrance to 'bombing around' was the impressively large 24-channel mixing desk that she'd acquired, and which immediately signalled 'studio' to new arrivals.

The Basement established a girls-only night (Gill: 'regularly gate-crashed by boys who would be quite disruptive') and worked with Traveller communities. All sorts came down, she said, not to become music masters, but to receive something unavailable elsewhere. 'What's in that "something"?' I asked her, digging back into the question that has come round so often. 'It's the small achievements. Playing a nice slow beat on the drums. Everyone got cheered, even if they were rubbish. Singing into a microphone and hearing it back. There's a pride in doing something of your own. It's a hard enough time between the ages of, say, eleven and sixteen, even if you've got a nice, safe home and support, but so many of the kids didn't have that. The teenage years, they're really formative, and these small things make a difference.'

Influential people in the surrounding neighbourhood recognised the value of what was going on, despite a recurring criticism that the project, which dealt with music of Black origin but was not based in a majority Black area, sucked up disproportionate levels of limelight and funds. However, an appreciation of what it did offer meant that issues could be resolved on a local level. Gill smiled as she recounted a specific example. 'The studio set-up I described, with the box that connected the computer to the reel-to-reel? It looked like a drum machine, and one evening someone stole it. We put out an alert to various people, saying, "Can you look out for this?" and within half an hour it was back. A taxi driver brought it up and said, "It's alright, we've sorted it. You don't steal from this project." I didn't know anyone knew about the Basement, but it had filtered out. When you see that the community respects what you're doing – that's a whole other level of love.'

It's hard to imagine now, with music-making technology in everyone's phone, how radical and rare this youth project would have been. Musician and lecturer Philip Kirby wasn't writing about youth clubs when he wrote his PhD thesis on the evolution and decline of traditional recording studios, but his work shines a light on the bigger picture. We caught up, and, without prompting, he immediately began talking about the Basement.

'With drum 'n' bass, when Roni Size started making it, in the early-to-mid-1990s, the gear is still quite expensive even though the technology was getting cheaper,' he said, explaining that digital equipment was becoming available as wealthy early adopters got bored or upgraded. 'When New Order bought their Akai S950, it was thousands of pounds. You haven't got eBay, but in the early 1990s you can start to find second-hand samplers.' A description of his own studio in the early '90s gives a sense of what was required: 'You had to spend about ten, fifteen grand to get a working set-up. You needed a mixing desk, your sequencing software, speakers and an amp, a computer, a keyboard, a sampler, some sound modules. Teenagers were unlikely to have fifteen grand available to put something together at home. If the youth centre had the gear and people to guide you on how to use it, that would have been a very attractive proposition to a teenager.'

Expert adults formed an essential part of the studio budget. Apart from the obvious aspect of being on hand to explain how things worked, a studio team brought attractive cultural cachet. Philip Kirby: 'It helps the kids take you more seriously, otherwise you're just a random punk that's telling them stuff. If you've actually done something, you've got more credibility, because kids will sniff you out super-quick if you're a fake. I mean, like much quicker than adults.'

His comment takes me back to a journalism project I ran for a group of incarcerated young people in the early 2000s, while working at *Live Magazine*. HM Prison Rochester housed eighteen- to twenty-one-year-olds, along with a flock of uniformed prison officers who looked like they were serving longer stretches than the inmates. At the same time as working as the editorial mentor at *Live*, I was writing for specialist music magazines and newspapers in the UK, had been appointed editor-at-large for *Fader* in New York, and had served on the jury of the Mercury Music Prize on four occasions. I brought copies of magazines, record company press releases and some CDs in through security, with the idea that the workshoppers could write record reviews or articles about music. One of the new releases was a comeback single from influential UK garage outfit So Solid Crew. We were a group of about eight, sat in a back room behind the prison library, just me and them. The energy levels would get a bit weird sometimes, but that's prison for you, where any new person becomes a blank screen upon which to project – and for me, as a woman in my late thirties, that meant I would simultaneously be their mum (good mum and bad mum), nan (good nan and bad nan), the girlfriend who was waiting for them, the girlfriend who'd dumped them, and all of their teachers, often in remarkably quick succession. One boy sat at the table, holding the CD, sussing me out. 'I've just got to ask,' he said, fact-checking like a pro. 'Are you really a journalist or are you a teacher pretending to be a journalist?'

By 1992, the Basement was officially award-winning, collecting prize money from the Working for Cities scheme, which was run by the Arts Council and British Gas. It was also beginning to galvanise funders: later that year, the *Bristol Evening Post* reported that it had taken a £16,720 share of the £1.6m handed out to clubs, schools, charities and voluntary bodies by the Pools Promoters Association, the pools being the form of everyday gambling that pre-dated the National Lottery. In 1994, the *Post* reported on a more pedestrian win: thirty tins of paint from Dulux in a community award scheme. Two National Arts Council awards followed, with memorable club trips to the ceremonies in Birmingham and Manchester. A 1994 survey commissioned by Avon county, Bristol and Bath councils and South West Arts found the Basement to be 'a model of good practice' offering 'tremendous expertise'. This expertise spanned different styles of music, from hip hop and jungle in the recording studio to rock in the live room. All sorts were being catered to, across the musical spectrum.

Another ahead-of-its-time Bristol youth project related to jazz, and not just because it was named Giant Steps after the John Coltrane album. Lasting three months in 1994 and described in the subsequent annual report as 'mammoth', it was run with Sefton Park, the Mill Youth Centre in Easton, the Basement, Salongo, Afrikan and Caribbean Dance and Music Resource Project, and South West Jazz. The idea was 'to generate an interest in jazz from young people', with a focus on girls and young women and those from global majority backgrounds.

Top-flight jazz musicians travelled from London to Bristol to make music with the Basement youth, with a photograph from the project showing young saxophonist Alice Perera playing alongside musician Jason Yarde, and another showing trumpeter Byron Wallen, almost out of shot. Alice attended the Basement and went on to volunteer in the studio, also running DJ workshops for young people in St Paul's. She has spent decades deep in Bristol's musical undercurrents, DJing under the name Alikat, writing and recording with influential producers Smith & Mighty, and working as a promoter and radio broadcaster. Now she works with vulnerably housed young people. Over time, she has kept and scanned thousands of flyers and has a remarkable archive of posters, recordings and typed-out rules for pirate radio DJs, along with various ephemera from the interface of Bristolian youth work and music culture. It's thanks to her careful keeping – and generously allowing me to drop round to her house one afternoon to flick through folders and read through letters – that I was able to access the Basement's annual reports and track the connections between UK jazz and youth clubs. One item she has kept is the poster for the culmination of Giant Steps: a showcase at the New Trinity Community Centre. It shows the Jazz Warriors at the top of the bill, 'their only appearance outside London this year', alongside Alice's band High Jinks, City Steppers and the self-explanatory Basement Posse.

Jazz and youth work made for a good fit. Aside from the long histories of musicians supporting the next generation at community level, Jazz Warriors' double bassist Gary Crosby had co-founded youth initiative Tomorrow's Warriors, in London, just a few years earlier. In 1996, Tomorrow's Warriors collaborated with another Bristolian organisation, Kuumba, which was based in St Paul's. It ran for six months, offering free workshops and a regular performance platform in the shape of an open jam session, which, usefully for emerging artists, would include an audience. 'The Tomorrow's Warriors' Jazz Project's overall aim is to nurture new talent and encourage a new generation of Jazz Warriors, and also to raise awareness of jazz music,' wrote Kuumba's Black Arts development officer in a letter to potential candidates. 'This promises to be a challenging and exciting project.' It would fulfil these aims, even if the results would take time.

Being involved with youth jazz projects opened doors for Alice Perera and others. Gaining funding from Kuumba to attend a three-day A&R course in London, she met top-flight managers working with Annie Lennox and Terence Trent D'Arby, as well as individuals and labels working with Bristol acts Portishead and Smith & Mighty, and doing so helped forge a pathway into a life of music in community. 'Of course, there weren't many women – just me and someone from Moles Studio in Bath. It gave me confidence and good insight, and I went on from there to work with Easton Community Centre, co-ordinating the Easton Festival line-up.'

Namechecking some of the other projects she was connected to, including Asian Arts Agency, BS5, Ashley Cabot Youth Centre, Docklands Community Centre and the Dockland Settlement, Alice reflected on the complications of telling one Bristol music story when there are so many others echoing around. 'I know you can't include everyone,' she said. 'There are hundreds of thousands of stories. It's too much for anyone to put together – the continuity of the youth services that were still relevant through the 1990s, and then carried on, in different pockets around the city. Obviously, the Basement was an important one, but there were others too.' The musical ecosystem at the time was, she said, 'totally dependent on the grassroots providing things for young people, based on peanuts funding'. It's a familiar observation, connecting so much of the work that underpins UK youth club culture.

Back in London, Tomorrow's Warriors would trenchantly advocate for grassroots music for decades, and are considered to be foundational to the wave of jazz musicians that emerged across the UK in the late 2010s. When, in a neatly circular moment, Tomorrow's Warriors alumni Ezra Collective won their own Mercury Prize in 2023, band leader Femi Koleoso made it his business to shout out youth clubs, and to celebrate 'the special people putting time and effort into young people to play music'. In this way, the Basement, and the grassroots youth projects that surrounded it in Bristol, can claim a connection to not just one Mercury Prize but two.

Mid-1990s youth projects in the south-west of England were holding tight in the face of a wholesale reorganisation of local government, whereby district councils were broken up to create new unitary authorities. This inevitably had a negative effect on youth work, not least because the service lacked, and continues to lack, meaningful statutory protection. This placed the Basement in what was described in annual reporting as 'a position of uncertainty', a phrase that conjures up sleepless nights and youth worker worry. However, in 1995, Avon Council still covered the running costs of the Basement and 50 per cent of the costs of one workshop organiser. Bristol City Council covered a series of afternoon workshops for young unemployed people and city-wide DJ workshops. South West

Arts contributed towards a project training sound engineers, while the south-west's Training and Enterprise Council, WESTEC, paid the Basement to train Black tutors. A family of interested parties were working together to try and keep things going, with the Arts Council, Bristol Safer Cities, the Calouste Gulbenkian Foundation and the Prince's Trust also on the list of funders. Having been on the ground in project-based youth work, I understand what all this would have meant on a practical level. Funding applications demand resourcefulness. Not just the labour of filling them out, but the effort required to bridge the gap between what funders want and work that is actually useful or acceptable to the kids. And, at the same time, being able to deliver broadly accurate reports – a virtuoso balancing act.

In 1996, Daddy G of Massive Attack became a patron of the Basement, describing it in the *Bristol Evening Post* as a 'real starting point for the diverse musical styles that come out of Bristol'. That summer, I saw the effects of the Basement's contribution myself. Writing for *Jockey Slut*, a magazine with a now-difficult-to-explain name that my friends had started, I spent three or four days meeting up with the DJs, producers and musicians behind Bristol's drum 'n' bass scene, almost all of whom had started out in the city's youth clubs. Roni Size told me that his Full Cycle crew were 'like Power Rangers'. In explanation, he went on: 'You've got all your individual strengths, and then when we come together we turn into that robot thing and try to take over the world.'

I don't appear to have asked about youth clubs specifically. Finding the article in a big pile of old magazines, it seems I was more interested in describing the dancefloor at their monthly club night at the Thekla, and the sonics and lineage of their music – but I did record comments relating to community and communality. '[Roni] talks about building an infrastructure in Bristol, commitment and the tightly knit nature of what they have at Full Cycle,' I wrote, before quoting him: 'This is our own small industry. It's our own thing. It's not necessarily the music, it's a lot deeper than that. Our relationship as people first and foremost is essential.' Quotes from DJ Krust follow, describing how the DJs and producers that made up the label came together from different crews around town, bringing locally distinct knowledge and influences: 'Full Cycle today is giving all of us the opportunity to recreate what we grew up on; the old school parties, the warehouse parties, the old days. What Full Cycle set out to do was to recreate some vibes.' The final word in the paragraph goes to Roni, in a line that I wish I'd dug into back then: 'Roni Size reinforces all of this when he says simply but passionately: "society is responsible".' By this, I took him to mean that local society – or, in other words, community – can and should provide spaces for the next generation's evolution.

The following year, youth clubs were considered vote-winners, at least at manifesto level. In the run-up to the 1997 general election, both the Labour Party and the Liberal Democrats committed themselves to the introduction of a statutory youth service. Once in government, Labour instead initiated a Youth Task Group. The results of their findings were not published, and an audit of the youth service was undertaken, which showed, unsurprisingly, great variation in what was being offered. The government wanted to focus on 'disaffected' or 'excluded' young people – the new 'unclubbables'.

*

I arrived in Bristol again, decades later, one hot July after-noon in 2023. The city formed part of a grassroots tour I'd self-organised around my book *Dance Your Way Home* which saw me running workshops and hosting talks with DIY venues and organisations. Jason 'Sweetpea' Ellis, from youth project the Cause, had asked me if I might be interested in taking part in one of their regular creative youth sessions, and I replied in the affirmative.

Jason and his co-founder, Jordan Davies, shared a deep back-ground in music, both having found entry points into their chosen styles of music through time spent in youth clubs, albeit at an age-generated time lag of a decade. Set up using their own money, the Cause was their attempt to plug the vast gaps that had appeared in the city's provision. They knew why it mattered first-hand.

The walls of the Full Moon and Attic Bar in Stokes Croft were covered in an ad hoc exhibition of creative community spaces in the city, made up of flyers, photographs and posters: a visual celebration of underrated spaces and cultural instigators. The event was warm and lively, and we got chatting. High levels of connectedness between people and place in the youth club story meant it wasn't a shock to hear that both Cause founders had attended Bristol youth clubs and music projects, including the Basement. What was surprising, though, was that Jason had also passed through the doors of Oxford House in Bethnal Green, where Errol Wynter ran higher-level youth club discos and drove young people to raves in the club's minibus.

'I was just a young person causing havoc,' he said, 'spraying paint on shops and vans. Excluded from school, even though I wasn't that bad. I just wanted to be heard. There was a lot of art in Oxford House, and music, DJing and MCing, and I was getting inspiration off the older people. It was a cool place to hang out, before I moved to Bristol.' He paused, remembering. 'Without being overly dramatic, youth clubs and some of the people in them changed my life. I was on a difficult path. I never thought I could do things. It was life-changing, being able to meet like-minded people that liked music and nurtured me. It was a safe place to go when life was quite difficult.' Having left London, he quickly found the Basement.

The space was also a favoured after-school spot circa 1994 for Cause co-founder Jordan, who'd play ping-pong, football and pool at the upstairs youth club, 'just catching a vibe, really', he explained. 'I did that for about a year, before I took an interest in the music side of things. Then, around '95, jungle and drum 'n' bass became popular with the kids in our school. We'd MC, we'd have tapes.' He chuckled, remembering that his interest in music started a few steps to the side of heavy basslines and razored breakbeats. 'Me and my friends had this dream of us forming a group, a boy band. Them lot were into R&B – Jodeci, Blackstreet. They'd go off singing on the benches with all the girls. And I would go into the Basement, with the mandem spitting bars.'

Success followed both tangents, with the BBC's flagship children's TV programme *Blue Peter* coming down to the Basement to film Jordan's friends, whose band Jelayju had been signed by Polydor and then, after a personnel split and renamed Triple 8, had enough success to end up on *Top of the Pops*. One member, Iain James Farquharson, went on to write songs for One Direction, Professor Green and Korean boyband TVXQ, before becoming a vocal coach on TV show *The X Factor*. Jordan himself became a prominent part of the city's grime community under his DJ name, Blazey, and in the mid-2000s set up the city's primo dubstep night, Subloaded, with influential DJ and producer Pinch.

'Throughout my whole entire life I remember being crap at football and not being good at anything in particular,' Jordan told me. 'Before, I was quite disruptive and distracted very easily. The youth club setting was good for people like myself, who'd be at school and didn't feel they were good at anything. It changed me as a person, made me feel part of something, made me feel worthwhile.' Self-confidence and the expanded horizons that Jordan is describing are, of course, important. These shifts are the bread and butter of youth clubs. They're also almost entirely invisible to any known accounting method, which perhaps says more about our methods of valuation than anything else.

Jordan's time at the Basement is on the record. A black-and-white photograph circa 1997 shows Andrew 'The General' Williams running a session in trainers and a Yankees baseball cap. There's a bank of Apple Mac monitors, shiny CDs scattered on the worktops and a line of headphones hanging from the wall, with leads collected into loops like inky spaghetti. Four boys are sat on chairs in a semi-circle, holding notepads. Second from the right is Jordan, looking, it has to be said, a bit cheeky. The image has been sent to me by current Basement youth worker Troy Tanska, a woman with enough energy to power a thousand lightbulbs.

'Jordan would have been one of the young people who taught me,' she told me, 'by turning out all the lights and jumping up and down. Me in my middle-class bubble going, "Shit! Are they safe?"' She paused, so that I understood she was play-acting her panic. 'Of course they were safe, even though they were rapping about stabbing people. That's a really important thing to understand.' Troy's experience will be familiar to those involved in youth-led music-making: of allowing access to space, and then listening, with muted concern, while young ones get stuff off their chests. The moments afterwards offer rare space for discussion. A current youth worker described a session in the Birmingham studio he works in. The kids had made a tune all by themselves, but with questionable lyrical content. 'I said to them, "Everything in this is disgusting – but I'm proud of you."' Bridges are built in this way, with tools not available to teachers or most parents. It is essential construction work, for individuals and for society, giving otherwise wobbly teenagers a chance to stabilise.

Arriving in 1999 after completing a degree in journalism, Troy had started out running community radio stations, including one managed by young people during the Glastonbury Festival. Between 2004 and 2010, she was working out of the Basement's new home at Bristol Beacon, then known as Colston Hall. The project has been at another venue, the Station, since 2012, open four nights a week for young people from every Bristol postcode and regularly working with those newly arrived in the UK. She explained to me the work she does now, which doubled up as a way of showing how youth clubs will shift and change in response to whoever is furthest out on the margins: today, this might mean working with young Kurdish MCs using Google Translate to, in Troy's words, 'process trauma and find out who they are, through music-making'.

Troy helped me understand what was going on beneath the youth club surface back in the late 1990s and into the early 2000s. 'As usual in life, there were a whole series of fairly chaotic forces at play,' she said, recapping the social, political and cultural forces that shaped the Basement at the end of the century. 'You had an explosion of opportunities based on new technology. Lots of young people who were part of the club scene, free parties and festivals were connecting through music, in spaces they'd made. Self-generated opportunities created a DIY ethos and reference point for young people. At the same time, a group of grown-up young people – youth workers – came in with this DIY ethos and were really motivated around dance music to connect with each other and develop those opportunities.' She paused to take a breath. 'It was a beautiful wave the Basement caught.'

There are, she said, shifting into the present tense, ongoing benefits to centre-based space, a familiar building that isn't home or school. 'You get a node of connection where every-one can continue to engage as a group, *while* they change. If you're lucky enough to be part of [this kind of environment or space], you get a natural framework for trusted relationships to develop, through shared experiences and over time.'

Evidence exists for those who wish to frame youth clubs in terms of combatting criminality or improving outcomes at school. Arguments for locally accessible physical space where generations of young people can hang out are easily related to notions of well-being, hope and having a stake in your locality. They're also useful on a deeper level, she explained. 'Another reason that centre-based youth work is important, and why it needs to be funded, is it gives young people and workers a real taste of what a healthy working environment is. That includes developing trust, sharing vision, winning through adversity, being flexible and critical learning.' It is a family environment, she said, emphasising 'family'.

Stable space, she added, offers support that short-term projects can't match, an important observation given the pro-liferation of projects that last only a few weeks or months.

'Some young people have all sorts of interruptions: family breakdown; being suspended from school; someone might have died.' Troy paused. 'I was really struck by that: "Oh, my uncle died. Five people in my family have died this year." I'd be like, "What?" Then you look at the National Index of Deprivation, health outcomes and infant mortality. There are lots of early deaths in disadvantaged communities. When you're working with young people who live in those areas, they're dealing with all that. A youth centre is like a heartbeat. It's just there, a held space.' Grief is a reality for many teenagers, with the Childhood Bereavement Network reporting that, each year, 46,000 children under the age of seventeen lose a parent. 'I've had young people come in, gone straight on the mic, spit a load of lyrics, and then they've sat down and said, "My mum died today in hospital. I've come straight here."'

We finished up our conversation with a final reflection. 'Music, particularly in the youth centre, is amazing,' said Troy, before she whizzed off to run another workshop. 'When young people can't verbalise, because they're so hurt, they can hit a drum or grab a mic. I've had young people who can't even say hello to me on the way in head straight to the studio, and then they'll come and have a cup of tea, a hot chocolate or a cheese toastie and tell me what's going on.' Teenage life is full of extremity, if only because of the shock of encountering the adult world or the challenges of making adult decisions for the very first time. In this context the youth club can be seen as a kind of antechamber, from which a young person can emerge into the adult world.

Received wisdom is that everything must be scalable or it's not worth doing. Growth only counts when it's profit-generating or visibly extending outwards. To offer a natural metaphor, growth also happens downwards, stabilising plant life and nourishing the roots. The Basement existed because of needs identified by young people and actioned by adults whose access to systems and structures could protect the project from the very same systems and structures where necessary. For over three decades the Basement has made days, weeks and months more enjoyable and healthier for the people who've passed through, with consequent improvements for them and everyone they have met. And, of course, there's the music too.

In October 1998, the *Bristol Evening Post* celebrated the Basement in its leader comment. The article explained that the youth project had 'helped launch [Size's] career' and noted that the money he'd promised after the Mercury Music Prize had come through. 'He's kept his pledge, proving that despite his success he's not forgotten where he started or who helped him.' A feature, the following day, was headlined 'Banging the Drum for Bristol'. It retold the basics: that Roni Size and Reprazent vocalist Onallee had started out at the city-council-funded project. Adding a new line, the writer explained that the money would be used to make a compilation album to showcase the musicians who'd used the studio over the previous decade, mixed by more established Bristol artists. Quoting Roni Size, the article located the youth club squarely within the ecosystem needed to support new music: 'The only place in Bristol which is set up to help musicians is the Basement Studio . . . Bristol has got a buzz about it, and we need to sustain that. We've got to get the new artists through.'

The donation, and the popularity of drum 'n' bass, brought wider awareness. New difficulties arrived with the spotlight, with thirty or forty teenagers from all over the city regularly turning up to a locality youth club aimed at disadvantaged youth, itself a phrase that does a lot of heavy lifting. Issues of territory and ownership can be amplified for individuals for whom space and money is tight, and all of this needed to be worked through. Another adult was needed, and the local authority was able to provide a youth worker, a simple act that in today's environment seems like it's come from another planet. Overall, though, the Basement was simply the highest-profile example of something occurring nationally.

There are significant youth work histories in UK music and culture, particularly those that relate to global majority creative expression. Think, for example, of the youth clubs across the UK that hosted reggae sound systems in the 1970s, or the widespread practice in the '80s of using the space as a practice pen for hip hop, dance, DJing or MCing. The youth club disco has been replaced by studios, adding to the discography of UK music.

30

2000: A NEW WAVE OF YOUTH MUSIC

By the end of the 1990s, hundreds of music projects had emerged at a local level. A major survey, *Mapping Hidden Talent: Investigating Youth Music Projects*, was published by Youth Work Press in 1999. The introduction was written by Jools Holland, who described the book as the 'first attempt to pin down youth music projects: where they are, what they are trying to do – and what they want to achieve'.

Authors Richard Ings, Ruth Jones and Nick Randell had recognised a broader cultural moment. UK music was thriving, with 'proliferating' genres and styles including rap, trip hop, speed garage, swingbeat, indie, ragga, easy listening and thrash metal. 'Our newly-minted Albion is visible and definitely audible,' they wrote, noting that many music projects were based in youth clubs. Excluding commercial and formal groups with higher levels of adult intervention – for example, youth choirs, brass bands and orchestras – the trio, who were also youth workers, focused on places where fourteen- to twenty-five-year-olds could access music-based opportunities, participate on an informal basis, and 'interact with their peers in a supportive environment'.

Desk research and publicity led to over a thousand projects, including the Basement, being contacted by post. A third replied and were sent questionnaires. Of these, 198 sent back their answers. I recognise the non-repliers, meaning to fill in the paperwork but instead being consumed by the streams of kids coming through the doors and everyone wanting a 'quick word', all the time. Luckily, some youth workers were well organised, and their responses allow us to get a sense of how things were.

Three quarters of the projects making up the data set had only been around since the start of the 1990s, and half were founded in the previous four years. Most were building-based, with rehearsal space and equipment, although funding deficits meant that space wasn't often accessible to those with disabilities. Half offered at least some free activities and many charged only nominal rates, the equivalent of a couple of quid. Around a third were local-authority-funded, with the rest split between charities and independent organisations, plus a few co-operatives or limited companies.

Midi Music in Deptford, south-east London, was included, established in 1995 by Wozzy Brewster (now OBE), who is quoted in the report: 'The main problem with youth music, music technology and multi-media is that young people don't have access to it if they come from a deprived background,' she said. With 40 per cent of users being female, Midi Music had a better gender parity than average. Girls were outnumbered in 88 per cent of the projects surveyed. As so often in this story, youth work became boys' work by default unless significant effort was put in to divert the gravitational pull of patriarchy.

Characterised, wrote the authors, by a lack of profile, limited networking and little research, the youth music sector was 'driven by demand and fuelled by enthusiasm and creativity'. Their conclusion was simple and understated, one that applies at any point in time, from clubs for factory girls onwards: the youth clubs and music projects they outlined contained 'many remarkable success stories', but had 'fragile infrastructure' requiring sensitive funding and support.

Case studies brought the facts to life: Access to Music in Leicester had 500 weekly users, while Bandwagon Studios in Mansfield took place in a 'big old mansion owned by the council' and countered the gender-skewed world of youth music with a Women and Music project. Bass Connection in Salisbury, open six days a week, with free membership, won funding from the Prince's Trust for their new DJ-based offering.

Belfast's Youth and Community Group had been set up a decade earlier, making it one of the earliest music projects featured in the research, and was run by fifteen volunteers across three floors of a city-centre building; open seven days a week, with 440 users a week, it included a relatively high percentage of girls. Lack of money was putting the project at serious risk, as were intrusive new demands from funders. Requests to ascertain and record the socio-economic background of club users were problematic everywhere, but were significantly so in Northern Ireland, where such questions needed to be carefully set aside at the front door. Belfast youth worker Petesy Burns was understandably scathing about the infiltration of bureaucracy into his hard-won space. 'We don't "evaluate",' he said, fury levitating off the page in the shape of verbal quotation marks. 'There is never a problem with the creative energy of young people. It is always there and always will be. As long as we can nurture and channel that energy there will be hope of a better future for everyone.'

In the year *Mapping Hidden Talent* was published, a new central organisation was launched. Youth Music, still in operation at the time of writing, would distribute National Lottery money to youth music projects nationwide. New sounds created in basement studios and locally funded spaces were reverberating, nationally. And while some alumni became success stories, the need for youth provision remained – and remains – essentially about creating a safe, useful and enjoyable place for young people to be, regardless of celebrity outcomes.

To appreciate the role and function of youth clubs as Northern Ireland embraced a fragile peace after the British and Irish governments signed the Good Friday Agreement in 1998, we'll need to understand that peace wasn't a given. It's time to return to the history. Our first route in comes through a thirty-page publication, *Your Process or Mine?*, which was available for sale on the Visit Derry website, alongside mugs featuring characters and classic lines from TV show *Derry Girls*, and Christmas cards where characters from British cop drama *Line of Duty* double up as Jesus, Mary and Joseph.

Made and published by four youth clubs in the city nearly two decades after the Good Friday Agreement, it provided a handy way to explain the background, in terms of both what it says and how it says it. Unlike most publications, it is not designed in a linear fashion with a front cover, a back cover and content in between. It has two front covers and contains two versions of events: one that takes up the first half of the book, with the other story printed upside down – until you flip it and start again. One cover has images of a large Unionist protest and a north Belfast Ulster Volunteer Force (UVF) mural containing three variations on the Red Hand of Ulster and the slogan 'Prepared for peace, ready for war'. It is subtitled, unsurprisingly, 'The Loyalist Story of the Peace Process'. The cover of the other swaps out one word, replacing it with 'Republican', depicting a protest against Orange Order marches and a photograph from the 1980s that crams in two murals (including the famous 'You Are Now Entering Free Derry'), a rendering of a road sign that places the letters 'RUC' within a no-entry sign, and a statement painted in blocky capitals on the end of a garage. It reads: 'War or peace? Britain has the choice!'

Author and youth worker Mickey Cooper wrote the foreword, which is reprinted identically at each version's beginning. It outlines the prehistory of peace, strands of which existed throughout the Troubles, and explains the role of youth clubs from different parts of the city in making the publication. Young people met and interviewed people directly involved in the peace process, including ex-prisoners, who told their stories and offered fact-checking for accuracy.

Your Process or Mine? takes the reader up to and beyond this point, describing decommissioning, paramilitary feuds and other forms of violence, and the complex stop–start of political power-sharing at the new Stormont Assembly. The Good Friday Agreement was the beginning of the end; a semi-colon, not a full-stop. The halting back and forth of cessation embedded itself into childhood for the under-fifteens, who comprised 41 per cent of the population, the youngest age structure in the UK. Intergenerational trauma would percolate through people's lives and into the next generation, aided by segregation. The 2001 census showed that two thirds of the population still lived in areas that were at least 90 per cent Catholic or 90 per cent Protestant. In an example of the built environment as loudspeaker, walls in interface areas continued to be built and made higher after the Good Friday Agreement was signed.

In Westminster, the Labour government decided not to bolster the remaining network of youth clubs, or the youth workers who welcomed teenagers through the doors and, as we've seen repeatedly, allowed them space to grow and evolve on their own terms and at their own pace. Instead, Labour created a new service, Connexions, which ran between 2001 and 2012. It was to offer careers advice, guidance and support for thirteen- to nineteen-year-olds, with a focus on sixteen- to eighteen-year-olds who weren't in school, didn't have a job or weren't on a training scheme. Personal advisors were created, with a remit to remedy the above in a service that prioritised measurable outcomes, information-gathering and activities that led to accreditation – although not necessarily qualifications recognised by employers or universities as equal to GCSEs.

I interacted with Connexions through the young people I worked with in 2000s south London. Unlike youth clubs, where there would be snacks, freeform hanging out and music, or even youth projects like our magazine office, young people were expected to attend meetings in an environment more like the dole office, with lurid purple branding. I remember Connexions as offering a very basic version of school careers guidance, with little else to recommend it. Even the Conservative Party agreed, said Mark K. Smith, in his Infed. org exploration of the service, with the shadow education secretary arguing that the government was 'driving young people away' from youth provision by making them focus on learning outcomes. In Northern Ireland, the effects were amplified.

Kwame Daniels has spent his life at the overlap between nightclubs and youth clubs. He's a DJ, promoter and the founder of creative not-for-profit Bounce Culture, who left east London after completing a degree in history to study music production in Northern Ireland. He arrived at the Nerve Centre in Derry in 1997, in the autumn before the Good Friday Agreement was signed. By summer 1999, his studies had become practical, and he started a popular club night, Bounce, playing funk, hip hop, R&B, soul and jazz at Sandinos Café Bar on Water Street.

While he hadn't yet brought together the adjacent worlds of club culture and youth work, his adopted city had: in the mid-1990s, the YMCA in Waterside developed a youth work scheme in a disused sports pavilion aimed specifically at marginalised young people. Hard and fast house and techno sounds known as hardcore were having an extended moment in Northern Ireland, with international superstar and Radio 1 DJ Fergie and clubs like Kelly's in Portrush or the Met Arena in Armagh attracting bus-loads of ravers week in, week out. A core group of young people on the YMCA scheme did something remarkable: supported by youth workers and the management committee, the newly named Garage Krew organised and ran a series of raves, running the door and clearing up afterwards. In August 1996, almost 600 young people attended one of their Infinity raves, including Kwame's future wife, Donna.

The groundwork for youth work that revolved around dance music had been done by young people, with the support of inventive youth workers and brave committee members who did the counter-intuitive thing of allowing moral-panic material on the premises. It worked. So when staff at Derry's Nerve Centre were developing a rural outreach programme for youth clubs in the early 2000s, it made sense to incorporate DJing and dance music into their offering, which was otherwise based around live music and multimedia. Kwame was a good choice to deliver this aspect of the programme: he was a well-known DJ and was already working for them. Stacking six Technics 1210s and mixers into his Ford Fiesta, he began delivering DJ workshops to whoever had showed up at youth club that night.

We caught up one evening online, each on either side of the Irish Sea. 'Being born in London, I knew that whole DIY ethos,' he said, describing the knowledge that underpinned his own love of music and community. 'You're too young to get into the clubs, so you start it yourselves, doing parties with mates or in the youth club, and that's how you start your thing.' Growing up in east London, he went to a youth club in Forest Gate, where he played five-a-side football with his multicultural primary-school mates; then, in his early teens, he attended the Lubavitch in Gants Hill, which was open to young people regardless of faith background.

By the time he was making the generationally familiar transition between the youth club and nightclubs, there were dance-offs to the tuff soul sounds of new jack swing, a popular early-'90s music style that emerged across the US and the UK. I asked him, what did he bring with him to Northern Ireland from his London youth clubs? 'I think it was just that sense of a space to socialise and understanding the importance of the space to the young people we were working with. Also, knowing the environment [in Northern Ireland], all the other stuff that was going on, and what we were trying to steer the youth away from . . . I knew it was important, simple as that.'

By the very early 2000s, Kwame was taking his car-load of Technics turntables across the border to Buncrana and Letterkenny in Donegal, or even down to Sligo. Other times it'd be Belfast way, or down the Glens of Antrim towards Cushendall. 'The mileage was madness,' he said. 'I was flat out, five days a week in the car.' He paused to call up memories of these early missions. 'I'm 6' 3" with dreads down to here,' he said, indicating past shoulder length, 'and carrying all this equipment. Pretty much everywhere, I was absolutely the first Black person they'd ever, ever met in person, possibly seen. That in itself is a very vivid memory and handling that took me a few years. Ten or twelve young people looking at you, the elbows and whispers and the sibilance of "*Jesus*". Coming from London, where essentially no one gives an arse, to being here and being very, very visible . . .' He paused, because the memory was causing him to remember the feelings. 'My stomach's doing a mile a minute!' he said, before continuing. 'I had to be able to go, "Okay, I'm setting up equipment, and we're going to engage in music." Once I'd set up, I'd find out what they were into, and we'd connect. It went from it being about a guy with dreads to being about tunes, and the next minute they're up on the tables, dancing.'

Gradually, Kwame grew out of Nerve Centre's programme and into his own, which he named Bounce Culture. Working closely with youth clubs and other community groups, he was using music and creativity to bring some light, freedom or just ten minutes of good times into people's lives. The experience of being in and out of youth clubs throughout the early 2000s gave him overview and perspective. He described committed youth workers engaged in a sometimes thankless task. 'They cared so much,' he told me. 'They were from the community they were in. Regardless of what side of the water you came from, people cared. They were probably born two streets down. They knew the other generation. There was a really deep love and care of the space and what it was doing, and the path the young people were on. It was their turf.' What he was saying, I think, was that the supportive bonds that can develop between young people and youth workers are amplified in locations that experience disproportionate levels of violence, a message that is useful on both sides of the Irish Sea.

While youth clubs were safe spaces that offered alternatives, they weren't magic. There were limits to what could be achieved. 'It wasn't always successful,' he said. 'There's youth clubs I was working with that were amazing, but you knew how precarious it was. There was still a fair bit of rioting going on. I remember walking through the Bogside, and even though they've got scarves wrapped round their heads, I know them. I see the eyes of two or three of them, and we stop and chat. They've been swept off in this wave and off they go. It's all kicking off and I'm walking through. They know me and I know them. That was the importance of the space – a way out of all the other madness by deep diving into music or other creative technology.'

As Kwame is talking, two strong memories of my own come up. One is of seeing a young woman I knew from *Live Magazine*. Let's call her Ameera. She worked on some of our photostories and was a regular in the office for a while, only taking off the niqab that covered her face when there were no boys in the room. One day I saw her down Brixton High Street and recognised her immediately, even though she was wearing a full body and face covering – a moment that taught me that you don't need to see someone's facial features to recognise them. The second memory that bubbled up during our conversation was of another young woman who'd become involved with *Live Magazine* in her mid-teens. Let's call her Renée. One of the other contributors had gone off to interview someone for a story about exiting gang culture, and we got talking. 'Thing is, you *can* leave a gang, you just have to leave strong,' she said, disabusing the generally held belief that gang membership was for life.

It struck me at the time that working on a magazine run by young people, where you got to interview artists who were street-famous in the morning and interview-them-in-a-hotel famous in the afternoon, probably counted as strong. Listening to Kwame, I had a similar feeling. For young people in Northern Ireland caught between paramilitaries and poverty, learning how to DJ with trusted youth workers might also have been considered strong, reason enough to swerve the magnetising power of quick money and street-level authority, and to give those holding the magnets reason to let you be.

EU aid flowed into the country in the run-up to the Good Friday Agreement and continued afterwards. In 1994, the European Commission had established a special task force to offer practical assistance to Northern Ireland and the six border counties of Ireland as an 'expression of the European Union's commitment to the peace and reconciliation process'. The following year, the initiative was formally established under the name PEACE 1, with a budget to match the ambition. Over five years, between 1994 and 1999, EU structural funds and national contributions came to €667m, with the intention, as described in the official PEACE overview, of reaching 'communities at the coalface of the Troubles'. This meant making funds directly accessible to groups on the ground, assisting over 15,000 projects, according to the PEACE 1 evaluation (2003). PEACE II followed, investing €995m over six years. Within the UK, the National Lottery New Opportunities Fund had provided grants worth £60.7m by 1999, and, of course, the Department of Education in Westminster had its own budget too. Problems were plentiful, but money wasn't one of them. Although, once again, cash did not flow freely into dedicated physical space for young people.

Sam McCready and Richard Loudon's phenomenal *Investing in Lives: The History of the Youth Service (1973–2017), Volume 2* was the follow-up to their first expansive history. 'Despite the paramilitary ceasefires, the Good Friday Agreement and weapon decommissioning,' they wrote, 'there was still a substantial legacy of the years of Troubles for young people.' Youth clubs were more necessary than ever, but more boys than girls were attending, they wrote, and girls were dropping off from the age of thirteen.

Their book contains an overview of youth provision in the year the Good Friday Agreement was signed. In 1998, there were 3,000 youth groups and over 1.8 million young people involved, with 122 full-time youth workers and forty-nine youth tutors, and another 2,793 youth workers in training. Another report, by the Youth Policy Review Group in the same year, noted 17,000 volunteers working in registered groups, with a further 12,000 in the statutory sector, representing a contribution worth £89m overall.

Once again, it's necessary to reckon with unpleasant realities, and I do so knowing the risk of flattening human experience into trauma stats. Violence was turning inwards, powered increasingly by drugs trafficking. A House of Commons report by Professor Liam Kennedy from 2001 speaks to the ways this impacted people who were young at the time. Titled *They Shoot Children Don't They?*, it undoes the legitimising language of 'punishment beatings', a phrase that shrugs off blame by suggesting that victims had done something wrong. Raw data tells only part of the story: paramilitaries of all persuasions shot 167 children under eighteen years old and assaulted 344 in the same age group between 1990 and 2013. It should also go without saying that not every bullet or beating would have shown up in the official figures.

While most of the individuals who comprise these statistics would have been boys or young men, they had sisters, girlfriends, mothers and aunties who undoubtedly picked up adjacent damage, fear and trauma. This sharp end of Troubles-related violence particularly affected young people from lower-income families. Notably, given all of the above, the percentage of pupils leaving school with five or more GCSEs was higher in Northern Ireland than in England and Wales.

Structures and spaces began orienting themselves around the needs of young men, even as they recognised the ways this further marginalised those gendered as female. Boys and men were seen as central to the violence, and therefore the peace, and they were more likely to be experiencing street-level political brutality than girls, whose experience of violence often tends towards the domestic – and not just in Northern Ireland.

YouthAction NI commissioned reports on male mental health, and academics including Sam McCready and Ken Harland began telling influential evidence-based stories about masculinity and how gender played out for adolescent boys across the country. By the early 2000s, the youth service was exploring how to shape itself accordingly, and in 2004 the Centre for Young Men's Studies at the University of Ulster was established. Set up by youth worker academics, it was designed to promote the voices, needs and interests of boys and young men through research that would then inform youth work practice, training and policy. Even outside of paramilitary or post-conflict violence, this was increasingly a matter of life and death. Suicide rates increased during the late 1990s and early 2000s, and by 2009 suicide rates for fifteen- to twenty-four-year-old males was 60 per cent higher than the UK average.

Running a youth service was complicated enough, given the circumstances. Doing so without a functioning government added yet further difficulty. The Good Friday Agreement legislated for Stormont, or the Northern Ireland Assembly, in east Belfast. Historically opposed political parties would theoretically make and scrutinise laws together, through a process known as 'power-sharing', now that direct rule from Westminster had finally ended.

The Assembly was regularly suspended in what the *Belfast Telegraph* described as 'an all-too familiar feature in the years after the Good Friday peace agreement'. Unionist parties required additional progress on the decommissioning of IRA weapons before participating in government alongside Republican party Sinn Féin, which led to devolution being mothballed for four months in 2000, and twice, in two twenty-four-hour suspensions, in 2001. Power-sharing was reinstated briefly, until October 2002, when Sinn Féin's offices were raided over allegations of an IRA intelligence-gathering ring operating from within Stormont. Three men were arrested, charges against whom were dropped within weeks. This proved a major political crisis, with the Ulster Unionist Party refusing to share power with Sinn Féin. London-based ministers would control affairs in Northern Ireland for the next five years, until 2007, when devolution was restored again.

With government business suspended, workarounds had to be found. One already existed, where youth clubs could be run through existing Education and Library Boards. They operated like subject-specific local authorities and dated back to previous eras of direct rule from Westminster. The ELBs had been given the designation 'community enablers' by the British government, and they ran provision alongside voluntary projects and clubs.

As conflict turned towards peace, international and UK-based charities and their staff had started arriving in Northern Ireland in greater numbers. Often, these offered projects that sat outside of the traditional youth club format – for example, Headliners, who used journalism as a way to engage young people and help them tell their stories.

Savvy outreach workers from one of the new youth organisations looking for clientele would have found them by tuning in to and following the basslines and breakbeats. From the early '90s onwards young citizens from low-income, high-peril neighbourhoods in all parts of the city had been filling Belfast's Ulster Hall or Maysfield Leisure Centre for the infamous Hellraiser raves. Belfast's streets might have been heavily policed but age limits weren't, and spending a little time in this pocket of youth culture will help us understand how subsequent projects honed in on dance music.

All of the above is painted with great clarity in the documentary *Dancing on Narrow Ground*. Directed by film-maker and academic Des Bell in 1995, it attempted to bring together two groups of dedicated ravers, drawing from two areas which had become highly segregated: Lenadoon in west Belfast and Orangefields Park in the east of the city. Footage shows buses packed with ravers on their way to Kelly's in Portrush, queuing up, having it large on the dancefloor and then exiting, wide-eyed, once the lights came up.

The credits for *Dancing on Narrow Ground* include the Glen Parent Youth and Community Centre, which had been set up in Lenadoon as a response to anti-social behaviour and solvent abuse. Des already had strong youth club contacts in some parts of the city from his time writing his book *Acts of Union* and making films exploring Loyalist youth culture, as well as lecturing on youth work courses, but there were limits to his access. 'It [the youth club] provides an initial point of contact between the film-maker, who has a fair degree of cultural familiarity – not parachuting in from outside Northern Ireland,' he told me. 'But at the same time, meeting particular kids, on their premises, where they felt very safe, and where they could see what we were doing, ask questions . . . You're always conscious that many of these young people had lost friends and family who'd been shot by the army or in sectarian attacks. Questions of confidence-building and trust were absolutely primary to being able to do any work at all.'

The youth clubs were particularly useful in majority Catholic west Belfast, he explained, 'where the kids were very reluctant to engage with film-makers, for a variety of reasons'. One youth worker, Marie, had helped Des find interviewees for his film, and she features briefly in the documentary, sat in the youth club minibus offering an overview on behalf of the kids. They haven't turned up for the planned rendezvous with the film-makers because it's the start of the marching season, which means there are concerns about increased levels of violence.

Interviewees uniformly describe raving as one of the few reliably good things in their lives. Youth workers at the time will no doubt have recognised the allure of club culture, but will also have been aware of the limits of what the youth club could legitimately offer. 'In the late '90s and early 2000s, some youth projects really took dance music on board,' I told Des, 'but it tended to be in informal settings, outside of education board provision. Would that have been because of the conflation of raves and drug culture?'

'I think that was the core of it really,' he replied. 'There was a recognition that rave culture did offer an umbrella for cross-sectarian mixing, which everybody thought was a good idea – but everyone knew perfectly well that a lot of this was done under the influence of E. Youth workers had to be very careful, not seen to be condoning illegal behaviours or turning a blind eye. They had their own ways of dealing with it and communicating to the kids what was acceptable in the club and what wasn't.'

The dancefloor, within and outside of the youth club, could only do so much. Des's voiceover for his now-cult film shared a careful adult perspective: 'Although the peace process had begun and the young of Ulster might dance together, scars caused by violence and mistrust would take a long, long time to heal.' His observations weren't heard by many viewers because the documentary was never broadcast on television. Des had previously made films for Channel 4, and had been encouraged to develop *Dancing on Narrow Ground* by his commissioning editor, who then left. Scrabbling together a small budget from the Community Relations Unit, which supported cross-community activity, he made the film on a shoestring, ran screenings for the participants and showed it at festivals. Until 2021, it quite literally sat on a shelf, at which point editor friend Connor Clements suggested posting it on YouTube. 'In no time at all it had 10,000 hits,' said Des. '*Vice* magazine took it up, and then people were asking me to screen it all over Europe.' He went to see the band Kneecap at Ulster Hall recently, not least because the band sampled *Dancing on Narrow*

Ground on their album *Fine Art*. 'It was very strange,' he said, with humour radiating through his voice, 'hearing my own voice booming out of Ulster Hall, with a band playing and kids jumping up and down. It's taken on a new life, completely.'

The conversation slipped back to youth clubs. It's important, he said, to connect the discussion to the political economy. 'They've been squeezed by austerity and marginalised, and the price that will actually be paid – that *is* being paid – is social disruption. Youth clubs, together with schools, are key institutions. Schools are protected because they're statutory, but youth clubs don't have that, so they've suffered.' He cited the importance of drama workshops and creative youth clubs, and their role in 'dealing with things culturally'. Their loss in Northern Ireland, he said, with the tonal version of a full stop, 'is an absolute disaster'.

I'd been chatting with a man named Cathal at a house party when I was in Cushendall, staying in the Curfew Tower. Now a boat builder and painter, he'd grown up raving at Kelly's in Portrush. His fellow ravers would often be wearing white gloves, he said, which was not a particularly surprising detail; images of raves across the UK would show the same thing. At Kelly's, he told me, some ravers would fill their gloves with a decongestant, typically Vicks, because the eucalyptus fumes were supposed to improve the quality of your Ecstasy rush. They'd then go up to fellow dancers and offer them the chance to take a sniff, he said, describing a friendly dancefloor act, similar to offering someone a swig from your water bottle. The image returned when watching a YouTube conversation between famous DJ Fergie and his brother, Ken, who is also a DJ. They were talking about their early teenage years, about going to youth club, including St Anthony's in Craigyhill, and another at the First Larne Presbyterian Church – the cultural affiliation of each being suggested by their names – and being part of marching drum bands. The uniform required by the latter included white gloves, a detail that caused me to real-ise with a jolt that elements from different parts of young people's lives leaked into nightclubs in ways that were occa-sionally emblematic.

Together, raves and youth clubs formed part of a street-level fabric. Woven together, they made it possible to realise aspects of peace that were available, particularly once politicians and political leaders began pulling roughly in the same direction. And so, in one more detour around the overlaps between the nightclub and the youth club, let's meet Dr Maria-Adriana Deiana. She is a scholar of international relations who has brought her experiences as a raver and club-goer into her academic work. Sardinian-born, she attended youth club in Italy and has lived in Northern Ireland since arriving as an Erasmus student in the early 2000s. Now based at Queen's University, Belfast, she published a paper in *Critical Military Studies* that described dancing in Northern Ireland and Bosnia as an 'everyday, embodied and multi-sensorial register of war'.

I first came across Maria's work when we met in Belfast record shop Sound Advice. I was doing a workshop on docu-menting Northern Irish club culture, and, a few months later, we caught up to chat. She began by telling me about the UN's Youth, Peace and Security agenda, which emerged in 2015, and which acknowledges the centrality of youth in ensuring inter-national stability. I asked about a line in her work, 'Dance as a Register of War', where she writes that dance music culture offers a significant space where 'peace and togetherness could at least be imagined'. 'Could the same be true of the youth club?' I asked.

She paused, perhaps aware that her academic profession requires caution when extrapolating. 'I think this could extend to youth clubs,' she said carefully, recalling raver friends who'd grown up in Larne and who'd talk about attending youth clubs that were some distance from their allotted place on the orange–green continuum. 'I can see the parallels. We probably wouldn't have had peace if it wasn't for all the connections and grassroots work that happened many years before the peace talks were even possible.' To paraphrase her work about dance-floors, youth clubs allowed people to feel and even resist the normalisation of war. Peace and togetherness could, in these spaces, be imagined. In this way, the youth club was – and remains – a space for negotiation.

There's another phrase in Maria-Adriana's work, 'easily discarded knowledge', that resonates with me. It describes the ways that material relating to ordinary life can be easily dismissed, something that 1940s youth worker Josephine Macalister Brew understood when she described fish and chips as culture. I broadly understand the dynamics but I wanted to get under the bonnet, and Maria-Adriana was the perfect person to ask. 'Why are the powerful effects of youth clubs so easily discarded and so invisible?' I enquired.

'It's to do with the narrative we want to hold about communities at the sharp end of conflict or violence or austerity,' she said. 'On the one hand there's a tendency to think of people as problems – of security, employment, of anti-social behaviour. The more benign approach is also damage-centred: to see people as someone we can help, to teach them how to be better youth workers or better women activists. The complexity gets squashed and the full humanity of people and communities gets completely missed. There is a lot of work now in feminist circles and in decolonial scholarship – why the everyday matters, why the full personhood matters whenever we're dealing with violence. People aren't just victims or problems of security.' Maria-Adriana's observation is relevant, I think, far outside the North of Ireland: on English housing estates and in the Welsh valleys; in low-income coastal towns and other places too.

Finishing up, she told me about a recent TV segment that showed a new music studio for young people in east Belfast, in which local kids were making hip hop tunes. 'One of the young people said they're doing it because they grew up learning about club culture and how important it was to their parents. They want to create something similar now. There's an intergenerational lineage that builds on from the punk legacy to club culture, not only through venues, but the sharing of knowledge and the sharing of equipment.' More was being shared between youth workers, DJs, clubbers and club members than perhaps was obvious at the time.

31

2002: YOUTH DJ SESSIONS, BELFAST AND BEYOND

A ferry appeared to be parked outside the Olderfleet Bar and Restaurant in Larne. Inside, people were gathering for one of DJ Fergie's reunion parties. One of the first superstar DJs, the Larne local had flown over from the US, where he holds down three residencies, including one at the opulent Hakkasan Las Vegas. As discussed on his YouTube channel, Fergie and his brother Ken had attended a range of youth clubs in their town and had started DJing young, after seeing Carl Cox at a Belfast Hellraiser event. By the age of fourteen, Fergie had been taken under the wing of another famous DJ, Tony De Vit, and was travelling the world. Between 2001 and 2006, he held down a flagship BBC Radio 1 dance show, and since then has regularly been voted onto *DJ Magazine*'s annual list of the Top 100 DJs.

Between 2002 and 2007, Fergie's mum, Alice Ferguson, and her friends ran youth project KeyMix, which organised itself around the massive popularity of dance music at the time. Fergie and his friends mucked in, bringing heavyweight kudos to proceedings. 'It seems more remarkable now,' he said, across a table in the Olderfleet's bar area, as we pieced together this story of ultra-grassroots DIY youth work. 'How many fucking years is it? A lot of my posts on Facebook or Instagram, it's a constant topic – people talking about KeyMix or talking about my mum. I knew it was a big deal and I knew it was important, because there was nothing like it, but as time's gone on, it's built up this legendary status. They all talk about it, and that's amazing for me.'

Also sat around the table with us was DJ and promoter Mark Dobbin, who caught the era of Blue Lamp Discos run by the RUC. 'In my younger days, youth clubs were a very big event for the kids all over,' said Mark. 'It kind of faded out, and then Alice came up with the idea of KeyMix, which was going down the road of cross-community, bringing the two sides of the community together, back into a youth club scene. It was the music. Young kids are into music, and especially dance music.' His understanding was that KeyMix existed to keep the kids off the street and give them something to do, especially those that didn't do sport. 'It worked,' he said. 'We went into some areas you probably wouldn't have wanted to go to, but whenever we arrived the kids just couldn't wait to get on the decks.'

KeyMix wasn't a youth club in the statutory sense, but it fits into my definition: a space where young people could engage with something they were heavily into without being graded on it, run by welcoming adults who made things possible. 'You have to look at KeyMix as really, really basic,' said Fergie, referencing a cultural tendency in Northern Ireland not to shout about your talents and to downplay your achievements. 'People didn't know about industry talk or putting themselves across. If you said "network" to them, they'd have thought it was a fucking club in Belfast.' As well as offering possibilities for talented individuals who'd otherwise lack industry connections, KeyMix attendees learned how to meet people and talk to them through the lens of their shared interests.

Youth work is often intergenerational, not least because those with youth-worker-type parents are likely to be familiar with communal life outside of work and family. Alice Ferguson grew up in a mill worker's house in Belfast, on the kind of street where everyone knew everyone. An only child, her dad worked in the shipyard, while her mum worked at the York Street Linen Mill. On the Monday after leaving school, aged fifteen, she started work at a shirt factory. In a move that applied a tiny bit of wriggle room to otherwise fixed and binary identities, Alice also joined the Salvation Army. 'I loved their approach,' she told me, when we first started talking, the spring before I went to Larne. 'It wasn't the very tight, structured, religious church that we have here, as you know. The Salvation Army seemed to be a mode or a model of Christianity, if you like, with its sleeves rolled up. We were always out there, in the thing, and that appealed to me.'

Fast-forward to the mid-1990s, and Alice was running a literacy programme for sixteen-year-old school-leavers in Belfast. 'They were great kids, but they didn't have any real skills in the area of reading and writing. They needed a bit of help,' she said, 'which they weren't interested in. They'd just got out of school. Freedom!' And, of course, there was the local context at the time. 'Some of those young lads, they'd go for a job interview and they'd be asked, "Do you have any hobbies?" And they'd say, "Ah sure, I was down at the corner on Friday night, throwing bricks at the peelers."' Another time she asked them to make a health-and-safety poster for an imaginary workplace, and they included info about safe usage of Molotov cocktails ('You know, the things you throw at the police'), including a pair of gloves and a ski mask. 'This was health and safety, telling us what to be careful of. I just had to say, "That's a very, very good poster, it's just not the content we're after."'

One day she made an offhand comment about the DJ Carl Cox, whom she knew through her DJ sons. The kids couldn't believe that she knew one of the biggest names in dance music, and their response gave Alice an idea. 'Within that moment of music,' she realised, 'I had some influence. I said, "You're going to be the promoter for a DJ event," and I incorporated their English and maths into this music focus.' She brought in catalogues full of DJ gear and incorporated literacy and numeracy into the task of organising a club night. Phoning up local record shops, recording studios and nightclubs, she wangled work placements for some of the young people. 'Back in the day, everybody wanted to be a DJ,' she said. 'I found the carrot, 100 per cent.'

Life took a few twists and turns and, after caring for her parents, Alice set up a company with her husband Bobby and friends Maeve Ferguson and Lesley Reilly, working in youth clubs and on youth employment projects. The idea for a series of DJ workshops solidified and, in 2002, the friends booked a room under the name KeyMix at the Brownlow community centre in Craigavon, just south of Belfast in County Armagh. In a replication of the previous generation's resourceful approach, Alice, Lesley and Maeve begged and borrowed six sets of DJ turntables and mixers, then Bobby set them up on pasting tables and crates, ready to be used by early-stage DJs who'd be supported by high-profile mentors including Fergie, if he wasn't in Ibiza or LA, and a host of his locally and internationally famous friends.

Hundreds of young people applied for the twenty-four places, sending in a 30-minute mix CD and written answers to a questionnaire that Alice had devised. It was a success, and sessions followed, offering a whole range of DJ skills, including club promotion and how to come across professionally. Varying locations were put to use, including an industrial estate behind the Europa hotel in Belfast and a derelict house on an estate in Limavady, which had been turned into a sort of youth centre for the kids.

DJ, videographer and graphic designer Leigh Swann had spent his early teens at the Craigyhill Methodist Church youth club discos in Larne, where he quickly homed in on the idea of DJing himself. Aged eighteen, he attended an early KeyMix session. It took place during the daytime at the Met Arena, a wedding venue that had been turned into one of Northern Ireland's most famous nightclubs, and which he'd been attending most Saturday nights for the previous two years, packed into buses from Belfast with hundreds of other young people. KeyMix, said Leigh, was new and unique, offering what he described as 'a bit of a stepping stone to get somewhere'. A DJ workshop at the Met Arena, it must be said, was comparable to a football fan being invited to an afternoon kickabout at the National Football Stadium at Windsor Park.

Unlike the National Stadium, the Met was in the middle of a field in Drumsill, a good two miles outside the city of Armagh. 'It was in the arse end of nowhere,' said Leigh. 'It wasn't in the town. You got let off on the side of the road and walked up to this complex.' KeyMix took over the club in the daytime, an arrangement made easier by the fact that it was owned by the family of DJ and mentor Mark Dobbin, who ran the place. KeyMix participants were on a rarefied daytime guest list, about to practise their mixing skills behind the decks of this famous club with a massive sound system. 'I remember sitting on the dancefloor, on these chairs they'd brought in for the workshops,' said Leigh. 'It was weird, properly out there, really surreal.' Having Fergie and his friends involved brought a whole other level to the exercise. 'It added a bit more magic. He was on Radio 1 at the time, really high profile. He was on on TV, on Comic Relief, doing boxing matches with Fatboy Slim and then talking to us. We all idolised Fergie, and having access to chat to him was magic. It was absolutely brilliant.' The daytime workshop also offered industry panels and networking opportunities to meet promoters or journalists at well-known music magazine *BBM*.

Being involved with KeyMix, he added, gave him confidence, or, to use his term, 'verification'. 'Back then I was really into graphic design, designing my own artwork for my CDs and tapes. Alice really nailed it home to me – "You're good at this." It's a lottery when you're that young and there's a lot of doubt in your head. If people like what you're doing, it makes a difference.' He's still DJing and getting work as a designer, and this could easily not have been so. It makes me think of what you might call the 'social sorting hat', or the way that some young people are so much more likely to become security guards than graphic designers, regardless of where their skills actually lie.

'I think it gave people the idea that there's an interest in these kinds of things,' added Leigh. 'It shook things up, created awareness that there was an opportunity and demand for people to make a living in arts and creative industries, which was pretty unheard of in our part of the world back then.'

For another alumnus, Cricky Lyttle, there wasn't much else on offer in the early 2000s. 'I grew up in west Belfast, and no one really left west Belfast,' he said to me. 'Maybe to get the bus to the Arena and back, but it wasn't very . . .' He paused. 'People weren't as open to meeting people from all walks of life. It didn't seem like there was much in the way of opportunity.' Luckily, his uncle told him about KeyMix, and he applied, successfully.

I told him about my experience, around the same time, of working with young people in south London, and how a big city can be very small when you're tied into an area full of street-level politics. It could be parochial, I said, despite knowing that the word 'parochial', with its religious roots – the parish – might have a different meaning in Northern Ireland. Cricky agreed. 'Especially in Northern Ireland with the age group I grew up with and the ones slightly older, they obviously lived through the tail end of the Troubles and there were certain areas you wouldn't go. Me coming through was kind of after that a wee bit, and I was far more comfortable with doing that sort of thing.' Perhaps, I think, KeyMix could only have existed in the early post-Good Friday Agreement context.

It was also a product of the emerging digital age. KeyMix and other dance-music-adjacent youth projects existed alongside the early days of message boards, and when social media meant Friends Reunited (est. 2000), which itself wasn't much use in a place where everyone still knew everyone they'd grown up with. Key moments in the online world stacked up alongside the operational years of KeyMix: forum host Usenet was bought by Google in 2001, Friendster launched the year after, with MySpace (2003) and Facebook (2004) arriving one after each other. The digital and the analogue were mixing in and out of each other.

In 2005, BBC Northern Ireland TV show *Inside Out* came along to interview KeyMix alumnus Jordan X, who was making waves as a big-name DJ while just sixteen and still at school, and who had already moved from participant to mentor. The camera switched to a small conference room with buzz-cut boys and hair-up girls facing a table at one end, which had been set up a little like a post-football-match press conference. Alice appeared next, sat at the controls of a radio studio, headphones laid out behind her. You didn't have to be fully grown to make things happen, she said, offering more cultural context: 'We don't like people to think they're good, and so when they do say, "I think I'm good at something," we tend to put them down. I think that's a trait we have in Northern Ireland.' Another shot shows someone in a Ralph Lauren sweater showing two girls and three boys how to scratch. Everyone's hard at work and having fun, in an environment where two qualities – focus and enjoyment – are not mutually exclusive.

In the years that followed, KeyMix used DJ culture as a way of engaging with a broad range of young people, including girls who had been brought up in care, single mothers, homeless communities and people with mental health issues, 'not for them to become DJs but to use that to engage', as Alice put it in another of our conversations. For these groups, it was less about gaining access to the music industry and more about creating confidence. 'We developed,' said Alice, 'from working with DJs to working with people in general, bringing DJing into it; not for the want of DJing, but for the want of connection.'

Connection brought KeyMix into the orbit of the Training for Women Network, who saw that they were opening up a new employment sector to young women who'd not otherwise have thought of it. Alice: 'It was amazing, honestly. Some of these girls were sitting in the corner, not connecting in any way. See, by the fourth week they were up and at the decks. We got them to create their own mix CD. Then they had to perform that to their family and friends. It was about "Look what happened. You never thought you could do something you never tried before. If you can do that, you can do other stuff." The single mums did the CDs. Then we had a teddy bear's picnic and they brought their kids, all bopping around. It was good craic.'

A girls-only strand allowed for conversations that were ahead of the cultural curve, instigated by co-founders Maeve and Lesley, who'd always be pushing the question – where are the girls? 'Why can a guy DJ in a black t-shirt, but a girl DJ has to have her things all hanging out?' said Alice, explaining that they'd bring veteran DJ Anne Savage, Lisa Lashes and locals Mandy Reid and Troya in to meet the girls. It provided acceptance for Alice and her contemporaries too. 'Nobody ever commented on the fact that we were all older women. It was always just "Alice, can I talk to you?" or "Lesley, can I talk to you?" It was amazing.'

KeyMix existed at least partly because of the decreasing age of youth club attendees nationwide, making the environment of less use to older teenagers and completely out of bounds to young people in their early twenties – who, let's face it, also need space and support. As well as building the confidence of those who attended, KeyMix acted like a youth wing of club culture, building from scratch a pipeline of DJs, promoters, graphic designers, artists and social strategists who'd go on to influence local and national culture in ways that are still unfolding. It achieved a lot, in acutely grassroots style.

'It was rough, it was ready. We weren't doing it very long, but we packed it in,' as Alice put it. In 2006, KeyMix was nominated for an award for its contribution to dance music at the Northern Ireland Dance Music Awards. 'When I look back, I can see it was as much about personal development as DJing,' said Alice. 'We talked about visualisation, creating road maps for where you want to get to, and action, how you move yourself forward. They coached each other. That's not just a skill for

DJing – that's a skill for whatever you're going to do in life.' One KeyMix regular, Boyd Sleator, is the co-founder, with DJ Holly Lester, of national campaigning organisation Free the Night, publishing research and advocating successfully for changes to outdated national licensing laws. The groundwork laid by dancefloor-adjacent youth projects across Northern Ireland has contributed to the emergence of dance music education businesses, including Sonic Academy, which opened in 2003 in Belfast and is now a global company.

One outcome, however, outstrips all others. 'The biggest thing for me was the coming together,' said Alice. 'It was the peace process starting. They came from everywhere. We never asked anyone what religion they were. Here we were, with these guys from Derry and flipping Boyne Square, and no – it was the music. That they came together absolutely was our contribution. We showed – quite apart from the drugs in the clubs, with everyone hugging each other – there was a common factor. That, to me, was a massive thing. And in flipping Craigavon. I mean, God, of all places, down there. D'you know what I'm saying?'

———

The Olderfleet dancefloor had filled up with a home-town crew with rave moves in their bodies, pumping arms and boingy legs. Fergie was playing anthemic hard house and trance, and Mark Dobbin was MCing, cutting tiny slices of the air with a staccato wave from the wrist. The night was drawing to a close, and I was having a lively conversation with a member of the KeyMix family, one who has a million stories, including some that illustrate the 'coming together' described by Alice. We were talking about how rich and deep the dancefloors here are: the most interesting in the world, he said, 'because of what we went through'. A big tune dropped and took over for a moment. 'You lot,' he said, in an aside that was not an aside, 'you had racism, but you fuckers grew up together. We never spoke to a Catholic. We were told their eyes were too close together or they had two arseholes.' It was a no-messing directness that indicated the realities of his own youth in the late 1990s and early 2000s, and perhaps something of the bigger picture too.

The final tune rolled out through the speakers, and Fergie got on the mic to wrap things up. He was shouting out the DJs, the bar staff and the crowd, when someone heckled from the back. In three words, they pointed to both the centrality of women and the communal, intergenerational nature of youth work.

'And your mum!'

32

2003: PASSING THE MIC WINS PRIZES

There are deep youth work histories embedded in UK music. Grime, a style of music and culture realised in a network of east London youth clubs and on street-level pirate radio in the early 2000s, offers a window into these realities. A Black British version of hip hop, it was a direct descendant of the men and women playing dub reggae, or controlling the mic, on late-1970s and early-'80s sound systems, and led directly to Dizzee Rascal's Mercury Music Prize win of 2003, as well as Mercury-winning albums by Skepta (2016), Dave (2019) and Little Simz (2022).

Richard Kylea 'Wiley' Cowie Jnr is considered a founding father of the genre. He had an outsized influence on all aspects of the music and culture as label owner, rave promoter and underground A&R; a pop star with Top Ten hits as a solo artist and with his crew Roll Deep, and an underground hero for his ground-breaking work as an MC and producer. A youth club attendee, he would go on to operate in a style that replicated the mentoring mindset: paying for high-quality studio space and making it accessible by covering people's taxis; offering practical encouragement to teenage talent while still in his twenties. While Wiley's position as a full-spectrum cultural instigator is solid, it could be argued that his reputation for an extreme sensitivity to perceived slights and for never backing down has been notable, even within a style of music built on lyrical war. During the first Covid pandemic lockdown, an online argument turned into a slew of comments offensive enough to get him banned from social media.

More grounded aspects of Wiley's work can be tracked back a generation. His musician dad, Richard Cowie Snr, ran workshops in youth clubs, contributing in tangible ways to the culture his son supersized and sent global. 'They really sparked young people perfecting their craft,' said Richard Snr, when we spoke. 'You could go and test your bars in the youth club, then progress to a radio station, Rinse FM or whatever.' Youth clubs are community space, he believes, suggesting that they're part of the backstory of almost every form of UK music. Even more than that, they perform a vital collective function. 'It's letting a community show its wares,' he said, 'and grow as a family.' Individuals whose parents were youth workers appear repeatedly in the youth club story, amplifying the idea of this space as a kind of family, with youth worker parents offering a unique and expansive dynamic to teens in their actual household.

Richard Snr became a youth worker by accident, through his background as a musician. 'I had a friend who worked at Poplar HARCA, and he'd bought some software to make music but didn't know how to use it, so he called me,' he explained. 'I volunteered to show them. But then I ended up going into the youth club to teach the stuff and record the young people. Then they offered me a post – "Could you do two hours a week?" Then it was four, then . . .' He laughed, not needing to complete the sentence. It's the magnetism of the youth club, I think. You pop in for one reason, and then, before you know it, you're involved, locked in even.

Back in the day, each area in the London borough of Tower Hamlets had a youth club, he explained, listing some of them out: Aberfeldy, Teviot, the Linc, HARCA. Within each building there were adults on hand to help out. 'An aspect of the youth club is that adults were encouragers,' he said, midway through our chat. 'You're into photography? Okay, let's get some funding, get some cameras. We'll buy a few computers and a keyboard, and we'll get you doing that. Youth clubs encouraged people to follow something. That's my personality too. If you wanted to take something seriously, you only need to tell me once. If I can hear your vibration and I can see you're serious, man, I will knock on every door for you. My son is exactly like that.' His reframing of youth workers in this way, as 'encouragers', rings true, fitting precisely as a character trait of so many of the adults involved in youth work. Richard Snr is still working in service of youth, running intervention programmes in schools.

We move on to the period of active destruction, when government policy played out as closures. 'It's a shame, the downfall,' he said, with his tone now resigned and serious. 'I saw it die. The story they gave was funding, facilities being under threat. But some of the sites they had as youth clubs were very good buildings. Community buildings, in my eyes, were being taken over or snatched by other situations.' I told Richard Snr about the origins of youth clubs in east London Settlements and Mission Houses and the long-term impact of these spaces, opened up initially by wealthy patrons and later being sold off in service of their demographic descendants in government. 'Just as an example,' he said, 'the school, Eton. That was actually built for poor people. It wasn't designed to be this exclusive thing. From the grassroots there's always a product that the world wants to get its hands on, whether it's music or sports.' He paused and dropped an understated truth:

'A lot of greatness has come from humble beginnings. And I'll leave it there.'

In a retrospective feature on the role of youth clubs in grime, *Trench* magazine spelled it out, explaining how key artists attended local authority clubs that survived into the early 2000s: 'Grime's history is built on the foundations laid in local youth clubs by titans of UK music like Wiley, Kano and Dizzee Rascal. "Growing up when grime was brand new, it was a talent exchange as much as anything else," says Reiss De Bruin, a journalist who grew up going to youth clubs in east London. "Nowadays kids just get given a library card by Tower Hamlets council or some vouchers for the cinema, and they're told to just be happy with that."' It's a view reinforced by detail peppered across the internet: MC Double O's auntie letting Lethal Bizzle, Tinie Tempah and Heartless Crew 'clash in the yard of her Leyton home', or artists including Dizzee Rascal, Tinchy Stryder and Ruff Sqwad accessing the Linc Centre, just off Devons Road, directing their considerable energies into MCing, productions or DJing.

Photographer Simon Wheatley's book *Lost Dreams* depicts four east London youth clubs still in operation between 2005 and 2007, presenting them as extremely lively and boisterous places where young teenagers would jostle each other – and the photographer – as they grappled for the microphone. The book was, he told me, both a record of the role youth clubs played in early grime and a protest against the funding cuts that followed after the Tories gained power by going into coalition with the Liberal Democrats in 2010. 'These places were effectively grime's original underground,' he said, adding that the youth club sessions were major events, especially for the younger generation coming up in the wake of Dizzee Rascal's Mercury Music Prize win.

'I don't know if there's a contemporary equivalent,' he added. 'Not just because of funding cuts but also the dominating role social media has come to play.' As he recalls it, youth clubs were places where young people could go and MC or experience what it was like to hear their tunes being played by a youth club DJ, or, indeed, to become the DJ.

What did he think was the value of places like those shown in *Lost Dreams*? 'At the time I was quite disturbed by the lyrical content I would hear in the youth clubs,' he said, adding that the location for most of his best-known photographs, Lansbury Youth Club in Poplar, had to close down because of violence. 'But,' he said, 'there was also a lot of fun and laughter, and people would mingle together in a safer place than the street where there were youth workers around who often would have been through trouble themselves and would be in an authoritative position to observe, advise and intervene.' I was reminded, talking to him, of safety as a relative quality: certain places can be both dangerous and still safer than other available locations, a difficult circle for official systems to square.

Generosity is evident throughout the youth club histories, with youth clubs supporting the music and, in turn, being supported by artists once they became successful. Numerous rappers and producers have used their success in service of next-generation youth clubs. In London alone there's Stormzy's set-up in Croydon; a community music facility established by Skepta at the Selby Space; Lady Leshurr's Rap College workshops; and the Ruff Sqwad Arts Foundation. West Londoner AJ Tracey, who has spoken about both starting out in youth clubs and the role of his youth worker mother, teamed up with a fast-food brand on a youth project.

Grime-powered crime drama *Top Boy* was screened first on Channel 4 in 2011, and then on Netflix in 2019, after Drake campaigned for its revival. Written by Belfast-born novelist Ronan Bennett and scored by Brian Eno and Michael Asante, it told a version of life as lived on the margins. I appreciated it for the successes, but I never loved it. Mostly, I put this down to my pathetically low tolerance for on-screen violence and depictions of peril, as well as some discomfort about the difference between the kids I knew at *Live Magazine* as graphic designers or photographers and the ease with which they would be read as 'drug dealers' by the outside world. I also wonder, now, where the youth workers were in the storylines. They would have still existed in the real-world equivalent – just.

Prominent *Top Boy* actors were also musicians with central roles in grime and UK rap. Kane 'Kano' Robinson, Ashley 'Asher D' Walters, Little Simz, Dave, Scorcher and Bashy took lead roles. Many other cast members had never acted before, having been scouted from schools, boxing gyms and, yes, youth clubs. Lead actors variously reported on the role of youth clubs in their own successes: Ashley Walters's original outfit, So Solid Crew, had attended Devas Youth Club in Battersea, while Little Simz had been vocal about the role of Mary's in Islington, a youth club which, in suitably circular style, existed because of support from a musician: in the late 1960s, megastar Yusuf Islam, previously known as Cat Stevens, had donated significant sums towards the building costs of St Mary's Neighbourhood Centre, which houses the youth club. Artists who benefited from youth clubs absorbed the undercurrent of instruction: to give back.

Again, though, youth club was not available to everyone who needed it. I once had a conversation with someone who has been influential in UK music that unpacks this assertion from a particular perspective. The youth club, they said, was for the nice kids, those whose lives benefited from some stability. 'We robbed the youth club!' they said, offering first-hand perspective on this particular occurrence. They regretted what had happened, wishing it wasn't the case. Later, they'd engage in youth work themselves, creating significant uplift for others.

In all of this, there's another remarkable point to be made. A functioning network of youth clubs in east London that existed well into the early 2000s, accessible by foot or bus, meant that young teenagers had multiple places to go. Maybe it's not just that warm, welcoming spaces and adults supported the new music. Grime may have emerged in east London *because* of the youth clubs.

33

2005: BRIXTON'S YOUTH-RUN MAGAZINE

Everyone has to make the transition from childhood into adulthood, just as most of us learn how to walk and talk, and, later, discover how to be old. Repeatedly, in the nations of the UK, adults and teenagers have worked together to create youth club spaces, which remained steady as waves of individuals entered, grew and exited into adulthood.

We are now about to enter our last location. We'll do so through a doorway cut into a metal shutter, just off Brixton High Street, at youth-run print publication *Live Magazine*, in the 2000s — a location I've touched on several times already in this book. However, given that I worked there as a mentor, and might have been the person that answered the door, I need to begin with a moment of soul-searching. Don't worry, it won't take long.

So, a basic principle: while a parent might display baby photos of their grown child, youth workers and mentors don't have the right to declare or divulge processes or moments witnessed from a trusted position, observed from established adulthood. No one buzzed the doorbell outside *Live Magazine* thinking that they'd later become 'material', which makes writing about any of this contentious, to say the least. How to include this rich, deep environment without compromising the relationships that made it possible? Even asking permission is complicated, given the power dynamics that remain, and which come from knowing someone when they were young and emerging. I remember that, even at the time, there was pushback from contributors when broadsheet journalists would come down to 'hear their story' without having the necessary connections to properly receive the information.

However, I made a decision. Becoming part of *Live* made me an accidental and untrained youth worker. I learned on the job, and I have memories and a cache of back issues that form one part of a bigger story. I was a small piece of a big and very lively picture, experiencing the joys and as aware of the flaws as the next person. In short, being at *Live* was a transformative and extended period in my life, which spanned over a decade in all. It connected my politics to experience, and grounded both in relationships that are ongoing and which continue to inform my beliefs and actions.

More importantly, as an example of the shifting, changing, locally specific environment, at a time when neoliberal economics began moving youth provision away from council-run clubs into a range of market-influenced projects, this place offers insights into universal dynamics. I offer my perspective, sat behind an iMac at the end of a trestle table, chatting about reviews with our sixteen-year-old music editor or wrestling an opinion piece out of whoever had walked in that day. I will handle this archive, which is both mine and not mine, as carefully as I can.

———

Live Magazine began on May Day 2001, when business partners Sam Conniff and Michelle Morgan set up a marketing agency that had an unusual starting point. Realising that brands spent huge sums on promoting basic products – for example, cornflakes – Livity would, in Sam's words, 'harness marketing and hijack it'. They didn't have to wait long for their first client. By the end of the first day in their one-room office, the phone had rung, albeit only the once. Someone at Lambeth Council was looking to promote the work of the borough's Youth Council, which was then disseminated through a brochure-type publication, and knew that Sam had a background in printing flyer packs handed out at clubs and raves. Ever alert to possibility, the pair responded to the request with an idea: what if Lambeth's young people did it themselves, presenting otherwise dry information in their own style, in the form of a revamped magazine?

The new agency now had a client. Sam and Michelle went into action, visiting local youth clubs to find an editor and contributors. They have told this story millions of times, and it goes something like this: Sam walked into the youth club assuming he was relatable, being only twenty-four years old and having grown up down the road in Streatham in a single-parent family, a notion of which he was quickly disabused when he stood in front of blank faces and heard a pointed comment from the back: 'Why are you wearing flares?' Luckily for them, fourteen-year-old Aziza Francis took Sam and Michelle up on their offer, and *Live* had its first editor.

Magazine covers are an art form, using images and text to sell the contents to potential readers. The first two issues of *Live* had been made in-house by Lambeth Council and were, let's say, a little underwhelming: coverlines included 'Mission Statement' and 'Interview with the Mayor'. Issue three, published in June 2001, came from a different planet, one inhabited by the all-new and all-teenage editorial team. Contributors would hang out, play music and put the mag together after school and during the holidays in the Livity offices with Sam's journalist friends, including newspaper reporter Kate Burt, *Dazed & Confused* editor Callum McGeoch and underground music blogger Gavin Weale as editorial mentors. *Live* was a rare entity: equal parts youth club, small business, social enterprise and magazine office; a parallel-universe version of early-'90s ITV comedy-drama *Press Gang*. It drew from, and distributed magazines to, a network of local authority youth clubs.

Workers in council-run clubs were having a hard time. Historian Sue Robertson has pointed out that, in 2001, Comprehensive Performance Assessment had been introduced for local authorities, which meant they were rated on key service delivery areas, including services for children and young people. Providing such data would have taken up valuable time and inevitably led to an executive focus on things that could be measured. 'Quick outcomes are demanded,' she wrote, 'with hard data, such as a fall in crime or better school attendance rather than soft data like making relationships with, or offering support to, young people.' In her book, Robertson quotes *Recognising and Recording the Impact of Youth Work* by Bryan Merton, Hilary Comfort and Malcolm Payne, relaying a sentence that helps illuminate the context: 'The risk is that the more that project work can demonstrate convincingly the outcomes of interventions, the more it feeds the decline of the work that cannot.' Youth clubs, increasingly, were in the latter category.

With a bold 3D logo over a compass, Rammellzee-style armoured tags and a digitally distressed shot of ruffneck grimey garage crew Dirty Dozen, the turbo-charged, now youth-run *Live Magazine* placed youth council business between articles on drug trafficking ('cussed, criticised and covered'), graffiti ('bombing the streets of Brixton') and a feature on making a career for yourself in fashion. *Live* had arrived and would soon run very early articles on artists who'd go on to national acclaim, including Dizzee Rascal and Ms Dynamite, as well as tackling social issues that included teenage fatherhood or the realities of having a parent who used crack.

It was the feature on drug addiction that first brought me into *Live*'s orbit, in early 2002. Aged twenty-nine, I was the parent of a five-year-old and had left my job at *The Face* magazine after a very difficult series of life experiences, including the death of my dad. In the aftermath of bereavement, I no longer wanted to write jibber-jabber. I wanted to do something proper.

A PR who worked for Sony and was promoting their FIFA PlayStation games tapped me up. 'There's something interesting happening in Brixton,' he told me. 'You should get involved.' I did as he suggested and walked along Tunstall Road, off Brixton High Street, past three terraced houses that had been knocked together and turned into offices. The outside walls were painted a flat terracotta, with windowsills and metal bars picked out in green.

Inside there was a courtyard that led to a small room with teenagers sat on the tables or at the computers, laughter and music audible as I walked up the metal stairs to the Livity office. Sam and Michelle said something along the lines of 'Hi, hello, come on in,' offered me a cup of tea and introduced me to everyone in a whistle-stop tour of the *Live* universe. Assigned two young writers, the three of us sat in a side room, getting to work. One of them had an addict parent, and she'd decided – or, more likely, had been encouraged – to write about it with her friend. I was used to working with new writers because my job at *The Face* had involved commissioning fresh-faced journalists, often for their first pieces.

At *Live*, though, I quickly learned a very important lesson. Ideas about quality or 'good writing', which I'd had to learn – the hard way – as a self-taught journalist on national newspapers and magazines, played out differently here. I was instead to be a kind of midwife, simply assisting with the delivery, making the process as safe and painless as possible. This seems a relevant metaphor, given that teenage pregnancy in Lambeth at the time was running at twice the national average. The article was published, emblazoned on the cover with the words 'My Teenage Crack Nightmare', alongside 'Nuff New Music Reviews' and 'Hair and Beauty Tips'. Overall, the borough skewed young in the Y2K, the first census of the new millennium showing that nearly 20 per cent of the population was under eighteen in the year *Live* launched as a quarterly print publication.

In 2001, Lambeth was topping a range of unhappy lists. The borough had the highest rates of street robbery in England and Wales and was experiencing a sharp rise in violent crime, according to Home Office figures. The Met Police's Lambeth Borough Operational Command Unit was over a hundred officers short of their 'budgeted workforce target' and, as a way of dealing with the shortfall, the Met introduced a short-lived pilot project. Under Lambeth's Cannabis Warning Scheme, people found with small amounts of the drug would be given a warning and their stash confiscated, instead of being arrested. The intention, according to a Met Police Authority report at the time, was to 'give officers more time to deal with the Borough priorities of robbery, burglary, violent crime, class "A" drugs and to respond to calls from the public'. It was some distance from *The Wire*'s fictional decriminalised drug-dealing zone Hamsterdam, but there was a predictable fuss from media commentators, and so the pilot was unceremoniously ended, with an exit plan put into place at short notice and at some cost to those caught up in the rule changes.

While the data doesn't give a sense of how street robbery and violent crime affected teenagers, including those who attended *Live*, it's reasonable to assume that much of the violence would have taken place in small pockets of the borough, and that young men were disproportionately affected, as those being robbed, doing the robbing, or both. Being around the risk of violence, in a stigmatised environment, would have been stressful for many of the borough's 52,000 under-eighteens, regardless of gender. A magazine that reflected a buoyant version of borough life, in which school-age readers could – often literally – see themselves, their friends or extended family members, may have been a small but welcome refutation of their area's reputation.

Another youth club in the borough shows how these spaces also act as a social or cultural archive, retaining information and context long after they fell out of general circulation. Marcus Lipton Youth Club, or ML Community Enterprise, as it is now known, was named after the Labour MP who represented Brixton in Parliament between 1945 and 1978. A few years after Lipton began working in Westminster, HMT *Empire Windrush* docked at Tilbury. The government had spent time, money and effort recruiting Commonwealth citizens, but hadn't created a national plan to accommodate workers when they landed. Consequently, over 240 of the new arrivals were temporarily housed in Clapham Common Underground station. *London's Newcomers*, by Ruth Glass, explains what happened next. The Colonial Office was 'by now seriously concerned' and asked the mayor of Lambeth if a welcome could be arranged. A group of forty '*Windrush* men' were invited on a Wednesday after-noon to a special event at the Astoria cinema in Brixton. Tea, cake and a cinema screening were accompanied by speeches by the mayor and the local MP, Lipton, who told the men that they should regard Britain as their second home. Glass's book connected hospitality to future histories: 'In the unknown and perplexing vastness of England, the Jamaicans now felt they could be sure of one place. Brixton was friendly. In Brixton they would make their homes.' Marcus Lipton's name lives on, through the youth club.

Journalist and presenter Jordan Jarrett-Bryan credits *Live Magazine* with his entry into broadcasting, first as a commentator for Channel 4's coverage of the 2012 Paralympics, and now as a staff sports reporter on *Channel 4 News*. Jordan joined *Live*, however, as a sports-mad teenager, a decade before the Olympics rolled into town. His mum had seen an advert in the *South London Press* and encouraged her son to go along. Writing album reviews or articles about video games and sneaking in the occasional sports-related item, he quickly became a key member of the team. Within a year he'd been offered the role of editor alongside Cleo Soazandry.

'Lambeth had a lot of issues with young people at the time,' said Jordan, when we caught up. 'I saw it as my job to produce a magazine but also to produce a safe space for people to come and hang out.' The team, said Jordan, were 'low-rent counsellors', and by 'team' Jordan means his teenage peers as much as the adults, who were mostly in their twenties or very early thirties. People would drift in, he said, before a mock-outraged tone entered his voice: 'There were young people who came to the office on a regular basis and didn't write anything for

Live! Didn't write a word! They took up our time and ate our food – but that was the whole point, and I think that's a beautiful thing. The council were paying for us to produce sixty-four pages of something. But *Live* was a conduit, a place young people could hang out. It was safe, fun and relevant. The ones who never contributed, they weren't on the street, they weren't being groomed by gangsters to go and shot on the corner. They didn't have to go home when home life wasn't really good. Having someone write an article was a bonus.'

I told Jordan that he was basically quoting 1940s youth worker Josephine Macalister Brew, and I pulled up her quote about young people who come along and never take off their white muffler, never get involved but keep coming back, and he laughed. 'It's true! The whole point of the youth club isn't the table tennis or the pool or the music; it's basically the young person's version of the pub. It's a community, a build-ing that young people want to go to, to forge friends, find a boyfriend or a girlfriend, or to talk about stuff that's happen-ing at school. The ping-pong is just honey, a tool to get you there. The bigger point with youth clubs and *Live Magazine* is: how do we give young people a place where they can just feel young?'

Hardcore professional development also took place after school. 'It gave young people who didn't have an easy route into the corporate world a sense of "I could be a record label boss or an executive producer or a film director," and not going through traditional routes. *Live* gave people confidence and skill, not theory, and it gave industry people who were empowered and confident.' Fast-forward to now, and he's a senior journalist, sometimes stepping in to deputise for anchor newsreaders. 'Everything I took with me to Channel 4 was honed and harnessed at *Live*: deadlines, expectations, writing style, interviewing techniques. I didn't get my Channel 4 gig because of *Live*, but I might not have got it without *Live*.' He's probably the only person in his newsroom, he said, who doesn't have a degree, and with an undercurrent of playfulness bubbling up into his voice, he continued: 'They let me read the national news on Friday! They let me read news about serious issues like the economy and wars and scandal! They let me talk to the nation!'

From the first half of the 2000s, I was part of the extended *Live Magazine* family, in their orbit as an occasional mentor or workshop facilitator. Come 2006, I took a permanent part-time role, running journalism workshops, helping with the print publication and, later, the website and YouTube channel. Livity's sister business Live Futures had secured European Union money to run a project for young people who were not in education or training. Between 2000 and 2006, London received around £90m per year through EU structural funds, mostly the European Regional Development Fund and the European Social Fund. The funds, under a marker known as Objective 3, were aimed at regions in the Union that were 'lagging behind in their development, undergoing restructuring or facing specific geographical, economic or social problems'. Lambeth – and *Live Magazine* – fitted the bill.

Contributors came from a range of backgrounds, although that nuance was easily flattened by structural racism and the assumption that all global majority south Londoners at the time lived on an estate, hiding Glocks in shoeboxes under their beds. Contributors lived in council blocks and in spacious houses on wide, leafy roads. Some did well at school, while others didn't.

Households came in various shapes, large and small, with strict mothers or fathers, or absent ones, and with grandparents who were born in the UK or had journeyed from afar. Families were of all faiths and none. Contributors were short and tall, straight and queer (or emerging as such), loud and quiet. What connected almost everyone, despite the differences, was proximity to deprivation and lived experience of racism.

While most contributors had lives that were south London ordinary, a few lived within extreme environments. An example of this took place one afternoon when the doorbell rang, and I answered it. On the other side of the steel shutters was a teenager. They'd come straight from prison, they explained, but they wanted to get involved, and could they find out about joining? They were welcomed in by the whole team, with as little fuss as if they'd come from school. 'There was no judgement,' agreed fellow mentor Rahul Verma, when we spoke. 'The ones who society deemed wrong 'uns were just as capable as anyone else, if you could find out what they were interested in. My number-one learning from that time was that every single human being, no matter who they are, has talent, and if you can give them a pathway through their interests, they can fulfil their potential.'

And yet the set-up didn't always work for everyone. Adults, many of whom were white, and who, mostly, had access to social mobility, were sharing space with young people who were negatively racialised, in a borough facing vast and deep social inequality. Teenagers were promised futures that just weren't feasible when, to quote one young person I worked alongside, 'everyone in your family is a drug dealer or a gangster'. This level of chaos was experienced by only a small handful of *Live*'s contributors, of course. But it's fair to say that broader society couldn't always match our ambition for talented young people whom schools, employers and criminal justice systems saw as dangerous or, at the very least, 'other'. In retrospect, some contributors were arguably harmed by our collective enthusiasm. We pulled them into a world which, outside the office doors, was not truly open.

Between my joining on the permanent part-time contract and 2013, when I left, a little burned out, I worked with thousands of contributors. I did so alongside many other mentors who helped out with design, photography, illustration or specific aspects of journalism, like sports. Some came down once or twice; others became embedded, part of the fabric that held us together.

Livity staff were also part of the mentoring picture, with the assumption that new hires at the marketing agency would be, at the very least, tolerant of this unusual workplace. In 2009, the company moved up the road to beautiful new offices in a regenerated Victorian warehouse turned co-working space, and, of course, *Live* moved too. In the earlier iteration, the magazine team had a separate room, but now everyone was in it together, sharing space and navigating the unique challenges of such arrangements – for example, some of us needing quiet because of phone calls with clients, and others needing to turn the music up or emote loudly when a beloved new friend walked in through the doors.

For me, every day was a million miles an hour, greeting new people and finding them something to do, working with section editors on their ideas and chasing copy, or meeting with trained youth workers who wanted to refer one of their young people to *Live*. When potential mentors or other adult professionals would visit for the first time, they often commented on the difference between what they were expecting and what was actually happening. 'Oh,' people would say, looking around at the big windows, framed copies of Andy Warhol's *Marilyn* and banks of computers. 'This is nicer than my office! I was expecting something much more grotty, maybe above a shop.'

Live offered, for some people, at least some of the time, radical friendship between those otherwise divided by factors including age or ethnicity, or simply between teenagers who went to different schools. The unusual structure – a youth club masquerading as a magazine office, existing within a somewhat renegade profit-making marketing agency – allowed for strongly bonded forms of friendship, support and relationship, and lasting responsibilities. The latter is important: knowing someone during a vulnerable period of transformation potentially gives you power over them, including, now time has passed, the risk of extracting reflected glory.

It is fair and accurate to say that young people accessed a very entertaining space that broadly kept them safe and which offered incredible opportunities unavailable elsewhere. Mentors got to work alongside people who were tapped into the source of next-generation culture, with all the personal and professional benefits such proximity offers. The agency that created and sustained *Live* offered contributors meaningful, high-quality space and support; the opportunity to be published as a writer, photographer, designer or editor; access to a wide range of contacts in the creative industries; and opportunities for pocket-money-type paid work. In exchange, Livity had access to gold-dust insights that brought the company, among other things, contracts from brands, local government, national bodies and the Big Lottery Fund, as well as executive production credits on TV show *Dubplate Drama* and multiple industry awards. It remains surprising to founder Sam Conniff that other businesses haven't replicated the model.

An exchange was taking place, changing everyone. Adults had made space that was brought to life by teenagers in ways that share common ground with rest rooms for factory girls or the Basement in Bristol, albeit in the changed, newly neoliberal context of the 2000s. Connections between *Live* mentors and magazine contributors, not always boundaried in the way they might have been if we were trained youth workers, had more in common with the youth club minibus excursions to the rave than the safeguarding era, which was about to begin.

Safeguarding, in the way we understand it today, began entering UK life after the Children's Act of 1989, which established several key principles about a child's welfare, placed a duty on local authorities to promote and safeguard the welfare of children in need in their area, and set out actions to be taken when staff had cause to believe a child might suffer harm. The Criminal Records Bureau (CRB) was set up in 2002 and processed checks on those working with young people. The Safeguarding Vulnerable Groups Act 2006 followed the double murder of two children in Soham by a school caretaker and established a legal basis for the Independent Safeguarding Authority (ISA), which then merged with the CRB in 2012. Criminal record-checking and the legal barring of individuals from working with children is now undertaken by the Disclosure and Barring Service (DBS).

Safeguarding is, of course, important. However, it can also be executive-facing, about protecting institutions instead of ensuring young people have the flexibility and freedoms they need. Society causes harm to young people. Where's the safe-guarding against that?

The south-east London borough of Lewisham shares a borough boundary with Lambeth, where *Live* was based. For certain teenagers in the mid-2000s, it might as well have been a different kind of border, with passport control staffed by peers caught up in street-level politics. Sian Anderson, however, made the cross-borough trek when she heard that her friend Mervin Martin had been interviewing major US R&B and rap artists, including Trey Songz.

Now a long-serving BBC DJ and broadcaster with a grime and electronic show on 1Xtra — listeners will be aware that her name is pronounced 'Sigh-Ann' not 'Shaarn' — she's been behind major moments in UK music. These include promoting Ed Sheeran's first EP, *No. 5 Collaborations*, during a period when Sheeran was still making the transition from MySpace to major-label deals, as well as handling Charli xcx's and Jess Glynne's first Top Five hits while working at Atlantic Records, and thus laying the groundwork for future successes. On top of her BBC show and about a gazillion other things, she also runs a restaurant, Octaves.

We met in a café on the edges of south-east London to talk about an article she engineered while editing the magazine, aged nineteen. The opening page of her 2009 *Live Magazine* feature, 'UK Grime vs UK Indie', showed five MCs — Bashy, JME, Griminal, Shorty and Ghetts — sat on the grass in Hyde Park. Members of Brixton rock band The Thirst stood in a line holding guitars and one of the footballs that would be used in this Sian-instigated five-a-side. Photographs show Ghetts — who would later earn BRIT, Mercury Music Prize, MOBO,

NME and *DJ Magazine* awards and nominations – as striker, making a break down the pitch. In another shot, he's in goal, mid-jump and successfully denying the guitar players a win. 'The day started off, ironically, with every single member of the UK Grime team arriving late to the meeting point,' wrote Sian, in her characteristically no-messing article, describing Griminal's and Shorty's tempers coming 'to a hot point' when the match remained goal-free five minutes before the end. Match coverage continued in a way that will be amusing to anyone with a passing familiarity with grime dynamics: 'Inevitably, JME scored,' she wrote, adding that the UK grime team 'perked up', with The Thirst's Kwame dropping out and deciding to film the rest of the match instead. The article ends with a pointed mention of website Grime Daily, which ran something similar.

Sian was on her way to becoming a central figure in UK music, able even as a teenager to get grime's biggest names to meet in Hyde Park, and to write about them without fear, favour or unnecessary reverence. Soon she'd be offered a radio show with fellow *Live* contributor Julie Adenuga, on Rinse FM. The space provided by a youth-run publication allowed talent and drive to flourish. 'What was the connection between *Live* and your life in the music industry?' I asked Sian. The answer was pragmatic. 'I didn't have internet. I didn't have Channel U,' she said. 'I'd heard about the grime legends through my friends, then I got a teardrop phone and got [foundational instrumental] "Functions on the Low". This was without the context. I'd never seen any of the artists. When I came to *Live* I was able to put a face to a name and interview all these people – Ruff Sqwad, N-Dubz, the hottest things the playground was talking about. I hadn't had a chance to be that exposed 'til I got internet, at *Live*. When [mentors] were asking me who I was into, musically, I was able to say, "These guys," and get interviews with them, which then shapes my career.'

Live contributed to the cultural ecosystem in the 2000s above and beyond inviting MCs for a kickabout in central London. Young writers could interview artists at the start of their careers, preparing them for scrutiny by journalists living at a remove from the experiences they chronicled. Articles and photoshoots held up a mirror, so emerging artists could see themselves reflected in a light that offered validation and a practical boost. Under the earlier mentorship of journalist Chantelle Fiddy, *Live* created pathways for numerous individuals to become writers, editors, photographers, videographers, graphic designers, music industry leaders and commentators, and many now have significant and influential roles in a range of media, music and cultural businesses and institutions. Contributors at *Live* didn't have to find out about the way the world was changing – for example, when phones became portable music players or when musicians and videographers began bending new digital platforms to their own ends. They were living, using and shaping newness, as it emerged.

There are many examples that I could use to illustrate the successes. One relates to the time *Live* interviewed SB:TV founder Jamal Edwards. Writer Rotimi Odukoya (known back then as James Rotimi, and later of popular climbing community Clmbxr) went over to Jamal's mum's house and interviewed him in the bedroom that doubled up as an early HQ for the teenager's YouTube channel. Jamal had attended Bollo Brook and Friary Park youth centres, and his channel had a new way of presenting the music. SB:TV presented UK grime artists showing off their freestyle skills in the F64 feature or being interviewed. We put Jamal on the cover, under the headline 'King of the World', in 2011, and he came into the office to pick up a copy the day it came back from the printers. I remember the excitement – 'This is my first cover!' – and a feeling we don't really have a word for in English, of being extremely happy for someone else's successes: positive *Schadenfreude*. Jamal had many successes, including an MBE (2015) and numerous brand partnerships, with Simon Frederick's 2017 photograph of him going on to be acquired by the National Portrait Gallery for their permanent collection. In 2021, a year before his accidental death, Jamal set up Jamal Edwards Delve, a project aimed at refurbishing and reopening youth centres. In this way, the youth club legacy would continue, underpinning mainstream society.

34

2007: MISSION HOUSE NIGHT RUNS II

Youth club roots are deep and long. Existing in recognisable shape since Victorian times, they provide extended family, a safety net and a place where young people can shake off some of the worries that surround them. Divested, even a tiny bit, of their individual troubles by playing table tennis or shouting into a microphone, teenagers have a better chance of getting on with living life.

But still, the value of youth clubs remains hard to explain. As with so many aspects of community, they exist in an economy of relationships and feelings where, to quote artist and youth-club-to-youth-worker alumnus André Anderson, 'the process is the prize'. Their impact is also hard to see because those with structural power probably didn't attend them, making them invisible, or at least abstract, to those who hold the purse strings. It's worth repeating that the connections between youth clubs across time and space are so numerous, though, that they seem rhizomatic: connected like elements of the natural world, entwined roots under the woodland of recent history.

According to DJ, poet, sports ambassador and writer Charlie Dark, youth clubs are a social network. 'At a time when there was no internet, the youth club *was* the internet,' he said, decisively, when we talked. Charlie, who was awarded an MBE for his role as founder of international running collective Run Dem Crew, could also be awarded medals for perfectly phrased explanations of what's what. 'If you demonise young people and don't provide spaces for them to come together, your future is going to be rocky,' he said. 'When you stop taking care of your young, you don't have a future.'

'Spaces for young people benefit all of us,' he added, warming to the theme. '"Community" has become a buzzword, but youth clubs are a mirror of what a good community should look like. If I feel taken care of by my community when I'm young, generally I will stand by that community as I get older. I'll want to give back.'

Charlie spent his twenties running DJ and poetry workshops in youth clubs, after realising that doing so meant access to turntables and record collections. He'd not been able to attend as a teenager because his mother forbade it. 'I'd be really interested,' he said, 'to know the amount of African kids in comparison to West Indian kids who went to youth clubs in the '70s and '80s. For the African community, the youth club was a place you tried to keep your kids away from, because you were aspiring for a future that was greater than what you were seeing coming out of that youth club environment.' Youth clubs had a reputation, he said, of not being safe, and instead young Charlie was bundled off to 5th Camberwell Cubs, church and cadets.

Recognising youth clubs as a key transmitter in music culture, he made up for lost time by joining as a mentor, aged twenty-one, initially at a youth music project in Brixton. At the same time, he was building success with his collective, the Urban Poets Society, and with the band Attica Blues. 'From 2000 onwards I got really into teaching poetry, creative writing, the music stuff. I was in schools, prisons, youth clubs, pupil referral units regularly, like ten years deep of that, every day.'

In 2007, he started Run Dem Crew. It spilled out of a number of genesis points that help illustrate the interconnectedness of so much in the youth club world, including *Live Magazine*, where he'd got involved as a mentor, and another Livity scheme, a youth-run record label called Live Recordings. '*Live* is where I realised the extent of the postcode wars between young people,' he said, describing increased levels of violence based on where an individual lived. The risks, or perceived risks, painted teenagers into ever-smaller corners of the city.

'I was rediscovering London, running at night, realising how amazing the city is,' said Charlie. 'I started thinking about turning this into an idea for cross-cultural, intergenerational mentoring. I've got graphic designers in Hackney and loads of 'hood kids from south London. Put them in running kit and we can get them safely from one area to another.'

'What are the youth club-esque qualities of Run Dem Crew?' I asked. 'It has the loose structure,' replied Charlie. 'It's agile. It has the spirit of it being the place people come; a home for as long as they need it. It has the sporting element that a lot of youth clubs have, and it's a place where people can test their strength and push their boundaries. A great youth club has space for everyone, including the vulnerable.' The youth club as a concept remains useful way beyond the second decade of life, I think. It's for life.

With Run Dem Crew, a group of creative professionals and young people still meet in east London every Tuesday to get changed into their running kit. Paired up with mentors, RDC members run five miles along a range of routes with evocative names like Murder Mile, referencing the pre-gentrification moniker for a stretch of Dalston High Street, or Three Bridges, which spans the Thames. Without knowing it, Charlie has been retracing the routes taken by the men behind the Etonian Mission Houses a century and a half ago, when public school old boys took teenage factory workers out on night runs to stop them smashing up the place. What of Run Dem Crew or *Live Magazine* or the Holyhead will be visible in a hundred years? The detail may well be erased by time. The effect, however, like in so many other cases, will continue like waves, energy moving forwards through the decades.

Youth clubs in the UK are a muddle, unique and various because of who we are as a nation. Sensing the connection between Eton Mission Houses and Run Dem Crew, surveying all the groups that sit between the two, makes me think that the state still doesn't know what to do with empire's echo. The youth club has this message for us too: reckon with your histories.

2010: AUSTERITY CANCELLED YOUTH CLUBS

In 2009, there were approximately 11,000 youth clubs across the UK. A few, around 20 per cent, were 'large and well-established', according to *Somewhere to Belong: A Blueprint for 21st Century Youth Clubs*. More than two in five were small, voluntary clubs 'struggling to survive on very limited funding and in buildings that need investment', while just over half operated on less than £10,000 a year. It sounds remarkably like the world depicted in 1960s books like *Razor Edge* or *Double Zero*.

A year before the 2010 general election, 40 per cent of young Londoners aged eleven to sixteen were still attending a youth club at least weekly. It's a remarkably stable figure, given all the ups and downs. Imagine if ad hoc groups had to keep schools going with no statutory basis and erratic, insufficient funding? I wonder how they'd fare.

No single party won enough votes to form a majority government in the May election. After five days of negotiations, the Liberal Democrats agreed to rule as junior partners in a coalition government with the Conservative Party. Austerity followed.

No risk assessment had been put in place for this measure, which resulted in more than half a trillion pounds of lost public spending, according to the Progressive Economy Forum. There was an absolute cut in youth service funding, with the exception of David Cameron's National Citizenship Service.

For youth clubs, the change in government was brutal. Spending on youth services was reduced by 73 per cent across the UK, to the eventual tune of £1bn. Open access clubs run by councils were hit the hardest, more likely to close than those run by charities and voluntary organisations. In the 1960s, a Conservative government paid for new and refurbished youth clubs, and invested in training for youth workers. The effects lasted for decades. Their Tory heirs in the 2010s did the opposite, destroying infrastructure. Their policy of austerity forced local authorities to sell off buildings and make youth workers redundant, so denying the next generation the incalculable benefits of going up the youth club.

The Institute of Fiscal Studies eventually did the calculations. 'Closing youth clubs was not cost-effective,' wrote economist Carmen Villa in *The Effects of Youth Clubs on Education and Crime*, presenting what she described as the 'first causal estimates of their effects on education and crime', using evidence from 2010 to 2019. Pages of statistical evaluation and economic equations showed that teenagers living near shuttered youth clubs performed worse in exams, were more likely to commit crime and committed *more* crimes. Additionally, these young people were less likely to attend extra-curricular activities and spent more time on screens, with the effects being stronger for those in receipt of free school meals. Evidence backed up her conclusion that these effects were not driven by general austerity, but specifically by the closure of what she described as 'unique amenities'.

Individual young people suffered, with knock-on negative effects for their friends and families – because no youth is an island – and to the wider economy, with an estimated £3 of societal costs for every £1 'saved' by closing youth clubs. Proximity to parks, sports centres or libraries did not mitigate the effects.

I caught up with Carmen for a chat, to better understand her findings. Before embarking on this research, she'd been working on the relationship between social housing and gang formation – during which the subject of youth clubs came up, very quickly. Having grown up in Spain, moving to the UK in her late twenties, she had to learn how these spaces operated here. 'It's difficult to answer what the youth club is, even within the UK,' she said. 'I was just working on the basis that it was free or low-price, that anyone can come and go, and that there has to be a non-formal complement to education.' 'What did you think of your findings?' I asked her. 'Firstly, the effects are large,' she said. 'The size of the effects were surprising. They are as large as those my colleagues find when they look at Sure Start Centres. Also, the longer you're exposed to youth clubs during childhood, the better your outcomes. In general economics literature, there is a perception that investments made early in life are more valuable than investments made later on. My paper, together with other recent research, challenges that.' Youth clubs illustrate hard-to-evidence value, she explained, describing their ability to offer 'education that doesn't happen in school, and community-building beyond the classroom'. We need to invest in young people, she said, explaining her view that adolescence matters, and that youth clubs are special because they offer after-school activities, for free. As part of her research, she visited a handful of clubs and was surprised to find 'how cool' some of them are. 'I'm a musician,' she explained, 'and a lot of them have these music studios that are really nice. Something else that isn't in the paper is that all the youth workers I met are very vocationally driven, very dedicated, really wanting to do the right thing. I found that very touching.'

Youth clubs hold up a mirror, showing us who we are and who we could be. They're defined by a set of characteristics, including resilience and resourcefulness, which strike me as useful qualities during times of crises relating to the climate, politics and the economy. They can protect against divide-and-rule, offering deep, long-lasting and protective relationships and training in togetherness. An in-between space, they're mutable, locally responsive to change and simultaneously able to create change. They're the embodied, actualised outcome of an intention – to make space for the next generation. For over 150 years, our pick-and-mix of youth clubs has illustrated that people will repeatedly try to create environments where youth can thrive – a history of community intervention. Lack of funding proves that governments don't usually prioritise the well-being of teenagers, perhaps because most of them can't yet vote.

Youth is transient and no one is young for long enough to articulate all of this from within the experience. But, luckily for us, enough people across the ages have left fragments behind them, like a youth club Hansel and Gretel: breadcrumbs of books, speeches, reports, drawings, photographs and films. Taken one at a time, they tell interesting individual stories. Together, they form an irrefutable chorus. Youth clubs are socially and culturally powerful, even as their full effects are impossible to measure.

An image comes to mind, of the cartoon *Scooby-Doo*. In each episode, nefarious adults would try to scare off the group of teenage friends and their titular dog. Each and every time, it was because these adults were up to no good, usually in service of private profit: trying to make a house look haunted so they could sell off the gold underneath it, or laundering counterfeit money. Pesky kids, I think, showing us the value of connection in community, a reminder that together we're stronger.

A SHORT OUTRODUCTION
BYE, TAKE CARE, SEE YOU NEXT TIME

Part of me wanted to avoid recommendations, because, really, that's a whole other book. However, I decided that I needed to offer something. I worked up these suggestions with a handful of young people, youth workers, thinkers and doers. Hopefully, they offer a useful starting point for ongoing discussions and action.

TO POLITICIANS AND POLICY-MAKERS, AT ALL LEVELS

You have real power. Please use it.

A few ideas: create an urgent fund to save the clubs, adventure playgrounds and skateparks that have clung on, administered so that maximum funds go to the grassroots. Prioritise an audit of surviving provision, created by youth-work experts, not bankers and accountants, and grow a network of open-access locality clubs nationwide, perhaps incorporating other key services. Prioritise knowledge on the ground. Find ways to recruit and retain youth workers and don't kill them with 'assessination'. Centre-based space is a community resource, generating deep social capital and mitigating against a wide variety of ills. Include these cultural and social assets in your strategic planning.

TO YOUTH WORKERS AND YOUTH CLUB COMMITTEES

Thank you for your incredible work. Don't give up.

Urban designer and researcher Akil Scafe-Smith describes 'collective, networked resource sharing', where the learnings of youth clubs in one place could address the problems of another through regular forums for sharing, open channels of communication and practical support. Useful questions might include: How are we connected to similar spaces, including and beyond the youth club? What could we offer to, and receive from, other clubs or projects, navigating the difficulties together? How could our young people connect with those in other projects? But mostly, huge respect. The fact that any of you still exist is amazing.

TO PARENTS, CARERS AND RESPONSIBLE ADULTS

As volunteers and voters, you can make a big difference.

Bear in mind that tiny organisations, run on a shoestring, might find it hard to reply to emails. Offer your support, but please don't take it to heart if no one replies. Build relationships by turning up to the AGM or fundraising events. Get to know people and see what's needed. Take on thankless tasks. Donate. If you benefited from youth club, leave them money in your will. On a totally informal level, you can always let your young people and their friends use the space you have. Oh, and please tell councillors and/or MPs that you won't vote for them if they close youth clubs or make youth workers redundant.

TO BUSINESSES, CHARITIES AND INSTITUTIONS . . .

You're perfectly placed to contribute – and you'll benefit too.

Make links with your local youth provision and find out how you might help. Perhaps you could offer equipment, mentors, pathways to employment, or food? Hand over space, unconditionally. Or find areas within your buildings that can be used by young people. Funders, please trust those you give money to, and find creative ways for organisations to report back. Businesses, what would happen if you invited young people into the office to run an after-school project? It has been done before, with incredible results.

TO SCHOOL GOVERNORS AND SENIOR LEADERS IN EDUCATION

You have a role too (sorry, I know you're already flat out).

It's in your interests that local youth clubs thrive. They support your students after hours. Young people having positive relationships with youth workers can support improved interactions with teachers and preparedness to succeed. You're being asked to deal with so many social issues, and collaboration with youth clubs could bring benefits all round. How could the relationship between your organisations, based on mutual respect, be built or improved? For further education colleges and universities, these spaces offer a pipeline to students. How could you extend taster sessions, mentors or workshops into the youth club?

TO YOUNG PEOPLE

You've had a rough ride. The youth club could offer a space to rebuild, together.

I'm sorry things have been so difficult. It's easy to feel disconnected from your peers, for all sorts of reasons. I would ask you to try out your local youth provision, and if there isn't one, or you don't like it, think about organising something simple with your friends. Many of the clubs in this book started small, with young people at the heart of the decision-making. Find people who have the keys to space and ask them to open it up. Ask parents, their friends or actual youth workers to support projects that you can lead. You are allowed to meet new people and make connections. And, of course, there's no point having youth clubs without you lot in them.

ACKNOWLEDGEMENTS

Many people went above and beyond the call of duty to help me with this book. Firstly, I want to thank everyone who agreed to be interviewed, many of whom had to deal with multiple follow-up questions. Having attended a youth club, or worked in one, generates precious life material and it's not always easy digging back into the past. I'm sincerely grateful to those who did.

Hassan Elmi supported with archive trips, transcription and invaluable insights. Katy Warren, Camelia Muldermans and Naomi Brown offered youth work knowledge. Thanks to Feargal Lynn, Clare Tavernor and Simon Lam, Emmanuelle Cottrell, Louis Hassan, Coral Poyser-Lindo, Dr Clifford Williams, Mark K. Smith and Bernard Davies for careful reading and patient responses to many requests. Millie Nightingale assisted with research. I own any mistakes, conflations or errors of nuance.

Others helped me navigate labyrinthine sidestreams, including Taylor and Reuben Cottrell, Dave Mills, Nathaniel Prescodd, Lou Jerzyszek, Krishan Singh, Viva Cummins, P Knowledge, Dion Stretch, Paul Bradshaw, Luke Billingham, Sally Baxter, Dempsie Earles, Rasheeda Page-Muir, John Burgess, Paul Benney, Joanne Wain, Kath McDermott, Karen Pearson, Joseph Patterson, Alanna Henry, Holly Lester and Boyd Sleator, Matt Anniss, Scott and Sophie McCready, J. N. Benjamin, John Sabapathy, Carolyn Roberts, Dannyelle

Mavour, Danny Byrne, Fleur Constance, Andy McHugh, Marion Hawke, Annalise, Cathal, Zippy, Sophie Nicol, Chris Waywell, Annette Richardson and Tania R. Thanks for additional help with the recommendations to Danny D, Nathan P, Polly, Petra R, Anja Ngozi, Tigs Ikkos. Much appreciation to the Tom ap Rhys Pryce Memorial Trust and anyone who ever attended *Live Magazine* or Woolwich Creative Club. If you helped but aren't named – you know who you are. Thank you.

Special gratitude to staff at Belfast's Linen Hall Library, especially Melissa Flynn; Mark K. Smith's Infed.org; Sanjida, Debbie and Richard at Tower Hamlets Local History Library and Archives; Fyza at Coventry Archives; Dr Christopher de Coulon Berthoud at the Medway Archives Centre; John Ryan and team at Oxford House; the custodians of the NAYC collection at the Cadbury Research Library, Birmingham; Paul Carlyle at the University of Manchester's John Rylands Research Institute and Library; the National Youth Agency archive at DeMontfort; Goldsmiths Library; Youth Work Ireland and Ann O'Toole, Lisa der Weduwe and Jamie Brett at the Museum of Youth Culture.

The team at Faber offered unending support. It was a real pleasure to have Hannah Knowles as my editor, and I'm grateful to Dan Papps, Rachael Williamson, Robbie Porter, Anna Hervé, Melanie Gee and Ian Bahrami. My agent Crystal Mahey-Morgan at OWN IT! is the best person I could hope to have at my side through all the ups and downs of being an author.

The Society of Authors' Foundation awarded me a grant at a time when it made a big difference. Thanks to Diva Harris at Caught by the River, who invited me to join the Curfew Tower residency, and Stephen Bass, who let me stay in his place in Margate.

ACKNOWLEDGEMENTS

Friends helped out with this and that: Emma-Jean Thackray, Neeru Rishi, Kevin Braddock, Kieran Yates, Richard King, Lexy Morvaridi, Mark James, Mark Gurney, Steve Yates, Tayo Popoola, Wendy Erskine, Paul Byrne, Kate Ling, Joanna Kirk, Jeff Barrett, Andrew Walsh, Timna and Tommo.

Big love to Meg, Detta, Nats, Karl, Callum and Bella, Jim, Katy, Ellie, Zac, Stella, Ruby, Edith and Jude, Kirstie and Anthony, Anne Davey, Peter Warren and Dawnie. But mostly, unending thanks to all the youth workers. This is for you lot.

NOTES

1

Maisons des jeunes et de la culture . . . Laurent Besse, 'Youth and
Community Centres versus Cultural Centers in France 1959–1980',
chmcc.hypotheses.org, 18 May 2016.

Tania is now a leading expert . . . Tania de St Croix, *Grassroots Youth Work:
Policy, Passion and Practice* (Policy Press, 2016).

youth work that refuses to disappear . . . Louise Doherty and Tania de St
Croix, '"Embers and Fragments": Social Haunting in Youth Work,
Impact Measurement and Policy Networks', *Journal of Education
Policy*, 1–20, 2024.

extremity unmatched by our European neighbours . . . Sue Robertson, *Youth
Clubs: Participation, Friendship and Fun!* (Russell House, 2005), p. 22.

starting employment, on average, at the age of ten . . . Emma Griffin, *Liberty's
Dawn: A People's History of the Industrial Revolution* (Yale, 2014), p. 60.

in no other town in Europe did the extremes of human existence . . . Sidney Bunt
and Ron Gargrave, *The Politics of Youth Clubs* (National Youth Bureau,
1980), pp. 11–12.

emerged largely out of the activities of evangelical Christians . . . Mark K. Smith,
'Methodism and Youth Work', Infed.org, 2024.

the Society in Scotland . . . Jamie Kelly, 'The Mission at Home: The Origins
and Development of the Society in Scotland for Propagating Christian
Knowledge, 1709–1767', *eSharp*, Issue 24, Spring 2016.

In Wales, educational entities known as Circulating Schools . . . Geraint H.
Jenkins, *The Foundations of Modern Wales, 1642–1780* (University of Wales
Press, 1987), pp. 370–81.

Sunday Schools, the first of which is recorded at St Mary's . . . Irene Smale, *The
Evolution of the Sunday School 1751 to the Present Day as a Paradigm for the
Church in Supporting Societal Crises* (Church of England, 2023), p. 1.

alternative history of the Industrial Revolution . . . Emma Griffin, *Liberty's
Dawn*, p. 179.

the Brighton Working Men's Institute . . . W. McG. Eagar, *Making Men: Being a
History of Boys Clubs and Related Movements in Great Britain* (University

of London Press, 1953), p. 129, quoted in Sue Robertson, *Youth Clubs*, p. 22.

daytime sewing classes . . . Gerald Schofield, 'Hard Times: The Cotton Famine', cottontown.org.

What was so dangerous about drapery? . . . Deborah Wynne, 'The "Despised Trade" in Textiles: H. G. Wells, William Paine, Charles Cavers and the Male Draper's Life, 1870–1914', *Textile History*, 2015, pp. 99–113.

The Reverend Arthur Sweatman presented a paper . . . Mark K. Smith, 'Arthur Sweatman: Youths' Clubs and Institutes', Infed.org.

his speech was included in a book . . . Henry Solly, *Working Men's Clubs and Institutes* (Simpkin, Marshall, Hamilton, Kent and Co., 1904).

harrowing detail of the lives of the very poor . . . Ernest Pilkington, *An Eton Playing Field by an Old Etonian: A Reminiscence of Happy Days Spent at the Eton Mission* (Edward Arnold, 1896), p. 24.

swimming in the filthy Hackney Cut . . . ibid., p. 36.

Shinpads were disallowed . . . ibid., p. 83.

'We had a good many "ructions"' . . . ibid., p. 76.

'When the fellows came back from a run' . . . ibid., p. 123.

Eton Manor . . . split with the Mission . . . John Few, *Eton Manor AC 1913–2013* (Eton Manor AC, 2013), pp. 4–6.

Harry Mallin . . . ibid., p. 8.

Roger Bannister . . . ibid., p. 11.

the positive effects of 'loving supervision' . . . Rev. Samuel Barnett and Mrs Samuel A. Barnett, *Practicable Socialism* (Longmans, Green and Co., 1888), pp. 100–1.

'habitable chambers' . . . ibid., p. 102.

what we'd now describe as youth provision . . . Sue Robertson, *Youth Clubs*, p. 23.

by 1911, there were forty-nine Settlements . . . John Gal, Stefan Köngeter and Sarah Vicary, *The Settlement House Movement Revisited* (Bristol University Press, 2021), p. 2.

a comprehensive school I'd been involved with . . . Thomas Tallis, in Kidbrooke, south-east London, which is proud to offer progressive education to young people in the area.

author of the highly readable . . . Jonathan Roberts, *Youth Work Ethics: Empowering Youth and Community Work Practice* (Learning Matters, 2009).

the Girls' Club Sectional Committee . . . Administrative History, 'Records of UK Youth, 1909–2015', Cadbury Research Library, Special Collections, University of Birmingham. MS227.

'The original intention of the NOGC' . . . ibid.

the growing number of clubs for these factory girls . . . 'Hearth and Home', *Manchester Times*, Saturday, 28 April 1888, p. 7.

'the spirit of Misrule is rampant' . . . ibid.

'an arrangement which proved exceedingly beneficial' . . . *Manchester Times*, 30 June 1888, p. 6.

'If rough girls or boys freely elect' . . . ibid.

'One is indignant to think of two children' . . . ibid.

where the average is twelve . . . www.penalreform.org/issues/children/ key-facts.

'Who gets to get away' . . . Yomi Ṣode, *Manorism* (Penguin, 2023), p. 1.

2

Parliamentarian and Royalist armies . . . Haydn Wheeler, *Clubmen 1645* (Haydn Wheeler, 2021).

If you offer to plunder . . . John Staab, *Riotous or Revolutionary: The Clubmen during the English Civil Wars* (Eastern Illinois University, 2002).

over a thousand Clubmen gathered . . . reproduced on Haydn Wheeler's blog, Clubmen1645.com.

'enforced to associate ourselves' . . . ibid.

3

'the vast reserve of loyal patriotism' . . . Robert Baden-Powell, *Scouting for Boys* (Horace Cox, 1908).

'getting recruits for the Territorials' . . . John Springhall, *Youth, Empire and Society* (Archon Books, 1977), p. 8.

'usually from the influential sector of society' . . . Louise Hurley, 'The Historical Development of Irish Youth Work (1850–1985)', p. 13.

'I promise to work for the independence of Ireland' . . . ibid.

Rebel scouts . . . Marnie Hay, *Na Fianna Éireann and the Irish Revolution, 1909–23: Scouting for Rebels* (Manchester University Press, 2019).

'pass on belief, values' . . . Louise Hurley, 'The Historical Development of Irish Youth Work (1850–1985)', p. 14.

4

'to liaise with educational bodies' . . . Sue Robertson, *Youth Clubs*, p. 25.

clubs had signed up . . . Administrative History, 'Records of UK Youth, 1909–2015', Cadbury Research Library, Special Collections, University of Birmingham, MS227.

Young Farmers' Clubs were formed in rural England and Wales . . . nfyfc.org.uk/history.

Urdd Gobaith Cymru . . . was established in 1922 . . . urdd.cymru/en/about-us/our-history.

fifty-two clubs in industrial areas such as the Rhondda Valley. . . Mark K. Smith, 2001, quoted in Sue Robertson, *Youth Clubs*, p. 25.

the first professional training course for youth leaders . . . Tony Jeffs and Mark K. Smith, 'Getting the Job Done', *Youth and Policy*, Spring 1993, Issue 40, pp. 10–32.

a grant from the King George V Jubilee Trust . . . Administrative History, 'Records of UK Youth, 1909–2015', Cadbury Research Library, Special Collections, University of Birmingham, MS227.

the Physical Training and Recreation Act . . . Sue Robertson, *Youth Clubs*, p. 25.

'significant expansion of clubs' . . . Administrative History, 'Records of UK Youth, 1909–2015', Cadbury Research Library, Special Collections, University of Birmingham, MS227.

'no youth clubs in one small rural area' . . . Sue Robertson, *Youth Clubs*, p. 128.

local authorities should offer 'leisure time occupation' . . . The Education Act 1944, Section 41(b).

the South African Aid to Britain Fund . . . Hansard, Vol. 445, 18 December 1947.

'as an expression of their deep sympathy' . . . ibid.

British governments would repeatedly . . . Sam Matthews Boehmer, 'Questionable Allies: British Collaboration with Apartheid South Africa, 1960–90', *The International History Review*, 24 August 2023.

900 new centres . . . Bernard Davies, *From Voluntaryism to Welfare State: A History of the Youth Service in England, Volume 1, 1939–1979* (Youth Work Press, 1999), pp. 25–6.

'the maintenance of essential facilities has been impaired' . . . Bernard Davies, 1999, quoted in Sue Robertson, *Youth Clubs*, p. 27.

an essential cornerstone of the literature . . . Bernard Davies, *From Voluntaryism to Welfare State: A History of the Youth Service in England, Volumes 1–3* (Youth Work Press, 1999).

Sally's parents . . . Celia Rose, *Touching Lives: A Personal History of the Clapton Jewish Youth Centre 1946–1976* (Youth Work Press, 1998).

5

a classic of the genre . . . Josephine Macalister Brew, *In the Service of Youth* (Faber, 1944).

'We all know the girl in the mackintosh' . . . ibid., p. 11.

'dance and listen to that horrible jazz' . . . ibid., p. 13.

'a great folk dance of the day' . . . ibid., p. 14.

'True culture is the appreciation of everything' . . . ibid.

an initial print run of 2,000 copies . . . Faber archives, E/9/29/3.

she wrote to her publisher . . . Faber archives, Letters, January 1943, E/3/38/1.

her Times *obituary* . . . S. H. Woods, 'Josephine Macalister Brew', *The Times*, 31 May 1957.

the iconic Creators not Consumers . . . Mark K. Smith, *Creators Not Consumers: Rediscovering Social Education* (UK Youth, 1981).

Jo had become chief outside consultant . . . Melanie Tebbutt, 'Listening to Youth? BBC Youth Broadcasts During the 1930s and the Second World War', *History Workshop Journal*, 2017, pp. 214–33.

a BBC internal circulating memo . . . BBC Written Archives, R51/7/1.

a talk entitled 'Youth and Tomorrow' . . . *The West Australian*, 18 September 1946, p. 12.

'besieged' by boys and girls at the YMCA . . . 'Thought Peculiar', *Sydney Morning Herald*, 10 September 1946, p. 6.

'seemed to have a Scottish grandmother' . . . ibid.

a campaign for 1,000 voluntary leaders . . . *Times Educational Supplement*, 7 October 1955.

<h1 style="text-align:center">6</h1>

The film is not exactly what it seems . . . Vic Pratt, *Police and Thieves: The COI Collection Volume One* (BFI, 2010), accompanying booklet, p. 9.

An NAYC leaflet from the era . . . The National Association of Mixed Clubs and Girls' Clubs, 'Growing-Up in Britain', undated. Cadbury Research Library, Special Collections, University of Birmingham, MS227/5/10/2.

'to help young people through leisure time activities' . . . *What CAYC Is*, undated leaflet. CAYC existed for groups located where there was no NAYC club nearby. Cadbury Research Library, Special Collections, University of Birmingham. MS227/5/10/2.

Newspaper cuttings compiled by the NAYC . . . Cadbury Research Library, Special Collections, University of Birmingham, MS227/4/3/1.

Karl Reinz's documentary . . . *We Are the Lambeth Boys*, dir. Karl Reinz, 1959. Screenonline.org.uk/film/id/444789.

a SCIF Christmas party . . . Rick Blackman, *Forty Miles of Bad Road* (Redwords, 2017), p. 52.

the celebrity-organised youth club lasted only six weeks . . . ibid., p. 63.

'most reasonably competent youth orchestras' . . . Johnny Dankworth, *Tom Sawyer's Saturday* (Oxford University Press, 1968).

7

Le Bal Masque . . . *London Evening Standard*, 28 January 1954.

He also wrote about Teddy Boys . . . Richard Hoggart, *Uses of Literacy* (Chatto & Windus, 1957).

Some 3,000 buildings went up . . . The Fairbairn-Milson Report, HMSO, 1969, paragraph 24.

'aimed to give young people' . . . Sue Robertson, *Youth Clubs*, p. 30.

Molly Lefebure was an active part . . . Oliver Gerrish, 'Molly O'the Morgue: My Grandmother', archmusicman.blogspot, March 2013.

a regular sight at Scotland Yard . . . 'Molly Lefebure', *Telegraph*, 17 April 2013.

Irish costermongers and the Teddy Boys . . . Mary Blandy, *Razor Edge: The Story of a Youth Club* (Victor Gollancz, 1967), p. 12.

under the pseudonym Mary Blandy . . . Mary Blandy was a historical figure, born in 1717, and convicted of murder for poisoning her father. She was hanged in 1752.

Razor Edge provides a sight-line . . . Molly's descriptions of early club life (pp. 12–14) offer a sense of the bigger picture, describing the youth service as part of the system of further education, supported at grassroots level by unpaid volunteers.

Molly's fellow management committee members . . . Mary Blandy, *Razor Edge*, p. 203.

'anti-social work' . . . ibid., p. 83.

'Youth-clubs are, of course, always being broken into' . . . ibid., p. 101.

'Indeed, I was later told the names' . . . ibid.

an encounter with a 'vitriolic old man' . . . ibid., p. 166.

it outlined the need for an emergency training programme. . . The Albemarle Report, HMO, 1960, paragraph 257. Paragraph 248 recommended that leaders be recruited from three main groups: teachers, social workers and 'mature persons with a natural gift for leadership'.

Charlie Parker played at Birdland . . . Ben Forrest, 'The Night Charlie Parker Blew Away Igor Stravinsky', *Far Out Magazine*, 13 January 2024.

8

focused on Withywood . . . 'A Blueprint Comes to Life: Model Youth Club at Bristol', *Times Educational Supplement*, 23 August 1963.

9

'Enter seven youths with shotguns' . . . David Collyer, *Double Zero* (Fontana, 1973), p. 7.

the Weekenders project . . . NAYC archive, Cadbury Research Library, Special Collections, University of Birmingham, MS227/5/10/2.

By 1967, there were 3,271 clubs affiliated . . . 'NAYC Facts and Figures', inside front cover, Annual Report 1967/8. Cadbury Research Library, Special Collections, University of Birmingham, MS227/5/11/1.

club rooms for the exclusive use of older members . . . Annual Report 1967/8, p. 18. Cadbury Research Library, Special Collections, University of Birmingham, MS227/5/11/1.

10

'surplus to requirements' and in poor repair . . . Coventry City Council, Education Committee minutes, 5 October 1992, p. 31. Coventry Archives and Research Centre.

The report describes approximately 700 youth organisations . . . Coventry Youth Services Report, 1971/2.

Holyhead received a significantly shorter entry . . . 'Report of a Working Party for the Review of Youth and Community Services', Youth and Community Services, April 1972, p. 78. Coventry Archives and Research Centre, JN369.4.

The West Indian Youth Club was granted one day a week . . . Gus John, *In the Service of Black Youth: A Study of the Political Culture of Youth and Community Work with Black People in English Cities*, Case Study 2, Holyhead (NAYC, 1981), p. 88.

Belgrade Theatre Company . . . ibid.

awarded Holyhead a £200 grant . . . ibid.

someone discovered a trap door . . . ibid., p. 91.

exhibited at Coventry Music Museum . . . 'Jah Baddis Before The Specials', Coventry Music Museum, November 2019.

Two neighbours led complaints about excessive noise . . . Gus John, *In the Service of Black Youth*, p. 82.

a new management committee was imposed on the club . . . ibid., p. 95.

'A youth club with a difference' . . . 'Youths' Club Dream Comes True', *Coventry Evening Telegraph*, 22 July 1976, p. 17.

decided it should become a standardised youth club . . . Gus John, *In the Service of Black Youth*, p. 97.

the local authority advertised a role . . . *Coventry Evening Telegraph*, 11 May 1979, p. 57.

reported on youth work in Coventry . . . HMI Inspection of Coventry Youth Services, 1987, pp. 2 and 26.

according to an evaluation by the universities of Coventry and Warwick . . . 'Coventry UK City of Culture 2021 Impact Evaluation: An Evaluation Report', University of Warwick and Coventry University, 2023.

11

social context is offered . . . 'Easterhouse Club Closure', 19 August 1970, BBC Rewind, discover.bbcrewind.co.uk/asset/62e14a3174bea30023918abb.

TAKI 183 . . . Inspired by election posters and stickers, TAKI 183 began writing his name all over New York City. An article in the *New York Times* in 1971 brought him to wider attention, arguably making him the father of contemporary graffiti. He remains anonymous (Taki183.net).

'knew virtually every police officer' . . . James Anderson obituary, *Glasgow Herald*, 26 February 2002.

NAYC launched Community Industry . . . Annual Report, 1980/1, p. 12. Cadbury Research Library, Special Collections, University of Birmingham, MS227/5/11/1.

Another clip, from 1972 . . . https://bbcrewind.co.uk/asset/634025ff1d6adf002371f126?q=youth%20clubs.

encouraged a community-based approach . . . Community of Interest (Scottish Education Dept., 1968), Tony Jeffs and Mark Smith, 'Getting the Job Done', *Youth & Policy*, 1993, p. 15.

the Alexander Report built on the idea . . . Gary Fraser, 'Community Education in Scotland, a Tale of Two Anniversaries: The Alexander Report (1975) and the Birth of the Performance Indicator (1985)', *Journal of Contemporary Community Education Practice Theory*, Vol. 6, No. 3, Winter 2015.

'adults must in future accept young people as social equals' . . . Department of Education and Science (1969), *Youth and Community Work in the 70s; Proposals by the Youth Service Development Council* (The 'Fairbairn-Milson Report'), London: HMSO, pp. 73–7. This quote was highlighted by Mark K. Smith on Infed.org, https://shorturl.at/duiuA.

12

when it comes to telling stories about Iran . . . Tara Fatehi Irani, *Mishandled Archive* (Live Art Development Agency, 2020).

Requiring the provision of facilities . . . The Education and Libraries (Northern Ireland) Order 1972, 14 August 1972, p. 2.

in 1972, the annual allocation . . . Sam McCready and Richard Loudon, *Investing in Lives: The History of the Youth Service in Northern Ireland (1844–1973)*, Vol. 1 (CDS, 2015), p. 421.

Between 1974 and 1979, funding increased . . . Desmond Bell, *Acts of Union: Youth Culture and Sectarianism in Northern Ireland* (Macmillan, 1990), p. 43.

There were 143 purpose-built youth facilities completed . . . Sam McCready and Richard Loudon, *Investing in Lives*, p. 421.

before 1975, less than one in ten clubs were state-provided . . . Desmond Bell, *Acts of Union*, p. 44.

'had little purchase on the activities of working class youth' . . . ibid.

In 1975, the Education and Library Boards identified 130 clubs . . . Sam McCready and Richard Loudon, *Investing in Lives*, p. 24.

The Open Door youth club . . . *Scene Around Six*, 18 December 1979, bbcrewind.co.uk.

he brought a message to his contemporaries . . . NAYC conference report 1977, Cadbury Research Library, Special Collections, University of Birmingham, MS227/5/10/1.

'borrowed a turntable from somewhere' . . . Sam McCready and Richard Loudon, *Investing in Lives*, p. 54.

ensuring paramilitaries didn't infiltrate . . . ibid., p. 129.

church youth clubs that were robbed . . . ibid., p. 128.

Some youth workers paid with their lives . . . ibid., p. 436.

13

celebratory history . . . Andrew Miles, *Birmingham PHAB Camps 1967–2017* (Birmingham PHAB Camps, 2017).

Elizabeth recalled the circumstances . . . Andrew Miles, *Birmingham PHAB Camps 1967–2017*, p. 36.

Tony Gray kept a diary . . . www.bhamphabcamps.org.uk/www/50years/volunteersdiary1969.shtml.

'It is a club' . . . 'Specialised Youth Clubs', *Where's the Sense? But What the Hell!* Annual Youth Conference Report, 11–13 July 1980.

a long-lasting and brilliant youth club . . . Richard Phoenix, in *Do Your Own Thing* (Rough Trade Books, 2023), conveys what he learned working at the club, which is run by creative arts organisation Heart n Soul.

Savile became honorary president of PHAB . . . PHAB obituary, https://web.archive.org/web/20111119234102/http://www.phab.org.uk

Jimmy Savile asked me if I would be president of PHAB' . . . 'All Together Now', *Nursing Standard*, 3 May, Vol. 14, No. 33, 2000.

individuals running the London Marathon described him . . . https://www.justgiving.com/fundraising/seanborejszo (2006) and justgiving.com/fundraising/Steve-Bussey (2010).

Harris was found guilty . . . Court of Appeal, Royal Courts of Justice, 7 November 2017. *Regina* v. *Rolf Harris*, 2014/3548/B2.

vice presidents of the NAYC . . . National Association of Youth Clubs Annual Report 1973, p. 11, and 1971–1972, p. 16. Cadbury Research Library, Special Collections, University of Birmingham, MS227/5/11/1/15.

'Tea-Rific Fun and Happiness week' . . . *This Is NAYC: Club Week 18–26 October 1974*, Cadbury Research Library, Special Collections, University of Birmingham, MS227/5/14/9.

'tea and "pep talk"' . . . 'NAYC Tea-rific Fun and Happiness Week with Jimmy Savile, OBE, Vice President' (programme), 1974, Cadbury Research Library, Special Collections, University of Birmingham, MS227/5/14/9.

a weekend and a 'mini-week' . . . 'Fun and Happiness', Annual Report 1976, p. 16, Cadbury Research Library, Special Collections, University of Birmingham, MS227/5/11/1.

Savile remained on the list of vice presidents . . . Youth Clubs UK Annual Report 1995–1996 and Annual Review 1996/1997. Cadbury Research Library, Special Collections, University of Birmingham, MS227/5/11/1/38.

'When Are We Old Enough?' . . . 'Conference Report, the National Association of Youth Clubs Annual Youth Conference, 7–9 July 1978, Earnshaw Hall, Sheffield University' (NAYC, 1978). Cadbury Research Library, Special Collections, University of Birmingham, MS227/5/7/1.

The conference agreed that police brutality was increasing . . . Conference Resolutions are listed on a separate document, within the same file as the main report. Cadbury Research Library, Special Collections, University of Birmingham, MS227/5/7/1.

O'Carroll was sent to prison . . . 'Child Sex Man Gets Two Years', *Daily Mirror*, 14 March 1981, p. 7.

A press statement . . . Conference Report, NAYC, 1978, op. cit. Cadbury Research Library, Special Collections, University of Birmingham, MS227/5/7/1.

a motion was proposed by NAYC members . . . The item, titled 'An Age of Consent', appears at the bottom of p. 1 of the Conference Resolutions, which are listed on the separate document, within the same file as the main report. Cadbury Research Library, Special Collections, University of Birmingham, MS227/5/7/1.

14

declared independence . . . Mick Lemmerman, islandhistory.wordpress.com, 7 December 2013.

the development that would become Canary Wharf . . . email conversation with Tony Westfallen, 14 December 2024.

renovated with the help of a group of local youngsters . . . Detail from club member Mike McSweeney, one of the original youth club members. Contacted via facebook.com/groups/theiodthenandnow.

clubbed together to buy Westfallen a gift . . . 'Isle of Dogs' Floating Youth Club', BBC *Nationwide*, 5 June 1974.

'diabolically skilled scrounging' . . . ibid.

'Most work in working-class areas' . . . ibid.

for every pound spent on education . . . MP Alan Haselhurst, debating the Youth and Community Bill, Hansard, 1 February 1974, Vol. 868, cc741–835.

'when cuts have come' . . . Hansard, 21 February 1975, Vol. 886.

'Say it a hundred times' . . . Hansard, 10 February 1978, Vol. 943.

the bill was 'talked out'. . . MP Cyril Townsend, debating the Youth and Community Bill, 9 November 1979, Hansard, Vol. 973.

15

the Multi-Racial Project . . . Multi-Racial Project Steering Committee, 6 September 1973, Cadbury Research Library, Special Collections, University of Birmingham, MS227/1/1/7/19–20.

At the second committee meeting . . . ibid., 15 November 1973.

Opened in 1973 . . . *Brockley Society*, Issue 154, March 2022, p. 1.

sucked out of communal ownership . . . ibid.

'mixed group of working-class kids' . . . John Goto, *Lovers Rock* (Autograph ABP, 2013), p. 114.

images from Lovers Rock . . . 'Then and Now', 2–3 Winslade Way, Catford Shopping Centre, October 2018.

16

RUC Box 1 Ephemera . . . Northern Ireland Political Collection, Linen Hall Library, Ephemera, RUC Box 1. Contents are not listed to item level and are intended for exploratory research. With more time, I would have also explored boxes titled 'Community Relations' and 'Community Groups'.

The RUC had been formed after partition . . . lrb.co.uk/blog/2020/june/what-happened-to-the-ruc.

Belfast poet . . . Martin Mooney, *Blue Lamp Discos* (Langan Press, 2003).

the RUC had acquired twenty-six 'disco units' . . . Royal Ulster Constabulary, Chief Constable's Annual Report, 1978, p. 39.

1,588 'well-supervised discos' . . . Royal Ulster Constabulary, Chief Constable's Annual Report, 1979, p. 20.

'activities in the field of community' . . . Report of the Advisory Committee on Police in Northern Ireland (HMSO, 1969), paragraphs 134 and 135.

'Blue Lamp youth clubs and discos' . . . '"Time" Say Blue Lamp Officers', *Belfast News Letter*, 2 October 1975, p. 2.

wrote a feature on the discos . . . Ivan Little, 'The Policemen Who Are on the Pop Beat', *Belfast Telegraph*, 14 January 1976, p. 10.

In 1979, the RUC engaged with . . . Royal Ulster Constabulary, Chief Constable's Annual Report, 1979, p. 20.

after Amnesty International called for an inquiry . . . 'Report of an Amnesty International Mission to Northern Ireland (28 November–6 December 1977)', Amnesty International, 1978. See also newspaper reports from decades later, including Ian Cobain, 'Inside Castlereagh: "We Got Confessions by Torture"', *Guardian*, 11 October 2010.

a widespread belief – later evidenced – of collusion . . . 'Report of the Independent International Panel on Alleged Collusion in Sectarian Killings in Northern Ireland', Centre for Civil and Human Rights, Notre Dame Law School, October 2006.

Sir Kenneth Newman batting off criticism . . . 'R.U.C. Criticism Less Than Fair, Says Newman', *Derry Journal*, 13 April 1979, p. 2.

discos in Armagh were being run . . . 'RUC Denies Disco Spy Bid', *Belfast News Letter*, 12 December 1975, p. 9.

The Gaelic Athletic Association turfed the event out . . . 'Red Light for Blue Disco', *Belfast News Letter*, 19 December, p. 1.

Blue Lamp Discos at Armagh Technical College . . . 'Close Disco Call from DUP Man', *Belfast News Letter*, 10 March 1976, p. 5.

community relations officer 'Paul Walters' . . . Northern Ireland Political Collection, Linen Hall Library, Ephemera, RUC Box 1.

'Every effort is made' . . . 'Terrorism – A Point of View', *Police Beat*, 1979, pp. 29–38. Accessed in microfiche room of the Northern Ireland Political Collection, Linen Hall Library, Belfast.

His memoir . . . Neil Trelford, *The Youth Club* (Austin Macauley, 2016).

the RUC reported that 1,116 Blue Lamp Discos . . . Royal Ulster Constabulary, Chief Constable's Annual Report 1981, pp. 20–1.

numbers stayed above a thousand discos per year . . . The stats in the Chief Constable's Reports are as follows: more than a thousand Blue Lamp Discos held (1982, p. 14), 1,051 held for 128,000 young people (1983, pp. 17–18), 871 held for 109,000 young people, plus 'several thousand entrants' to the Blue Lamp Disco Dancing Championships (1984, p. 28).

Cherry recreated a Blue Lamp Disco . . . Lesley Cherry, *Blue Lamp Disco Sessions*, The Station, June 2010, in association with the University of Ulster and Platform Arts. lesleycherry.wordpress.com/about/the-blue-lamp-disco-sessions.

In 1986, the RUC claimed . . . Royal Ulster Constabulary, Chief Constable's Annual Report 1986.

the CRB was replaced by Community Affairs . . . Royal Ulster Constabulary, Chief Constable's Annual Report 1993, p. 61.

17

Her obituary . . . Peter Tatchell, Rose Robertson obituary, *Guardian*, 26 October 2011.

famous newspaper agony aunts . . . Claire Rayner, *Sunday Mirror*, 9 May 1982, p. 23.

The Cork Examiner *was quoting Rose* . . . 'Would Like Law Changed', *Cork Examiner*, 27 June 1980. Posted on the Irish Queer Archive Facebook page, shorturl.at/SCHNr.

the House of Lords decided in summer 1921 . . . Hansard, 15 August 1921, Vol. 43, cc567–77.

nineteen-year-old John Holland tried . . . Clifford Williams, *Courage to Be: Organised Gay Youth in England 1967–1990* (The Book Guild Ltd, 2021), pp. 1–2.

In Liverpool, in 1972, members of CHE . . . ibid., p. 10.

Channel 4's youth culture show . . . Gary James, *Spangles, Glam, Gaywaves & Tubes* (The Book Guild, 2019), p. 56.

Philip Cox believed that a teenage group . . . Clifford Williams, *Courage to Be*, pp. 26–7.

Renowned choreographer . . . Sir Matthew Bourne discussed LGTG with Jo Whiley, BBC Radio 2, 25 January 2018.

influential 1983 documentary . . . Dr Ieuan Franklin has published fascinating research: 'Taking Liberties: Framed Youth, Community Video and Channel 4's Remit in Action' (2014) and 'Precursor of Pride: The Pleasures and Aesthetics of Framed Youth' (2019). It was, he said, 'an underground form of video art which itself anticipated contemporary remix culture in its imaginative and satirical use of footage "ripped" and recycled from film and television'.

The subject line stated 'rare footage' . . . The film was posted on YouTube by Martin Collins: youtube.com/watch?v=No1fIjUUQos.

'a clear illustration of institutional prejudice' . . . Lorraine Trenchard and Hugh Warren, *Something to Tell You: The Experiences and Needs of Young Lesbians and Gay Men in London* (London Gay Teenage Group, 1984), p. 162.

Leaders from the Scouts made the effort . . . Clifford Williams, *Courage to Be*, p. 55.

18

Phil Cox initiated Gaywaves . . . Gary James, *Spangles, Glam, Gaywaves & Tubes* (The Book Guild, 2019), p. 100.

Cox describes the joy of making the shows . . . John Hind and Stephen Mosco, *Rebel Radio: The Full Story of British Pirate Radio* (Pluto Press, 1985), pp. 72–7.

A poster and info pack was sent . . . Lorraine Trenchard and Hugh Warren, *Something to Tell You*, p. 19.

19

the FBYO will campaign for change . . . The Federation of Bangladeshi Youth Organisations, Tower Hamlets Archive I/SSP/4/9/9, 360 Box 2.

Bradford-born, before moving to Brick Lane . . . independent.co.uk/arts-entertainment/obituary-haroon-shamsher-1106287.html.

'A Young Generation Begins to Fight Back' . . . Ansar Ahmed Ullah sent me the clipping of this article, which did not include the date, page or publication title. Another story on the page, about the killing of two men in a Drogheda restaurant, ties it to 1987.

'Migration happened' . . . https://www.theguardian.com/world/2018/feb/07/ambalavaner-sivanandan.

MIC . . . Dr Christopher de Coulon Berthoud at the Medway Archive Centre noted that while officially the Medway Indian Centre, it was generally referred to as the Medway Indian Club.

who wrote in compelling style . . . Vic Templar, *The First Night of the MIC Club*, published online 28 June 2017: https://shorturl.at/GadvH.

20

'a more violent version of school' . . . Thanks to Robbie Wojciechowski
for this gem.

pamphlets on screen printing . . . Cadbury Research Library, Special
Collections, University of Birmingham, MS227/5/15/1/1.

NAYC launched a new Arts Festival . . . NAYC Annual Report 1984/5,
p. 7, Cadbury Research Library, Special Collections, University of
Birmingham. MS227/5/11/.

Kevin Kennedy, who played Curly Watts, was an adjudicator . . . ibid.

NAYC gained funding from the Gulbenkian Foundation . . . ibid.

Commercial sponsors got on board . . . ibid.

a three-day workshop in Rhydywaun County Youth Centre . . . NAYC Annual
Report 1984/5, p. 8, Cadbury Research Library, Special Collections,
University of Birmingham, MS227/5/11/1.

In Gloucestershire, an arts team was formed . . . NAYC Annual Report 1985/6,
p. 7, Cadbury Research Library, Special Collections, University of
Birmingham, MS227/5/11/1.

they approached Eagle House . . . . It should be noted that there were many
other youth clubs in Bristol at this time. Special mention to youth
worker John Nation and his graffiti wall at the Dug Out in Barton Hill,
where artists including Inkie, Cheo and Banksy passed through. 'My
Bristol Favourites: John Nation', Bristol247.com, 28 February 2015. Also
Lee Moran, 'The Revolutionary Street Art Project That Inspired Banksy
and Empowered a City's Youth', *Huffington Post*, 27 June 2017.

Conservative minister Norman Tebbit's response . . . Speech at Conservative
Party conference, 15 October 1981.

reported that there were 1,180,500 unemployed young people . . . NAYC Annual
Report 1983/4, p. 8, Cadbury Research Library, Special Collections,
University of Birmingham, MS227/5/11/1.

the NAYC had initiated Community Industry . . . NAYC Annual Report
1980/1, p. 11, Cadbury Research Library, Special Collections, University
of Birmingham, MS227/5/11/1.

money was found to open youth club doors . . . Sue Robertson, *Youth
Clubs*, p. 36.

The NAYC launched the all-caps DAYSPACE . . . NAYC Annual Report
1983/4, p. 8, and Annual Report 1984/5, p. 6, Cadbury Research Library,
Special Collections, University of Birmingham, MS227/5/11/1.

Unemployment was the highest in the UK . . . 'Economic Inactivity in
Northern Ireland' (Pivotal Public Policy Forum Northern Ireland,
2024), p. 14.

Practical Action's presence at the 1985 Youth Festival . . . *Belfast News Letter*, 14 January 1985, p. 15.

Sir Keith Joseph, then education secretary . . . National Youth Archive, DeMontfort University. Contained within folder 24951.

21

Becoming an adult can be a difficult . . . HMI Inspection of Coventry Youth Services, 1987, p. 3.

unemployment for under twenty-fives went up 167 per cent . . . Hansard, Vol. 80, 11 June 1985.

schoolkids rebelled against a government plan . . . Steven Johns, 'The UK School Students' Strike 1985', libcom.org, October 2015.

The NAYC's affiliation statistics . . . NAYC Annual Report, 1985/6, Cadbury Research Library, Special Collections, University of Birmingham, MS227/5/11/1.

Goulistan Girls Group . . . russellboyce.com/Peterborough.

in 1986, 10 per cent of eleven- to fifteen-year-olds in England smoked . . . ash.org.uk/resources/view/young-people-and-smoking.

'A cigarette for the beginner' . . . ash.org.uk/uploads/ASH_625.pdf?v= 1648213606.

'the creative industries' generated . . . 'Contribution of the Arts to Society and the Economy', House of Lords, 26 January 2024.

22

An ILEA List of Registered Youth Groups in 1986 . . . Tower Hamlets Local History Library and Archives, ref. 360, Box B2.

an ILEA report had landed . . . 'Report: Boxing in the Youth Service: Current Position', ILEA London Youth Committee, 14 May 1986, Tower Hamlets Local History Library and Archives, I/SPP/5/41 (2/2).

The NAYC's Girls' Work Unit had been set up . . . This detail is also included in an informative blog post by Ryan Aslett: history.ox.ac.uk/article/ gender-dynamics-and-feminist-intervention-in-youth-clubs-in-late-twentieth-century-england.

reporting on their formal Girls' Work policy . . . NAYC Annual Report, 1983/4, p. 3, Cadbury Research Library, Special Collections, University of Birmingham, MS227/5/11/1/26.

23

videos shot by a tech-savvy teenager on 8mm film . . . Peter Godfrey's YouTube
Channel contains the video in question: @PeterJG100.

a three-part programme for Thames TV . . . *Who Believes in Orpington?* Thames
Television/ITV, 14 March 1988.

a corrugated-iron building known as 'the tin Tabernacle' . . . 'Orpington
Methodist Church: Brief History': shorturl.at/Hwdzf.

A short history written for the Orpington Methodist Church magazine . . . Mr
C. W. Eade, 'The Romance of Methodism in Orpington', *Orpington
Methodist Church Magazine*, February 1952.

24

opening their West London Mission in 1887 . . . The London Archives,
West London Mission Administrative History, N/M/002: https://
shorturl.at/VoQhu.

In the beginning, there was just a Friday-night Bible class . . . Walworth
Methodist Church's website was useful here, as was the short
documentary *Loyalty and Service*, dir. James Steel, viewed via the
Southwark Local History Library and Archive and the London Screen
Archives Network.

Methodists already had a significant foothold . . . Mark K. Smith, 'Methodism
and Youth Work', 2019. Infed.org.

one of the largest church-based youth organisations in Europe . . . 'Youth Work',
A Dictionary of Methodism. shorturl.at/lsWHq.

Hope was mobbed . . . Gaumont British News, British Pathé, 1951,
shorturl.at/HjvwQ.

TV show This Is Your Life . . . The show was only a few months old
at this point, but was already hugely popular. bigredbook.info/
james_butterworth.

Christmas newsletter of 1960/1 . . . 'Clubs That Cannot Proceed with Their
Application', John Rylands Research Institute and Library, University of
Manchester, GB113 DDEy/47.

Correspondence between the MAYC's youth officer . . . ibid.

The Temple Street Methodist Church in Keighley . . . ibid.

Dexion Ltd produced beautiful leaflets . . . ibid.

Guidance from Staffordshire . . . ibid.

each received government grants . . . ibid.

a documentary special . . . *Candid Caine: A Self Portrait of Michael Caine*
(LWT, 1969).

Caine called the Reverend Jimmy Butterworth . . . John Butterworth, Jenny Wain and Sir Michael Caine, *The Temple of Youth: Jimmy Butterworth and Clubland* (JB Club Press, 2019), p. viii.

a retrospective mini-doc . . . *Loyalty and Service: Jimmy Butterworth and Clubland* dir. James Steel, 1998, London Screen Archive, LSA/4406.

Committees all over the country successfully applied . . . John Rylands Research Institute and Library, University of Manchester, GB113 (1960–70), DDEy/47.

Methodist Leadership Race Awareness Workshops . . . 'The Origins of Walworth Methodist Church', walworthmethodist.org.uk.

on Grosvenor Terrace, open seven days a week . . . A KidsCo alumnus told me that core opening hours in the early 2000s were five days a week, plus Christmas Day.

25

if you wanted to boost your number . . . Karen Maychell, Shalini Pathak and Vivienne Cato, *Providing for Young People: Local Authority Youth Services in the 1990s* (National Foundation for Education Research, 1996), p. 97.

Bernard Coard and his damning 1971 book . . . Bernard Coard, *How the West Indian Child Is Made Educationally Sub-Normal in the British School System* (independently published, 1971).

In the debate, MP Simon Hughes . . . Hansard, Vol. 130, 28 March 1988.

Simon Hughes, in a 1991 House of Commons debate . . . 'Youth Service (Inner London)', Hansard, Vol. 196, 17 October 1991.

The bill was debated a month later . . . Hansard, Vol. 495, 18 April 1988.

In 1990, a series of ministerial conferences . . . Karen Maychell, Shalini Pathak and Vivienne Cato, *Providing for Young People*, p. 98.

contracts with the Department of Health . . . Hansard, Vol. 202, 22 January 1992.

One, titled 'Managing the Youth Service in the 1990s' . . . Accessed through the Oxford House Archive.

performance indicators were necessary . . . Coopers & Lybrand Deloitte, *Managing the Youth Service in the 1990s* (DES, 1991), reported in Jon Ord, 'Youth Work Curriculum' PhD, University of Wales.

British National Party (BNP) won a council by-election . . . 'Shock as Racist Wins Council Seat', BBC *On This Day*, 17 September 1993.

his fifteen-year-old ex-girlfriend listened . . . The information about the racist attack and the subsequent trial of one attacker was reported widely at the time, with Nicky Fuller's girlfriend suffering a great deal of abuse for her brave actions.

Streel-level repair work was required . . . Oxford House Annual Report 1993/4, p. 12.

26

building-based versions of an endangered species . . . Mark K. Smith and Tony Jeffs were arguing that youth work was in deep crisis. Mark K. Smith, *Developing Youth Work* (Open University Press, 1988).

seven million viewers were regularly tuning in . . . 'Byker Grove Gay Kiss Criticised', *Shields Daily Gazette*, 15 December 1994, p. 9.

purchase the freehold of The Mitre . . . Via Matthew Robinson, and reported elsewhere: 'Pearl Calls Tyne on Byker', *Property Week*, 1 October 2008.

the first same-sex kiss on British children's television . . . 'Parents Seethe at Gay TV Kiss', *Belfast Telegraph*, 15 December 1994, p. 3.

right-wing TV campaigner Mary Whitehouse . . . 'Byker Grove Gay Kiss Criticised', *Shields Daily Gazette*, 15 December 1994, p. 9.

'Avid Fan Convention' . . . Matthew Robinson sent me the video of the first *Byker Grove* 'Avid Fan Convention'. Another film, of the 1993 Convention, is online: shorturl.at/BYPTr.

27

in the Saturday teatime slot . . . *What You Looking At?*, written by Trix Worrell, produced by Humphrey Barclay for Humphrey Barclay Productions and broadcast on LWT.

'a hit with both critics and kids' . . . *Daily Mirror*, 30 April 1994, p. 49.

Ofcom relaxed the rules . . . James Robinson, 'Ofcom Confirms Product Placement on UK TV', *Guardian*, 20 December 2010.

Thatcher and her sell-off of school playing fields . . . In 1981, Regulation 909 gave education authorities the right to sell school land they considered surplus to requirements. 'Margaret Thatcher "Never Really Understood Sport"', bbc.co.uk, 10 April 2013.

hadn't been commissioned for another series . . . *Daily Mirror*, 30 April 1994, p. 49.

28

two thirds of young people had been involved . . . Sue Robertson, *Youth Clubs*, p. 40.

the youth service was working with some five million young people . . . Karen Maychell, Shalini Pathak and Vivienne Cato, *Providing for Young People*, p. 1.

Youth clubs comprised part of the picture . . . ibid., pp. 62–92.

from forty to fifteen full-time youth service staff . . . ibid., p. 7.

'we've become very entrepreneurial' . . . ibid., p. 35.

Nearly £4million was allocated . . . Sue Robertson, *Youth Clubs*, p. 37.

'grasp the nettle of evaluation' . . . David Smith and Ian Paylor, 'Reluctant Heroes', *Youth and Policy*, Summer 1997.

working out the cost of their centres . . . Karen Maychell, Shalini Pathak and Vivienne Cato, *Providing for Young People*, p. 12.

'In order to evaluate' . . . ibid., p. 18.

regarding the youth service as catering for 'problem kids' . . . ibid., pp. 22–7.

a community youth worker and film-maker who'd made his own documentary . . . The documentary, *Sound System*, is available online: https://www.youtube.com/watch?v=E6Z5Q3_OG34.

the resulting drama . . . *Blazed*, dir. Jonnie Turpie (APT Films, 1995), shorturl.at/Cj7Hi.

satire on gang affiliation . . . *Tissue Paper Crew*, youtube.com/watch?v=6Wn5z4WUCp4.

A timeline of 'known gangs' . . . Simon Harding, *The Street Casino: Survival in Violent Street Gangs* (Bristol University Press, 2014), p. 312.

Lambeth Council launched a five-year strategy . . . Corin Williams, 'Lambeth Aims to Slash Youth Custody Rate Through Gang Plan', *Community Care*, 31 July 2008: https://www.communitycare.co.uk/2008/07/31/lambeth-aims-to-slash-youth-custody-rate-through-gang-plan.

29

Young members went on the hunt . . . Ben Farrin, 'Roni Size', *The Student Pocket Guide*, May 2005.

his PhD thesis on the evolution and decline of traditional recording studios . . . Philip Kirby, 'The Evolution and Decline of Traditional Recording Studios', PhD thesis, University of Liverpool, 2015.

By 1992, the Basement was officially award-winning . . . *Bristol Evening Post*, 31 January 1992, p. 19.

it had taken a £16,720 share of the £1.6m . . . *Bristol Evening Post*, 22 December 1992, p. 13.

thirty tins of paint from Dulux . . . *Bristol Evening Post*, 19 August 1994, p. 13.

Two National Arts Council awards followed . . . *Bristol Evening Post*, 8 June 1993, p. 37.

'*a model of good practice*' offering '*tremendous expertise*' . . . The Basement Annual Report 1995, p. 2, courtesy of Alice Perera.

'*The Tomorrow's Warriors' Jazz Project's overall aim*' . . . From a letter to potential participants, courtesy of Alice Perera.

in 1995, Avon Council still covered the running costs . . . The Basement Annual Report 1995, p. 9, courtesy of Alice Perera.

Daddy G of Massive Attack became a patron . . . 'Studio's Star Boost', *Bristol Evening Post*, 12 July 1996, p. 21.

*his Full Cycle crew were '*like Power Rangers*'* . . . Emma Warren, 'Bristol Responds to Bass', *Jockey Slut*, December 1996, pp. 41–3.

committed themselves to the introduction of a statutory youth service . . . Sue Robertson, *Youth Clubs*, pp. 41–2.

celebrated the Basement in their leader . . . *Bristol Evening Post*, 21 October 1998.

the money would be used to make a compilation album . . . Julie Cross, 'Banging the Drum for Bristol', *Bristol Evening Post*, 22 October 1998, p. 62.

30

'*first attempt to pin down youth music projects*' . . . Richard Ings, Ruth Jones and Nick Randell, *Mapping Hidden Talent: Investigating Youth Music Projects* (Youth Work Press, 1999).

Our first route in comes . . . Mickey Cooper, *Your Process or Mine? The Story of the Peace Process* (Gasyard Trust, 2016).

the complex stop–start of political power-sharing . . . See the Institute for Government's 'explainer' article 'Direct Rule Northern Ireland', Factcheck.ni, and Luke Sprule, 'NI Peace Deals: A History of Northern Ireland Political Agreements', bbc.co.uk, 4 February 2024.

walls in interface areas continued to be built . . . Teresa García Alcatraz, 'Belfast Has More Peace Walls Than 25 Years Ago', theconversation.com, 10 May 2023.

'*driving young people away*' . . . Mark K. Smith, 'The Connexions Service in England', Infed.org, July 2014.

'*the European Union's commitment to the peace and reconciliation process*' . . . The Peace Platform website contains PEACE I and II budgets and evaluation: shorturl.at/UXvl1.

the National Lottery New Opportunities Fund . . . 'Report by the Comptroller and Auditor General: Grants Made by the National Lottery Charities Board' (National Audit Office, 2000), p. 12.

'*there was still a substantial legacy*' . . . Sam McCready and Richard Loudon, *Investing in Lives: The History of the Youth Service (1973–2017)*, Vol. 2 (Youth Council for Northern Ireland, 2020), p. 148.

In 1998, there were 3,000 youth groups . . . Sam McCready and Richard Loudon, *Investing in Lives*, p. 215.

17,000 volunteers . . . ibid., p. 176.

A House of Commons report . . . Professor Liam Kennedy, *They Shoot Children Don't They?* (Queen's University Belfast, 2001).

five or more GCSEs . . . Sam McCready and Richard Loudon, *Investing in Lives*, p. 147.

by 2009 suicide rates . . . Ken Harland, *Masculinity and Mental Health* (HPA, 2009).

'an all-too familiar feature' . . . 'Brief History of Stormont Suspensions', *Belfast Telegraph*, 11 January 2017.

painted with great clarity . . . *Dancing on Narrow Ground*, dir. Des Bell, 1995: youtube.com/watch?v=dzo-42PpFLQ.

Fergie and his brother, Ken . . . *Kitchen Confidential*, May 2023: youtube.com/watch?v=UadF17ciKUQ.

'everyday, embodied and multi-sensorial register of war' . . . Maria-Adriana Deiana, 'Dance as a Register of War: Following Unruly Bodies, Affects, and Sounds in Conflict', *Critical Military Studies* (Queen's University, Belfast, 2022).

32

reinforced by detail peppered across the internet . . . Jack Mills, 'A Psychogeographic Guide to Grime', Medium.com, 15 December 2016, and Sam Diss, 'Nowhere to Go: The Crisis in Local Youth Club Funding and Access to Music', *Vice*, 19 October 2016.

depicts four east London youth clubs . . . Simon Wheatley, *Lost Dreams* (Simon Wheatley, 2022).

Grime-powered crime drama Top Boy . . . Channel 4 engaged Livity to ensure the first season reached a diverse audience, through a mix tape curated by Chantelle Fiddy, mixed by Charlie Sloth, distributed with *Live*.

had attended Devas Youth Club . . . Aurelia Foster, 'Youth Club Keeping Kids Off Streets Marks 140 Years', bbc.co.uk, 2 September 2024.

Little Simz . . . Nicola Haynes, 'Youth Club in Islington "the Place Where It All Began"', nelondoner.co.uk, 27 November 2023.

Yusuf Islam . . . majicat.com/Charities/hughprimary.

33

they were rated on key service delivery areas . . . Sue Robertson, *Youth Clubs*, p. 119.

'the more that project work can demonstrate' . . . Bryan Merton, Hilary Comfort and Malcolm Payne, *Recognising and Recording the Impact of Youth Work* (National Youth Agency, 2005), quoted in Sue Robertson, *Youth Clubs*, p. 117.

teenage pregnancy in Lambeth at the time . . . Abdu Mohiddin, Lucinda Cawley, Yimmu Chow and Ruth Wallis, 'Life as a League Table Bottom Dweller: Teenage Pregnancy in Lambeth', *Journal of Public Health*, Vol. 28, Issue 4, December 2006, pp. 304–8.

the highest rates of street robbery . . . 'Lambeth Worst Hotspot for Robbery', bbc.co.uk, 19 July 2001.

the Met introduced a short-lived pilot . . . 'The Lambeth Cannabis Warning Pilot Scheme', Metropolitan Police Authority, 26 September 2002.

Marcus Lipton Youth Club . . . The club would later form the basis of writer and youth worker Ciaran Thapar's influential book *Cut Short* (Penguin, 2021).

A group of forty 'Windrush men' . . . Ruth Glass, *London's Newcomers* (Harvard University Press, 1961), pp. 46–7.

London received around £90m per year . . . London Assembly, Members Question Time, 28 April 2004.

Jamal set up Jamal Edwards Delve . . . Nosheen Iqbal, 'Jamal Edwards Gives Back to Youth Clubs That Helped His Career', *Guardian*, 3 November 2019.

34

a youth-run record label . . . Live Recordings was run with Mark Gurney, and Burial remixed an early release. Another Livity project, Music4Good, successfully sent young people into apprenticeships at record labels.

35

In 2009, there were approximately 11,000 youth clubs across the UK . . . Amelia Gentleman, 'Youth Services: Lost in Nowhere Land', *Guardian*, 15 July 2009.

A few, around 20 per cent, were 'large and well-established' . . . Julia Hargreaves and Helen Garner, *Somewhere to Belong: A Blueprint for 21st Century Youth Clubs* (Clubs for Young People, 2009).

More than two in five were small . . . Carmen Villa, *The Effects of Youth Clubs on Education and Crime* (Institute of Fiscal Studies, 2024), p. 7.

more than half a trillion pounds of lost public spending . . . Rob Calvert Jump, Jo Michell, James Meadway and Natassia Nascimento, *The Macroeconomics of Austerity* (Progressive Economics Forum, 2023).

David Cameron's National Citizenship Service . . . 'MPs Attack Citizen Service Cost as Youth Funding Cut', bbc.co.uk, 23 June 2011.

Spending on youth services was reduced . . . Joe Lepper, 'Council Spending on Youth Services in England Falls by 73 Per Cent Since 2010', *Children and Young People Now*, 29 January 2025.

'Closing youth clubs was not cost-effective' . . . Carmen Villa, *The Effects of Youth Clubs on Education and Crime*, p. 42.

SELECTED BIBLIOGRAPHY

Baroíd, De Ciarán, *Down North: Reflections of Ballymurphy and the Early Troubles* (Ogham Press, 2010)

Bell, Desmond, *Acts of Union* (Palgrave Macmillan, 1990)

———, *Ireland Through a Critical Lens* (Cork University Press, 2023)

Blackman, Rick, *Forty Miles of Bad Road: The Stars Campaign for Interracial Friendship and the 1958 Notting Hill Riots* (Redwords, 2017)

Blandy, Mary, *Razor Edge* (Victor Gollancz, 1967)

Brew, Macalister J., *In the Service of the Youth* (Faber, 1943)

———, *Youth and Youth Groups* (Faber, 1957)

———, *Informal Education: Adventures and Reflections* (Faber, 1946)

Bunt, Sidney, and Gargrave, Ron, *The Politics of Youth Clubs* (National Youth Bureau, 1980)

Butterworth, Jimmy, and Waine, Jenny, *The Temple of Youth* (JB Club Press, 2019)

Campbell, Julieann, *On Bloody Sunday* (Monoray, 2022)

Collyer, David, *Double Zero: Five Years with Rockers and Hell's Angels in an English City* (Fontana Books, 1973)

Cooper, Mickey, *Your Process or Mine: The Story of the Peace Process* (Gasyard Trust, 2016)

Davies, Bernard, *From Thatcherism to New Labour: A History of the Youth Service in England* (National Youth Agency, 1999)

———, *Threatening Youth: Towards a National Youth Policy* (Open University Press, 1986)

———, *From Voluntaryism to Welfare State: A History of the Youth Service in England* (Youth Work Press, 1999)

———, and Gibson, Alan, *The Social Education of the Adolescent* (University of London Press Ltd, 1967)

Glass, Ruth, *London's Newcomers* (Harvard University Press, 1961)

Gus, John, *Blazing Trails: Stories of a Heroic Generation* (New Beacon Books, 2023)

Hay, Marnie, *Na Fianna Eirann and the Irish Revolution, 1909–23: Scouting for Rebels* (Manchester University Press, 2021)

Hedges, Sid, *Youth Club Programmes* (Cox and Wyman Ltd, 1961)

SELECTED BIBLIOGRAPHY

Holman, Bob, *Kids at the Door Revisited* (Russell House Publishing, 2000)

Ings, Richard, Jones, Ruth and Randell, Nick, *Mapping Hidden Talent: Investigating Youth Music Projects* (Youth Work Press, 1998)

Irani, Tara, *Mishandled Archive* (LADA, 2020)

James, Gary, *Spangles, Glam, Gaywaves and Tubes* (The Book Guild Ltd, 2019)

McCready, Sam, and Loudon, Richard, *Investing in Lives: The History of the Youth Service in Northern Ireland (1844–1973)* (Youth Council for Northern Ireland, 2015)

———, *Investing in Lives: The History of the Youth Service in Northern Ireland (1973–2017)* (Youth Council for Northern Ireland, 2020).

Mooney, Martin, *Blue Lamp Disco* (Lagan Press, 2003)

Nicholls, Douglas, *For Youth Workers and Youth Work: Speaking Out for a Better Future* (The Policy Press, 2012)

Roberts, Jonathan, *Youth Work Ethics* (Learning Matters, 2009)

Robertson, Sue, *Youth Clubs: Association, Participation, Friendship and Fun!* (Russell House Publishing, 2005)

Rose, Celia, *Touching Lives: A Personal History of the Clapton Jewish Youth Centre 1946–1976* (Youth Work Press, 1998)

Smith, Mark K., *Creators Not Consumers, Developing Youth Work* (NAYC, 1980)

Springhall, John, *Youth, Empire and Society* (Archon, 1971)

Staple, Neville, and McMahon, Tony, *Original Rude Boy* (Aurum Press, 2009)

Target, DJ, *Grime Kids: The Inside Story of the Global Grime Takeover* (Trapeze, 2018)

Thapar, Ciaran, *Cut Short: Why We're Failing Our Youth – and How to Fix It* (Penguin, 2022)

Trelford, Neil, *The Youth Club* (Austin Macauley Publishers Ltd, 2016)

Trenchard, Lorraine, and Warren, Hugh, *Something to Tell You: The Experiences and Needs of Young Lesbians and Gay Men in London* (London Gay Teenage Group, 1984)

Wheeler, Hayden, *Clubmen 1645* (The Minster Press, 2021)

Williams, Clifford, *Courage to Be: Organised Gay Youth in England 1967–1990* (The Book Guild Ltd, 2021)

Wynter, Errol, *On the Other Side of the Fence* (Spitalfield Books, 1980)